Understanding Violence

The causes of violence and conflict are often left untheorised, or they are discussed as an existent problem assumed to be an inevitable part of human interaction. This book seeks to examine, interpret and analyse a wide range of approaches to the causes of violence and conflict. Adopting an accessible approach, it presents readers with a clear understanding of these by highlighting their evolutionary roots and illustrating them with in-depth case studies and examples.

Tim Jacoby addresses the fragmented nature of the literature on conflict theory by drawing upon a wide range of disciplinary traditions. This text seeks to reflect the fact that international relations, history, economics, development, politics and sociology all share a longstanding interest in the study of conflict and violence, and that common concerns make interdisciplinary approaches stimulating and productive. It is, therefore, intended for students and scholars across these disciplines.

Tim Jacoby is Senior Lecturer at the Institute for Development Policy and Management at the University of Manchester, UK.

Understanding Conflict and Violence

Theoretical and interdisciplinary approaches

Tim Jacoby

Routledge
Taylor & Francis Group

LONDON AND NEW YORK

First published 2008
by Routledge
2 Park Square, Milton Park, Abingdon, Oxon OX14 4RN

Simultaneously published in the USA and Canada
by Routledge
270 Madison Ave, New York, NY 10016

Routledge is an imprint of the Taylor & Francis Group

© 2008 Tim Jacoby

Typeset in Sabon by Prepress Projects, Perth, UK
Printed and bound in Great Britain by Antony Rowe Ltd, Chippenham,
Wiltshire

British Library Cataloguing in Publication Data
A catalogue record for this book is available from the British Library

Library of Congress Cataloging in Publication Data
Jacoby, Tim, 1969–
Understanding conflict and violence: theoretical and interdisciplinary
approaches / Tim Jacoby.
p. cm.
Includes bibliographical references and index.
ISBN 0-415-36911-8 (hardback: alk. paper) – ISBN 0-415-36910-
X (pbk.: alk. paper) 1. Social conflict. 2. Violence. 3. Conflict
(Psychology) 4. Interpersonal relations. I. Title.
HM1121.J33 2007
303.601–dc22
2006016940

ISBN10: 0-415-36911-8 (hbk)
ISBN10: 0-415-36910-X (pbk)
ISBN10: 0-203-02882-1 (ebk)

ISBN13: 978-0-415-36911-4 (hbk)
ISBN13: 978-0-415-36910-7 (pbk)
ISBN13: 978-0-203-02882-7 (ebk)

To my parents

Contents

Figures

Tables

Acknowledgements

Much of the research for this book was undertaken in preparation for the lecture programme of a postgraduate course entitled *Conflict Analysis* which I teach at the Institute for Development Policy and Management at the University of Manchester in the UK. In devising this course, I owe much to Keith Webb, who introduced me to many of the ideas included in this book during my time at the University of Kent at Canterbury in 1997 and 1998. I also received a lot of support from my colleague at Manchester, Sam Hickey, who, especially during my first year, was particularly selfless with advice and support. In running the *Conflict Analysis* course, I have learnt a great deal from my students. On the basis of this, I have tried to revise and (hopefully) improve my treatment of each of the following topics. If this has proven to be the case, then I owe much to their enthusiasm and endeavour and for that I am very grateful. I am also indebted to Roger MacGinty, Eric James and Jonathan Goodhand for taking time to comment on a partial draft of the manuscript and to Routledge's anonymous reviewers for their corrections, criticisms and a raft of helpful suggestions. In addition, I am indebted to Harriet Brinton and Heidi Bagtazo, from Routledge, who have made the writing of this book as easy and pleasurable as such an undertaking can be. My biggest vote of thanks must, however, go to my family: to my mother, my father (who has meticulously proofread my prose and ironed out some of its errors) and my wife and our three children, all of whom have contributed immensely to this book and all of whom deserve a considerable share of whatever merit it deserves.

1 Introduction

This book aims to bring some order to the vast and fragmentary literature concerning the study of conflict and violence. It considers a diverse range of perspectives, models and theories that share a common attempt to explain why people engage in conflictive behaviour in general and violence in particular. In doing so, it presents nine broad headings under which an eclectic body of material is covered. By focusing on theories rather than theorists and on one overarching issue rather than a disparate array of topics, it hopes to encourage readers to compare various factors and mechanisms, to appraise common analytical themes and to develop a deeper understanding of the current landscape of conflict studies. To this end, a wide assortment of academic enquiries is presented, examined and illustrated with case studies, data and examples drawn from various times and disciplines. Research ranging from 1950s functionalism to the latest explanations of civil war, on the one hand, and from ethology to constructivism, on the other, informs the discussion of each interlinked approach. Inevitably, the book is selective in the sources it chooses and, deliberately, it claims neither to offer exhaustive analyses of each topic it handles nor to cover every scholarly tradition. Rather, it intends to bring a degree of lucidity and connectivity to a disjointed and frequently abstruse corpus of literature drawn from the explosion of academic interest in conflict studies since the Second World War. With this in mind, the chapter to follow endeavours to locate the themes that will be addressed in the rest of the book within a broader socio-historical context by taking in some of the more significant changes that have marked both the practice and the study of violence.

Conflict and violence

For much of history, human strength or muscle power has determined the forms that conflict and violence have taken. The development of basic tools around 200,000 years ago and rudimentary projectiles such as spears and arrows about 160,000 years later may have augmented Pleistocene peoples' capacity to injure one another, but it was not until the Neolithic period

– approximately 13,000 years ago – that clear evidence of weaponry be-comes apparent (Barash and Webel 2002: 67–72). Between 5000 and 3000 BCE, ecological differences across areas managed by riverine flooding and rain-watered irrigation began to generate economic surpluses within the Euphrates Basin, offering increased employment opportunities, urbanisation and the growth of political centralisation. Trade between centres of alluvial agriculture and the wider region centred on particular communication and exportation lines for tools, weapons and other manufactured goods pre-dominantly produced in the core and traded for labour and raw materials (Jacobsen 1970). As the exchange of a growing agricultural and manufactur-ing surplus increased, defence of these trade routes became more important, especially for economically dominant urban groups. City-states constructed fortified walls, created infantries equipped with bronze armour and weapons and intensified the use of animal haulage. Broadly concurrently, elites, pos-sibly elected by temple oligarchies for combatant functions in time of war, emerged with institutionalised political power. Around 2310 BCE, one such leader, King Sargon, succeeded in gaining control over a large area of Meso-potamia, founding what Michael Mann calls 'the first empire of domination' and establishing 'one of the dominant social forms for three thousand years in the Near East and Europe, and even longer in East Asia' (1986: 131).

Changes in patterns of collective violence occurred under each subse-quent era of imperial contraction and expansion. Iron was introduced, and ships were used to extend the power of maritime states, such as Phoenicia and Greece, and to organise small raiding parties on coastal settlements. Horses were deployed – both to draw vehicles rapidly across the battlefield and to carry archers – and production became increasingly committed to the material demands of warfare, not least as part of Rome's legionary economy (Carter 2001: 10). These innovations extended localised conflicts far beyond the boundary disputes of broadly contiguous groups that characterised early history. Eventually, wars extended over great distances as the cavalry-based formations of central Asian nomadic groups enlarged their range into the Middle East and on to the Mediterranean, while improvements in maritime technology facilitated the projection of military might across seas previously not traversed. By the early sixteenth century, the use of cannonry brought Asian horsemen to the gates of Vienna and the seafarer countries of western and southern Europe to the untapped endowments of a 'new world' on the other side of the planet.

The result was a new era of 'industrial' violence based on advances in chemistry, first in China and then in Europe. Explosive powders allowed commanders to replace mechanical devices reliant on muscle power to prime and make effective – such as the catapult and crossbow – with instruments, such as the musket and cannon, that could fire projectiles comparable dis-tances without the need for large inputs of labour. The consequent prolifera-tion of small arms during the fifteenth century reduced the effectiveness of mobile cavalry tactics already under pressure from pike-phalanx formations and the longbow (Rogers 1993). The inexpensive and easily produced bullet could penetrate costly suits of armour and, like the detachable bayonet which gradually replaced the longer pikes, kill valuable, highly trained horses. Consequently, considerable impetus was given to refining firearms, particularly with regard to rates of fire and accuracy. The former was greatly improved by the replacement of the matchlock with breech-loading flintlocks in around 1650, the spread of pistols and the adoption of percussion cap magazine-fed munitions in the nineteenth century. Accuracy slowly increased with improvements in barrel technology, culminating in the abandonment of smoothbore arms in favour of the rifles that are the primary weapons of infantry today.

In response to these changes, new defensive battlefield strategies became apparent from around 1540 onwards – such as the reintroduction of infantry lines now armed with muskets and protected by land-workings (Parker 1988). This had a number of important consequences, including prolonged campaigns, increased labour intensities and comparatively complex training programmes. High concentrations of standing troops also rendered armies more vulnerable to disease and malnutrition. The unprecedented size of logistical deployments (close to a quarter of million men under arms combined with a retinue of perhaps one million camp followers) during the Thirty Years' War (1618–48), for instance, provoked outbreaks of plague, typhus and dysentery so severe that they may have contributed to a reduction in Germany's population by as much as one third (Outram 2001). By this time, campaigns were so expensive to initiate, sustain and replenish that siege warfare became largely the preserve of Europe's wealthiest courts. Around the same time, naval costs rose exponentially as developments in cannonry obliged monarchs to refit and retrain their fleets. English state revenue, for instance, increased from £126,500 per annum in 1505 to £2,066,900 in 1688 (it had only increased from £12,200 to £54,400 per annum between 1166 and 1452), much of which, Mann observes, was due to the costs of warfare. 'All these changes', he concludes, 'led to a greater role for capital-intensive supplies and, therefore, for centralised, orderly administration and capital accounting which could concentrate the resources of a territory' (1986: 454).

So, despite the fact that military mobility remained extremely limited during this period (ground forces were still reliant on three days of plunder for every nine days of marching), smaller states that could not finance large-scale siege warfare tended to give way to bigger, more centralised administrations better able to raise the necessary revenues. Internationally, this gave rise to a warlike system of Great Powers rooted in Europe and underpinned by the region's growing economic strength (Levy *et al.* 2004: 17–19). France, for instance, has, according to Jack Levy, participated in 47 per cent of the 2,600 battles he records between 1495 and 1975 (1983). Domestically, too, the implications of warfare's new format were considerable. Now that monarchs could batter down the fortresses of their recalcitrant gentry, greater infrastructural reach into civil society was possible. This led to the gradual institutionalisation of a civil-state reciprocity, in which the court became both a mechanism for disbursing royal favours through a system of client–patron relationships and a forum for the raising of direct taxes and deficit borrowing. Such a widening of vested interests in the instigation and conduct of warfare had the correlative effect of instilling organisational routines and rendering policies, once embarked upon, more difficult to adjust and reverse (Iklé 2005).

The dilution of dynastic power in Europe gathered pace during the eighteenth century when considerable increases in literacy placed the courtly circles of the 'old regime', as well as the leadership of the armed forces, under increasing pressure from an ascendant bourgeoisie. As Marshall Foch said of the Battle of Valmy's conclusion in 1792, 'the wars of kings were at an end; the wars of peoples were beginning' (quoted in Osgood 1967: 52). Indeed, by 1804, only three of Napoleon's 18 marshals were from the nobility, and over half his officers had been recruited from the ranks of enlisted men – a situation that the restored Bourbon monarchy later found impossible to reverse fully (Mann 1993: 426). Notions of collective morale and camaraderie came to be emphasised as campaigns imposed comparable levels of privation on officers and men – both now governed by the same codes and regulations. Administrative innovations in the handling of maps, communications and timetables, particularly by the Germans, enabled commanders to co-ordinate soldiers' lives much more thoroughly. The enlisting of mercenaries declined (along with desertion rates) as professionalised armed forces became imbued with concepts of national statehood. Welfare provisions for soldiers were introduced, wages (now paid on time) kept abreast of civilian occupations, long-service military personnel were used to train the expanding ranks of short-term conscripts and reservists, and economic development became increasingly tied to, and in some cases reliant upon, military production (McNeill 1984).

As military sectors have grown, industrial production has generated weapons of ever greater destructive power, and an international system based on the perceived importance of power balances has emerged (Fuller 1992). During the modern era, the result has been an overall decrease in the number of Great Powers (although there has been a rise since 1945) and a fall in the total number of very large conflicts. Concurrently, however, there has been an increase in the destructiveness of warfare (perhaps doubling every 110 years or so). These changes reached an apogee in the two world wars of the twentieth century in which a relatively small number of powerful countries committed cultural, scientific, industrial, military and political resources on an unparalleled scale and comprehensiveness to a 'total' war effort that enveloped a large number of other states. Governments introduced legislation giving themselves more executive authority, levied supplementary taxes (many of which have lasted to this day) and created new ministries to increase their supervisory and extractive powers. They also greatly enlarged their share of the gross domestic product. During the First World War, for instance, this rose to around 50 per cent in Germany, France and Britain (where conscription put three-fifths of the eligible men into uniform) (Winter 2005). By the Second World War, the Allies were, despite suffering much greater casualties than the Axis Powers, generally able to outproduce their enemies; Germany produced 19 per cent and Japan 7 per cent of the world's munitions, while the United States produced 47 per cent, the United Kingdom and Canada 14 per cent and the Soviets 11 per cent (Goldsmith 1946). To achieve this, new workers (particularly housewives, students and the retired) were recruited to simplified jobs previously the reserve of the highly skilled. Germany compelled millions of prisoners of war and labourers to staff its munitions factories, while the Allies rejected the complex and highly engineered innovations of their enemies in favour of low-cost mass production techniques based on standardised models and logistical efficiency. In addition, every major state imposed a system of rationing, price controls and censorship as well as a sophisticated propaganda programme designed to boost the war effort and stifle dissent (Overy 1995).

Unsurprisingly, such a massive effort produced unprecedented destruction – confirming Winston Churchill's prediction that Foch's 'wars of peoples will be more terrible than those of kings' (quoted in Gilbert 1994: 3). For 10 months during 1916, for instance, the battle of Verdun in northern France occupied in excess of three million soldiers within an area not larger than 10 square kilometres and, despite no territorial gains, resulted in over 800,000 casualties, rendering the area agriculturally useless for decades (*ARRC Journal* Winter 2005). Similarly, the German encirclement of the Soviet's south-western front at Kiev in the summer of 1941 is estimated to have cost the Red Army 700,544 casualties (including 616,304 killed, captured or missing), resulting in the near total destruction of 43 divisions (Erickson 1999). In the First World War, a total of over 35 million people were killed, wounded or listed as missing (in the United Kingdom alone, 160,000 widows were created, 300,000 children lost their fathers and over 2.5 million men died or were injured), producing a worldwide sense of loss and anger that found expression in extreme politics, nihilism and anti-modernism (Havighurst 1979). The Second World War was more destructive still with deaths alone estimated to have exceeded 60 million, including 32 million civilians. This reduced the population of countries such as Germany, Latvia, Lithuania, Poland and the Soviet Union by over 10 per cent. Elsewhere, it killed around 10 million Chinese people, 2.5 million Japanese and 500,000 Americans (Ellis 1993). Such unequalled bloodshed was, in fact, only brought to an end by the first (and so far only) wartime use of a nuclear device which, in two deployments, killed almost 300,000, mostly non-combatant, residents of Hiroshima and Nagasaki and confirmed the start of a new period of conflict and violence dominated by the threat of weapons of mass destruction.

In fact, the potential of industrial science to produce a means of rendering the assembled ranks of mass troop deployments instantly vulnerable (and perhaps ultimately obsolete) was first realised (although rudimentary chemical weapons were probably used as far back as the Peloponnesian War of the fifth century BCE) during the First World War. The German chemical conglomerate IG Farben, for instance, developed a byproduct of their dye manufacturing system to create a chlorine gas which was used in April 1915 to open a 6-kilometre-wide breach in the Allied lines at Ypres and then to kill more than 5,000 (mainly Canadian) reinforcements. Refinements followed rapidly as the French replaced Germany's open canister methods with a non-explosive artillery shell containing the nearly odourless compound phosgene and the British developed a large-bore mortar that could fire gas cylinders up to 1,500 metres, thereby deploying higher concentrations of gas. Later, these techniques were used to deliver mustard gas – a corrosive agent first manufactured by the German company Bayer AG from thiodiglycol and hydrochloric acid. This was again first deployed near the city of Ypres, before being taken up by the British in September 1918 initially as a way of breaking the Hindenburg Line and then to attack Bolsheviks in 1919 and Iraqi rebels in 1920. In all, a total 50,965 tons of chemical agents were deployed by both sides during the First World War, hospitalising over a million troops and generating approximately 85,000 fatalities (Haber 1986). Since then, around another 70 chemical compounds have been stockpiled for use in warfare. The respiratory and blistering agents of the First World War have been augmented with nerve action weapons such as sarin and vx, asphyxiates such as the arsines and cyanides, cytotoxic proteins (ricin for instance) and incapacitants (agent 15 and the like), as well as defoliants (not acutely toxic, but associated with chronic health conditions – of which agent orange is the best known). Incendiary chemicals such as napalm, phosphorus and fuel–air explosives can also be considered weapons of mass destruction if their impact is of sufficient scale.

Alongside these, many states have used biological phenomena – particularly disease and infection – as a second type of mass destruction weapon. These, too, have a long history. Corpses have been catapulted into cities or dumped in water supplies during sieges, venomous snakes have been hurled at adversaries and, on at least one occasion, British officers attempted to infect the indigenous American population with blankets that had been exposed to smallpox (Dixon 2005). Like chemical weapons, though, it was not until the industrialised, total wars of the twentieth century that these techniques were exploited on a significant scale. In the Sino-Japanese War of 1937–45, for instance, imperial troops carried out extensive experiments on prisoners of war using bubonic plague- and cholera-infected foodstuffs and water, causing perhaps as many as 500,000 deaths. Germany, the United States, the United Kingdom and Canada also initiated biological weapons programmes focused on anthrax, brucellosis and botulism toxins during this period. Other pathogens thought to have been developed for military use since the Second World War include Ebola, rabbit fever, Q fever, Bolivian haemorrhagic fever, California valley fever, glanders, Whitmore's disease,

Shigella, Rocky Mountain spotted fever, typhus, parrot fever, yellow fever, Japanese B encephalitis and Rift Valley fever (Eitzen and Takafuji 1997).

Associated with this type of 'dirty' warfare is the use of radioactive material – the third type of mass destruction weapon. This can be employed in two ways. The first is to spread contaminants using conventional explosives with the result, intentional or otherwise, that those in the vicinity are harmed. Despite the fact that the likelihood of directly killing large numbers of people is remote, mass civilian casualties may result from panic and relocation, thereby rendering, in theory at least, powerful states vulnerable to such an attack. For this reason, debates concerning how much nuclear material should be left as residual fall-out as well as the efficacy of producing incendiaries 'salted' with cobalt remain a part of contemporary military strategising, as does the need to respond to the possibility that an irredentist group might plant such a device (a bomb defused by Russian security forces in Moscow in 1995, for instance, was reported to have contained a quantity of caesium-137 taken from medical equipment (*New Scientist* 2 June 2004)). Many states are also using radioactive material as a means of hardening projectiles. Although such weapons are not expressly intended to cause mass destruction, a growing body of literature associates the aeration of uranium isotopes with widespread health problems (http://www.umrc.net/).

Second, weapons based on thermonuclear fusion have been stockpiled. By the 1960s, both Superpowers had tested deliverable forms of such weapons many hundreds of times more destructive than the fission bombs dropped on Japan. With the development of ballistic missiles (based on wartime German rocket designs) shortly afterwards, the strategic potential of a nuclear attack – from silos, lorries or submarines – enlarged greatly and, in many ways, came to define geopolitics during the postwar era (Rhodes 1995). Since the end of the Cold War, however, the control the two blocs exerted over their nuclear deterrence has, partially at least, broken down. Consequently, the first generation of states to admit to developing nuclear weapons – the United States, the United Kingdom, France, the Soviet Union and China (Israel, despite an official policy of silence, should also be included here) – has been joined by a number of others. India and Pakistan, for instance, are both thought to have initiated uranium enrichment programmes during the late 1960s or early 1970s (the former tested a 'peaceful' device in 1974) but, under Western pressure, did not carry out overtly military testing until 1998. The latter is believed, by some, to have supplied material and data to North Korea, Libya and Iran (*New York Times* 12 February 2004).

Indeed, the spread of nuclear technology over the last 20 or so years may be regarded as part of a broader proliferation of weapons since the end of the Cold War. Although registered arms sales have not increased greatly worldwide, most major suppliers enlarged their focus on the South during the 1990s. The United States, the United Kingdom, France and Russia, for instance, advanced the value of their (completed and registered) weapons sales to the developing world from 61 to 66 per cent, 85 to 87 per cent, 69 to 88 per cent and 67 to 78 per cent, respectively, between 1993 and 2000 – part of an overall rise of 11,500 million dollars. Particularly affected was the continent of Africa where the total worth of registered arms transfers grew from 2,680 million dollars for the years 1993–96 to 8,896 million dollars for the years 1997–2000 (Grimmett 2001). Given that these 'legitimate' sales represent only a fraction of the actual quantity of weapons transferred over this period, it is perhaps no surprise that the United Nations estimates the numbers of small arms 'beyond the control of [African] states' to have now reached 30 million, fuelling a disproportionate share of the steady rise in civil wars that has emerged since the Second World War (Qoma 2004: 1; Travaglianti 2006). Indeed, the indiscriminate, lawless and plunderous nature of such conflicts, frequently within environments marked by a feudalisation of political authority and an internationalisation of economic exchange, have led some to conclude that contemporary warfare is moving towards a period of 'medievalisation' (Ahorsu 2004).

Understanding conflict and violence

In each of the three periods outlined in the previous section – those of muscle power, industrial production and mass destruction weaponry – sophisticated treatises analysing the roots of conflict behaviour have been produced and have, to varying degrees, influenced the way that violence, in all its forms, is considered today. These have not only focused upon the causes of conflict, but also included notions of peace. In one sense, an implied connection between peace and violent conflict is inevitable. After all, 'to account for knowledge, we must assume a reality that is wider than either subjects or objects, because it comprehends both, and neither is except in relation to its opposite' (Jones 1915: 239–40). Consequently, we tend to 'conceptualize all events, processes, and entities . . . as having an opposite and excluding (dual) meaning in relation to its opposite event, process, or entity' (Kronlid 2003: 122; Warren 2000). Conceptually, then, peace, like all things, is only comprehensible through a process of antonymic comparison. Similarly, in phenomenological terms, war is, 'in some sense, a necessary prelude to peace' – how else could the latter be experienced and identified (Tuzin 1996: 24)? Indeed, as Francisco Muñoz points out, in attempting to 'establish how violence and peace manifest and recur, . . . we know that both possibilities are closely related, so much so that they nearly always arise through the same social matrix' (2005: 2).

Understandings of this matrix fall into three broad and overlapping categories. The first, strategic studies, is, as John Groom notes, 'concerned with the manipulation and application of threats either to preserve or to change the status quo'. Assuming that 'all actors seek to dominate and only some can', researchers in this field, Groom continues, aim 'to ensure safe and orderly rules for this struggle'. The second, conflict research, proceeds from the premise that violence and warfare are a consequence 'not of intent per se, but an unwelcome result of pursuing goals that are incompatible with others' (Groom 1988: 105, 108). By analysing the costs of attempting to attain these objectives, the aim of the conflict researcher is thus to steer actors towards a less deleterious course of action. The third, peace research, rejects such an emphasis upon actors and their preferences in favour of a broader concern with structures and values. Rather than companionably facilitating incremental change, peace researchers therefore work towards 'the presentation of proposals, even whole blueprints, . . . that bring about a new world' (Galtung 1975: 256).

Most accounts of conflict and violence, however, share the basic premise that, while 'knowledge does not guarantee a political solution to public problems, without knowledge there can be little reasonable expectation for the amelioration of perennial problems such as war' and therefore tend to blend various elements of the above approaches (Vasquez 2000a: ix). Perhaps the earliest such example is Sun Tzu's (circa 544–496 BCE) *The Art of War*. This reminds us that 'war is of vital importance to the state. It is a matter of life and death, a road either to safety or to ruin. Hence it is a subject of inquiry which can on no account be neglected' (cited in, and translated by, Giles 1910: 1). Like Chanakya's (circa 350–283 BCE) *Arthasastra* a century or two later, this not only offers a complex account of battlefield strategy, but also studies the social impact of war, concluding with a passage on how best to mitigate its destructive effects and, ideally, avoid it altogether. In particular, Tzu's argument that, of the five 'fundamental factors' underpinning the course of warfare (the weather, the terrain, leadership, doctrine and morality), those under human control – the last three – must be combined and balanced to produce effective command. Such a distinction between the rational assessment of decisional outcomes and what Francis Kane later called 'intuition' or Morris Janowitz described as the 'heroic' demonstrates the long tradition of attempting to calculate the effects of logical and emotional elements in wartime decisions (Hables Gray 1997; Sion 2006). Of these, Clausewitz's unfinished work compiled following the Napoleonic Wars is arguably the greatest. For him, war is:

> composed of primordial violence, hatred, and enmity; which are to be regarded as blind natural force; of the play of chance and probability within which the creative spirit is free to roam; and of its element of subordination, as an instrument of policy, which makes it subject to reason alone.
>
> (1993: 101)

Around the same time as Tzu was writing, but on the other side of the world, the notion of rational human volition as a motive conceptually separable from the influence of fortune or divine preordination underpinned the work of many Athenian thinkers. Thucydides' (circa 460–400 BCE) account of the 27-year Peloponnesian War between Sparta and Athens, for instance, is widely considered to be the first work in which the past is analysed independently from the supernatural intervention associated with the earlier work of Herodotus (circa 484–425 BCE) and others. Thucydides, like Plato (427–347 BCE), drew a clear distinction between the use of violence in the pursuit of foreign policy objectives and the growing public disorder that was increasingly characterising this period (Price 2001). For both Plato and his student Aristotle (384–322 BCE), such civil unrest had its roots in growing levels of factionalism within Athenian society. The latter suggested that it may be a result of three fundamental causes, all of which remain pertinent today: the unequal nature of Athenian society, frustration with the weakness and incompetence of Athens' leaders and the desire for the wealth and privilege that holding political office may entail (Kalimtzis 2000).

For many Roman writers seeking to explain the causes of similar social problems, such dissent could best be dissipated through reform at the higher echelons of political society. In rejecting what he describes as 'the slave's ideal of a good master', Cicero (106–43 BCE), for instance, advocated a *concordia ordinum*, a harmonious alliance between the senators and the equites in which conflict would be resolved by selfless and honourable rule, consensus and the extension of a fraternal *omnium bonorum* to all citizens (Everitt 2001). Appian (circa 95–165) shared a similar concern to incorporate the views of the masses. His 24-volume historiography represented the perspectives of the defeated as well as the victorious by organising its narrative thematically around the histories of Rome's conquered peoples. In doing so, he succeeded, like his Greek predecessors, in demonstrating a major discontinuity between the social impact of Rome's internecine strife and life during the expansionist phases of imperial development. This not only had a profound impact on subsequent Roman historiographies (such as Cassius Dio's (circa 155–229) 80-book text), but has, in addition, influenced contemporary historians and sociologists attempting to compile synchronic accounts of the past based upon more 'bottom-up' discourses on war (Osgood 2006).

Hellenistic and Roman social commentaries were also influential in Persia under the Sassanid kings (226–650). There, a prevailing emphasis on the moral over the natural (derived from the teachings of Zoroaster) gave rise to a pronounced and eclectic interest in learning. Cities such as Gundeshapur proved an attractive centre for some of the world's foremost scholars, including eminent Jewish thinkers, Neo-Platonists displaced from Athens by Justinian in 529 and Nestorian Christians who brought Syriac translations of classical Greek works (Durant 1980). The resultant dissemination of philosophical and scientific research was extended by Muslim institutions such as the *Bayt ul-Hikma* (or House of Wisdom) founded by the Abbasi Caliph Abu Jafar al-Mamun ibn Harun (786–833) in 832. Through the work of academics, such as Al-Shaybani (?–circa 804), Al-Tabari (circa 838–923) and Al-Mawardi (circa 972–1058), codified limits (*hoddod*) to definitions of self-defence and upon battlefield behaviour were elaborated. The sciences of *tafsir* (understanding the Qu'ran) and *fiqh* (jurisprudence) emerged along-side research into the *sunnah* (the life and example of the prophet) and the lives of the *sahabah* (companions of the prophet – especially the *Khulafa ur Rashidun* or the 'rightly guided' leadership of the Caliphs Abubakr, Umar, Uthman and Ali) to produce sophisticated moral treatises on the use of violence. A Muslim was, for instance, prohibited from attacking non-combatants, destroying physical infrastructure and mistreating prisoners. Similarly, war, it was said, could be legally declared only if it was waged in defence of the faith, against a tyrant or to rescue others from repression (Hussain 2003: 51–8). These are comparable to the classical Jewish categorisation of just warfare into obligatory (those undertaken at God's behest), defensive (including the use of pre-emption) and optional (those pursued for a good reason) (Solomon 2005). Like all normative conventions, religious injunctions have, of course, been widely flouted. Nonetheless, their enduring efficacy has been demonstrated repeatedly in a wide range of contexts – from the refusal of Muslim Hutus to participate in the 1994 Rwanda genocide to the careful targeting and penal policies of some *mujahadeen* guerrilla units in Chechnya during the Russian war of the 1990s (*The Seattle Times* 9 August 2002; Yule 2000).

Similar ideas emerged within the Christian tradition. As the religion grew and gained more power in Rome, it was realised that it might become necessary to use violence to protect the innocent. Clement of Alexandria (circa 150–215), for instance, argued the need to defend the empire and to guard the position of the emperor – just cause and rightful authority in other words (Johnson 1987). These precepts were expanded and brought into contact with the work of Cicero by Saint Ambrose (circa 339–97) who helped to establish the idea that a just war could be undertaken to defend life as well as religious orthodoxy (Johnson 1987). The five-million-word corpus of Saint Augustine (354–430) – a convert from the Manichaean sect of Zoroastrianism – extended the definition of just cause to include repelling aggression, retaking something taken dishonestly and punishing wrongdoing, implying that war should be proportional, a last resort and aimed at achieving peace. During the medieval period, writers such as Gratian (circa 1140), Moses Maimonides (circa 1135–1204), Huguccio (?–circa 1210) and Saint Thomas Aquinas (1225–74) built on Augustine's voluminous work to establish an extensive revival of Roman thought (Swift 1973: 382).

The controversies of the later crusades and, particularly, the introduction of firearms towards the end of this period augured a new era of battlefield horrors which, accentuated by a rise in religious zealotry and polarisation across Europe (illustrated in the brutal subjugation of the New World and, later, the Thirty Years War), prompted a renewed interest in notions of the just war from scholars more associated with secular humanism. Here, Aquinas' suggestion (drawn from Saint Ambrose) that, even between warring parties, certain rights and covenants should be observed proved to be profoundly influential. Francisco de Vitoria (1492–1546) and Hugo Grotius

(1583–1645), for example, argued that sovereigns (ruling, as Francisco Suarez (1548–1617) propounds, not by divine right, but by the consent of the masses) should act in concert to prevent war's excesses. This should, it was suggested, be accompanied by limiting offensive war to just interventions defined by natural law and reason rather than simply by religious difference – a key premise of the modern Church's discourse on warfare today. The Holy See has, for instance, repeatedly condemned the use of religion as a justification for violence and apologised for the persecution of heretics, apostates and non-Catholics in the past. Through an unconditional condemnation of nuclear weaponry (issued by Pope John XXIII in 1963) and a recurring call for diplomacy in place of violence (most notably in Pope John Paul II's implacable opposition to Great Power policy in the Gulf), the Church has significantly narrowed its definition of what constitutes a 'just' war (Duncan 2003).

Taken together with the earlier work upon which they build, these propositions represent the philosophical underpinnings of much of what the West currently defines as the legitimate use of force in the international arena. They contain, in other words, the essence of *jus ad bellum* and *jus in bello* (Walzer 2006). The former is normally construed as the idea that sovereign states (not private armies) directed by a legitimate authority can, once all other means of redress are exhausted, use proportionate violence in response to aggression. This may be in self-defence or in the assistance of another state (or, in some extreme cases (such as genocide), a group within another state) aggressed against and must have the aim of returning to a peaceful status quo. The latter is generally understood to consist of a set of core principles guiding the conduct of warfare. Typically, these include a responsibility to distinguish between soldiers and civilians, to deploy a level of force commensurate with the tactical goal sought (thereby prohibiting certain weapons) and to adhere to generally agreed rules regarding the treatment of prisoners of war. As with other moral traditions, of course, Western states have regularly flouted these conventions (and continue to do so), but discussions of warfare remain closely connected to notions of justice (Frost 2004).

Indeed, as economic interdependence has grown during the industrial era, the kind of pooled structure of sovereignty, which could replace the signing of ad hoc peace treaties with a pacific federation of states, implied by renaissance writers and articulated more fully by Immanuel Kant (1724–1804) has gained popularity and come to underpin modern ideas of liberal internationalism (Reichberg 2002). For writers such as Norman Angell, who presciently pointed out the imminent folly of the First World War, the fact that the wealth of states is no longer held by absolute monarchs relying on the extraction of tribute renders redundant the idea that war can reduce an opponent to an inferior position. Instead, he concludes, force should be used only to increase international cooperation, in the same way as police are needed because thieves refuse to observe the normative structures of domestic communities (1910). The human and material costs of the Great War's industrialised combat convinced many that Angell (who received a Nobel Peace Prize in 1933) was correct, and his concept of collective security was, partly at least, embodied in the League of Nations and, later, the United Nations. His work also helped to establish the first chair in International Relations at Aberystwyth to investigate the 'causes of war, and the conditions of peace' in 1919, the British Institute of International Affairs in 1920 and New York's Council on Foreign Relations in 1921 (Groom 1992).

Not only did the First World War increase the attention given to the causes of large-scale conflicts, it also provoked numerous efforts to moderate the ways in which modern warfare was conducted through humanitarian intervention. Although such activity during periods of combat has a long history, the conflicts of the mid- and late Victorian age (of which the First World War was the culmination) showed an increasingly internationalised European middle class that the technical means of killing had far outstripped any sense of restraint in their application (Lawrence 1997: 31). Through the work of the Red Cross (founded in 1863) and others, conventions (especially that signed in Geneva in 1864) institutionalised battlefield access for non-combatants to organise medical treatment, to monitor the conduct of the conflict (including the use of certain types of weaponry) and to arrange prisoner exchanges. During the First World War, for instance, the Red Cross was permitted access, on the basis of its demonstrable commitment to impartiality, neutrality and independence, to over 500 penal camps where it recorded the identity of more than two million captives. In the Second World War, the Red Cross (along with Red Crescent societies) carried out nearly 13,000 such visits and, despite failing to reach an agreement with the German authorities over access to their camps, maintained a database of around 45 million prisoners of war (Wylie 2002). Since then, the size and scope of non-governmental and multilateral organisations involved in humanitarian work have, along with charitable donations and high-impact televisual reportage, enlarged considerably. The United Nations, for example, has taken on an increasingly interventionist role in world politics – from dispatching an observer mission to Palestine in 1948 to deploying an armed contingent of 28,000 'peace enforcers' to Somalia in 1993 (Jeong 2000). Today, its Office for the Coordination of Humanitarian Affairs has some 860 staff and a budget of around $110 million.

As the joint award of the 1901 Nobel Peace Prize to Henri Dunant (the founder of the Red Cross) and Frédéric Passy (the anti-war campaigner and co-founder of the Inter-Parliamentary Union) illustrated, such efforts frequently coincided with broader endeavours to prevent violence altogether. These, too, have a long history. The *Pax Dei*, or 'peace of God', for example, prohibited (from the mid-eleventh century onwards) violence in or upon consecrated people, places and occasions and was gradually extended to include women, children and other days. During the Middle Ages, the Dutch humanist and theologian Erasmus (circa 1466–1536) set out a reasoned case against warfare of all kinds, while Christian groups such as the Waldensians, the Mennonites and elements of the Religious Society of Friends (the Quakers) have continued to renounce all forms of violence – as have organisations from all other faith groups (Barash and Webel 2002). While some writers, such as Søren Kierkegaard (1813–55) and Leo Tolstoy (1828–1910), rejected organised resistance in favour of a pacifism based on individual reflection and God consciousness, other individuals have mobilised religious sentiment to achieve a considerable political impact. Prominent here have been Ghandi's *swadeshi* movement, Martin Luther King's Southern Christian Leadership Conference and the Dalai Lama's Tibetan government-in-exile. Alongside such organisations, others have achieved high levels of popular support through a non-ecclesiastical peace agenda. These include the Industrial Workers of the World (created in Chicago in 1905), the Women's International League for Peace and Freedom (founded in Washington, DC, in 1915), the War Resisters League (established in London in 1923) and the World Peace Council (convened simultaneously in Paris and Prague in 1949). Both secular and faith-based civil peace organisations – as well as the sentiments they represent – remain, as the examples of Desmond Tutu and Aung San Suu Kyi testify, profoundly influential today.

Since warfare entered the age of mass destruction weapons in 1945, the anti-nuclear movement has arguably been the largest and most vociferous of these. Early dissent took the form of a 1955 statement, signed by 11 intellectuals led by Bertrand Russell and Albert Einstein, which suggested that 'whatever agreements not to use H-bombs had been reached in time of peace, they would no longer be considered binding in time of war, and both sides would set to work to manufacture H-bombs as soon as war broke out'. Two years later, this became part of the founding charter of the Pugwash Conferences on Science and World Affairs – an international forum of scientists committed to disarmament. Having received a Nobel Peace Prize in 1995 for 'their efforts to diminish the part played by nuclear arms in international politics', it has now convened nearly 300 meetings involving over 10,000 delegates. In the United Kingdom, the Campaign for Nuclear Disarmament (established in 1958) has maintained a membership of over 50,000 for most of the last 25 years and currently claims to be Europe's biggest single-issue peace campaign (Hudson 2005). In global terms, the Nobel Peace Prize-winning (1985) International Physicians for the Prevention of Nuclear War (founded by American and Soviet cardiologists in 1980) represents one of the most internationalised movements with a membership of more than 200,000 people from over 60 countries (Wittner 2003).

However, while these organisations and the broader peace movement have been highly influential within the academic study of conflict and violence, policy making has remained dominated by the belief that reducing a state's level of war preparedness is not the most effective way to minimise the possibility of large-scale conflict. The idea of deterrence, and the school of realism that underpins it, is grounded in a clear distinction between a forceful geopolitical state and a passive domestic polity that can be traced back to the work of Dante (circa 1265–1321), Machiavelli (1469–1527) and Clausewitz (1780–1831). For strategic studies researchers such as Hans Morgenthau (1948) and George Kennan (1982), the gravest danger of war emerges not from an aggressive assertion of sovereignty, but from misperception and imbalances in the distribution of power between states. As we shall see in Chapter 9, a nuclear arsenal, along with alliances and conventional weapons, is regarded as having the potential to reduce uncertainty about a state's position and to ensure conforming behaviour in others. A hierarchy of states may emerge in which the hegemon maintains a stable and 'realistic' distribution of destructive power and alliances – ensuring, as Chapter 10 outlines, that large-scale conflicts are restricted to a (possibly cyclical) pattern of contest over the leadership position. The Hobbesian conservativism of seeing states and individuals as immutably conflictive (and therefore favouring robust precautionary and remedial measures) derives its motivational premise from a view of human beings as having an innate drive to aggress and dominate (see Chapter 5), which can be understood in terms of Darwinian biology, evolutionary psychology or settled socio-historical cultural legacies.

Such a position differs greatly from the behaviourist view of conflict, discussed in Chapter 6, as socially constructed, gendered and changing (Císař 2003). As the foundation of modern peace movements, this tends to see violent behaviour as primarily driven by environmental factors, and thus possible to extirpate. To do so, it was suggested that realism's emphasis on the Cold War's East–West balance of power as the basis of, and a threat to, global peace had to be replaced by a concern to reveal the frequently subliminal conflict between the global North and the South. As Chapter 3 explains, Marxist-influenced writing emerged in Europe and moved definitions of conflict beyond a focus on overt, behavioural hostility towards an understanding of violence as part of the normal, yet unjust, operation of the international system (Callinicos 2003). This questioned the notion that 'peace' in a world of such injustice was an objective worth pursuing. It also contained a broader definitional challenge: that relying on the narrow perceptions of actors to define their own situations inevitably obscures broader concerns and restricts the analyst to dealing with extant power relations (Lopez 1989: 69). The tension between such subjectivism and the potential dangers of its objectivist alternatives is pertinent to the social sciences in general and, along with associated debates over the different levels of investigation available to conflict analysts, is thus this book's initial point of enquiry as the primary concern of Chapter 2.

The idea that conflicts can be understood and compared at various levels of analysis – from the macro-economic forces of the global system to the limited awareness of the individual – questions another of realism's fundamental tenets: that the domestic polity is conceptually separable from international geopolitics. As increasing numbers of states in the world system produced a considerable rise in the frequency of civil wars following the Second World War (Singer and Small 1982), interest grew in the relationship between concurrent processes of modernisation and decolonisation, on the one hand, and enlarging expectations, inequality and grievance formation, on the other (Dos Santos 1970; Blum 2003). Building on the frustration–aggression model developed by social psychologists in the 1940s and prior studies on human needs, the notion of relative deprivation, the focus of Chapter 7, emerged as a key means of explaining the civil unrest of the period. This prompted a re-evaluation of earlier work dealing with the functionality of conflictive behaviour, particularly political elites' use of conflict – both domestically as a means of identifying an 'other' through which an enhanced sense of 'self' may be constructed and internationally as a similarly specious method of distraction. The causes of conflict, as Chapter 4 demonstrates, may thus be found in rulers' desires to maintain their domestic authority (Miller 1999). Indeed, the mobilisation of individuals into social movements, national groups or bands of insurgents (to be considered in Chapter 8) may be regarded as a better way to explain the causes of collective violence than motivational studies of unrealised expectations or perceived frustrations that do not account for power differentials and individuals' rational calculation of costs, benefits and probabilities of success (Buechler 1999).

Interest in a section of this latter body of work – the so-called 'greed' thesis – has, to the detriment of other theories of group mobilisation, been sharpened by the perceived 'end of old-fashioned war between states' in favour of 'new wars' (Kaldor 2001: 1). These are characterised as deliberately focused upon civilians as a source of revenue (whose share of total fatalities has increased from around half during the 1960s to over 90 per cent by the early 1990s) and organised by avaricious conflict 'entrepreneurs' (Collier *et al.* 2003). Recent studies have therefore tended to place responsibility for such bloodshed largely upon the shoulders of local agents. This has, in many cases, produced depictions of contemporary conflicts 'as explicable simply by reference to the narcissism of violence', leading to absurd portrayals of 'perpetually recidivist societies' where 'torture is exciting, rape is fun, and looting is profitable' and which can only be salvaged through the 'imposition of imperial order' (Gray 1999: 277; Shawcross 2000: 169–78; Cooper 2005: 464–5). The result is a partial abandonment of the intellectual pursuit of 'why' conflicts start in favour of 'how to' organise a response.

This book is, in many ways, an attempt to return to 'why' questions as the bedrock of conflict analysis. At the heart of preserving a wide-reaching and independent discipline is the maintenance of a rich theoretical tradition and, in particular, a broad understanding of the range of approaches to analysing conflict instigation. What follows, then, is not intended to be a mere list of possibly relevant topics. Instead, it is nine inter-related – and sometimes oppositional – ways of theorising the causes of conflict and violence (italicised below) which, together, constitute a comprehensive (though not exhaustive) account of why different conflictive phenomena arise. Based on around 900 academic sources drawn from more than half a century of research within numerous academic traditions, this study proceeds by initially considering the *dimensions*, and difficulties, of defining conflict at various levels of analysis, before examining the notion of *structure* as a fundamental challenge to the way in which conflict and violence is commonly understood. The idea that the normal operation of the international system is intrinsically violent leads to a more thorough treatment of who benefits from conflict – its *functions* in other words. A key element in both the functional creation of enhanced in-group coherence and the legitimisation of aggressive foreign policies is the idea that there is an *innate* basis to ethnic or national solidarity born of the immutably conflictive nature of the human condition.

Alternatively, understanding conflict and violence as essentially *learnt* could reveal the ways in which individuals and groups are organised into conflictive entities by elites. Neither of these approaches, however, explains why the masses should wish to follow elites. Here, participation in organised forms of conflictive behaviour may be determined by the presence of *grievances* born of the unequal division of material wealth and social status or by the *mobilisation* of individuals' rational assessment of the prospective benefits that conflict and violence might offer. Indeed, the distribution of resources through the international system can also be understood to be the fundamental cause of conflict and violence. Just as individuals perceiving themselves to be threatened seek to improve security and lower their isolation levels, so states respond to geopolitical pressures – particularly *crises* – by acquiring weapons and forming alliances. These patterns of interaction have produced hierarchical power blocs within and across which warfare has been used to attain or defend *hegemony*, producing ever more severe instances of violent conflict and raising the possibility that the next great contest over global leadership may be the last.

2 Dimensions

Explaining why people engage in violent conflict has, as the previous chapter outlined, absorbed academic thought for a great many years and has given rise to a wide range of deliberations. Not least among these are the problems of comparing conflicts at an abstract level, identifying conflicts' component parts, defining what a 'conflict' means and locating conflicts at various levels of social interaction. This chapter proposes to introduce the reader to some of the more significant elements of these discussions. It first presents some ideas surrounding the problem of approaching conflict *generally* by looking at the evolution of the literature concerning conflict dimensions. Here, there continues to be considerable debate. Analysts disagree over how conflicts can be identified, their origins, their consequences and even whether or not they necessarily involve violence or aggression. Second, it will discuss issues surrounding the definition of conflict. This is subject to a broader divide within the social sciences; namely, between approaches that emphasise the importance of actors' perceptions and those which argue that conflicts and other observable social phenomena can be present and influential without the self-awareness of those involved. Third, it will consider the 'levels of analysis' issue in conflict studies, first put forward by Kenneth Waltz in 1959 in his book *Man, the State and War*. It will deal with the different analytical implications of examining conflicts from various viewpoints, from intrapersonal dissonance to interpersonal disputes, civil unrest, interstate war and global conflagrations. As such, looking at these three topics – generalising about conflict, definitional debates and the unit of analysis – will help to introduce concerns that run right through the rest of the book.

Generalising about conflict

A truly *general* model necessitates the development of analytical categories into which *all* examples of conflicts, regardless of whether or not they evoke violent behaviour, can be placed. A common attempt to do this, outlined in this section, is the triangular typology developed by Christopher Mitchell (1981a) from the work of one of the pioneers of conflict studies, Johan

Galtung, who first presented it to the Peace Research Institute in Oslo during January 1968. This breaks conflicts down into situation, behaviour and attitudes, with each heavily influencing the others (Figure 2.1). Under Mitchell's definition, a conflictive situation is considered to be 'any situation in which two or more social entities or "parties" (however defined or structured) perceive that they possess mutually incompatible goals' (1981a: 17). From the subjectivist perspective (to be discussed further shortly), this remains a common definition. For instance, Louis Kriesberg defines a conflict as occurring 'when two or more persons or groups manifest the belief that they have incompatible objectives' (1998: 2).

Fundamental to this type of approach is the inclusion of non-violent forms of conflict. Both the above definitions could apply to parent–child relationships, competitive sport, contact between ethnic groups or a breakdown in diplomatic affairs between two states. In all these instances, a crucial component is *incompatibility*. This means that individuals or groups, commonly called 'actors' or 'parties', think that the realisation of one or more of their goals is being, or will be, thwarted by another party. These may be *positive* in that they refer to a desired outcome or *negative* if they relate to the avoidance of an unwanted future. The value of these goals to the actors involved determines the *intensity* of the conflict. The number of goals that each actor perceives to have been thwarted demarcates the *scope* of the conflict (although, of course, the perception of these goals within the constituent elements of each party may be very different). If others become involved in the conflictive situation or the value of the goals in dispute increases, then the conflict will *escalate* and its *domain* will be extended – an important process in the development of international crises (to be discussed further in Chapter 9).

Conflictive situations need not, however, be grounded upon actual issues or events. While *realistic* conflicts are based on past occurrences that have led to the perception of incompatible goals and conflicts of various intensities and scopes, *unrealistic* conflicts may emerge from misperceptions and confusion, or may be pursued for the sake of conflict participation rather than any particular goals. Evidence suggests that the majority of conflictive

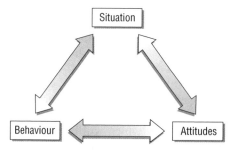

Figure 2.1 The structure of conflict. Source: Redrawn from Mitchell (1981a: 16).

situations contain both realistic and unrealistic elements. They also tend to involve the expectation of *zero-sum* and *variable-sum* outcomes. The former relates to circumstances in which the total benefit to all actors always adds up to zero. In other words, no gain can accrue to one party without an equal loss to another. It is typified by conflicts perceived to be based upon limited resources, such as land in Palestine or diamonds in Sierra Leone. The latter involves conflicts over goods which are not, inherently, in short supply – such as status, legitimacy, religious expression and dignity – and so do not, theoretically at least, inevitably mean that one actor must lose in order for another to gain. In this sense, perceptions of scarcity within conflictive situations may be over *material* goods like oil, lootable objects and so on or *positional* goods such as access to political representation and economic management.

There are also qualitative differences in the type of goal pursued which determine the nature of a conflictive situation. Different *interests* may lead to conflict, although parties basically concur about the value of some position, role or resource and the various factors that may have led them to disagree. Conflict here arises over issues of distribution within a broadly agreed framework. Examples might be a husband and wife arguing without considering divorce or academics discussing their profession while agreeing that higher education provisions are worthwhile. Consequently, a compromise is usually possible. On the other hand, conflicts of *value* exist when parties differ fundamentally about the nature of desirable end-states or social and political structures. The conflictive relationship between the goals of the World Trade Organization and the Anti-Globalization Movement is an example of this, although, as Anthony de Reuck points out, 'the distinction is rarely clear-cut' (1984: 97). Within the latter, there is liable to be a conflict over what has given rise to the set of circumstances from which a dispute or problem has arisen – the question of *attribution*. Here, parties may hold each other or a third party responsible. Protagonists are also likely to disagree over the best *means* of dealing with the problem – often stemming from a different view of its causes. The ways in which interests, value, attribution and means interrelate within a conflictive situation are illustrated in Table 2.1.

Conflictive attitudes are closely related to conflictive situations. Mitchell defines them as 'common patterns of expectation, emotional orientation and perception that accompany involvement in a conflict situation' (1981a: 28). Here, anger, resentment and suspicion are common, as are cognitive processes such as stereotyping and selective approaches to new information. These frequently become self-perpetuating in the sense that previous experiences of a conflict will reinforce or exaggerate conflictive attitudes in the future. As a source of conflict, attitudes, in the form of internal drives and thoughts, may push individuals towards conflictive behaviour. In this sense, there is a fundamental division (which will be looked at in more detail in Chapters 5 and 6) between analyses that focus upon actors' response to their

Table 2.1 Aspects of conflictive situations

Conflict aspects	Agreement on basic values and ends	Agreement on causes
Value	No	No
Interest	Yes	Yes
Attribution	Yes	No
Means	Yes	Either

Source: Mitchell (1981a: 42).

environments and studies which emphasise inherent physiological, psychological or cultural states – between, in other words, writers who hold the attitudinal point of Mitchell's triangle over the situational point as the prime causal location of conflictive behaviour. Indeed, such a division has major consequences for the way in which conflicts are approached both theoretically and practically. If conflicts are considered to be driven by the cathartic release of inherent drives, for instance, then there may not be clearly defined interests and values amenable to analysis. It may thus be concluded that the conflictive situation is largely unrealistic and, as discussed towards the end of Chapter 1, the search for causality may ultimately be futile.

In keeping with the inter-related nature of Mitchell's model, conflictive attitudes are also acutely influenced by conflictive situations and behaviour. As conflicts progress, changes in group identity are common, as we shall see in Chapter 4. As individuals tend to seek security and prestige in identifying with others, threats to the values of the group frequently become a threat to the individual. In this way, group affiliation can help individuals to rationalise their behaviour and to dismiss contra-information. In the case of violent conflict, a commonplace consequence of such attitudinal change is the legitimisation of *transference* and *displacement*. The former occurs when violence becomes directed at an object or actor resembling the perceived source of goal incompatibility. This may be highly illogical and turn inwards towards members of the group itself. Following the German football team's defeat of England during the European Championship of 1996, for instance, German brands of automobile belonging to other England supporters were deliberately damaged near locations where the game was being watched in the UK. Displacement, on the other hand, is where violence is directed at any convenient object/person regardless of their connection to the perceived source of goal incompatibility (however tenuous). An instance of this is the old circular adage of domestic violence where a delay in social security payment leads the claimant to beat his wife, who then slaps her children, who then kick the dog, which then bites the postman, who then does not deliver the husband's social security cheque, and so on and so on. Here, conflictive behaviour, driven by an initial source of goal incompatibility, is focused on the handiest rather than the most culpable, thus ensuring the future occurrence of the same goal incompatibility and perpetuating the conflictive situation.

Reciprocally connected to changes in conflictive attitudes is conflictive behaviour. This is defined by Mitchell as 'actions undertaken by one party in any situation of conflict aimed at the opposing party with the intention of making that party abandon or modify its goals' (1981a: 29). It may also originate in an intention to punish an opponent for a real or perceived previous action. The way that intention is measured, however, is highly problematic. This is because each of the three parties who may make such an evaluation is extremely unlikely to do so in any unbiased way. The actor, an observing third party and the target of a conflictive act all tend to have a vested interest in the dynamics, or outcome, of the conflict itself. Intentions observed by any of these three parties may, themselves, be realised by a combination of three strategies. First, threatening or imposing an unacceptable level of costs upon another actor will succeed if the intimidation is credible, if something of value is imperilled and if there is no obvious way of ignoring, or circumventing, the pressure. The overwhelming form that this strategy takes is coercion – either verbal or physical. A second form of conflictive behaviour involves offering or proposing alternative courses of action. This typically entails the use of *persuasion*: pointing out, in other words, favourable outcomes to a certain course of action that the opponent may not have considered or, alternatively, showing that agreement is to *their* advantage. A third type of conflictive behaviour is the abandonment of some or all of the actor's own goals – often through the involvement of bilateral or third-party brokered negotiations.

Thus, it may be seen that a general model of conflict frequently takes the occurrence of goal incompatibility as the starting point from which a conflict becomes manifest and each of three elements – situation, attitudes and behaviour – begin to interact. Conflictive behaviour (particularly if very violent) can, for instance, harden attitudes, increase in-group cohesion and widen both the issues at stake and the number of actors involved, thereby altering the conflictive situation. Equally, conflictive situations tend to alter behaviour as frustrated goals lead to enlarged efforts at goal realisation or, as new issues and actors increase, mistrust and suspicion. Conflictive attitudes also affect behaviour as increased wariness strengthens defensive preparations and plans which, in turn, modify the situation by lengthening the duration of the confrontation. As such, resolving conflicts must involve all three aspects. Actors achieving attitudinal integration will develop a consensus, those attaining behavioural integration will conform and those accomplishing situational integration will realise goal compatibility.

Defining conflicts

General models also tend to contain three elements apparent before the manifestation of conflictive behaviour. In the case of Mitchell's work, these are, as Figure 2.2 illustrates, incipient, latent and suppressed conflict (1981a: 51). The first can broadly be regarded as a situation in which a conflict is not recognised by one or both parties. The second emerges when goal incompatibility is perceived, but not sufficiently motivating to give rise to observable conflictive behaviour. In the third scenario, one or more parties are aware of a conflictive situation, but the costs of pursuing their goals are too high to produce conflictive behaviour. In Mitchell's model, these three elements are not, however, theorised. Broadly speaking, he and others who adopt a subjectivist approach to identifying conflicts argue that actors must not only *believe* that they are in a conflictive situation, they must also *manifest* this belief in a way discernible to others. This position is subjectivist in the sense that it relies on the actors, or *subjects*, involved in the conflict to define their situation as conflictive.

An alternative approach to relying on the actors' own perceptions is to define what constitutes a conflictive situation itself – the *object* as opposed to the subject. It is often argued that this offers a more inclusive way of identifying conflicts as it takes into account the frequently imperceptible formations which surround actors. In this sense, conflicts are 'not seen as a matter of subjective definition but as determined by the social structure. In other words, conflict is incompatible interests built into the structure of the system where conflict is located' (Schmid 1968: 226). Such a 'maximalist' agenda includes 'the effects of social and economic exploitation' within a definition of a conflictive situation – regardless of whether or not this is perceived by those involved (Rogers and Ramsbotham 1999: 744). A slave may not, for instance, be aware that she is in a conflictive relationship with her mistress. This may be particularly well hidden if the mistress defines the role of the slave and teaches her that being a slave is part of the normal or natural way of the world. The slave is unlikely to question its legitimacy so long as the mistress reinforces the structure of their relationship with kindness and

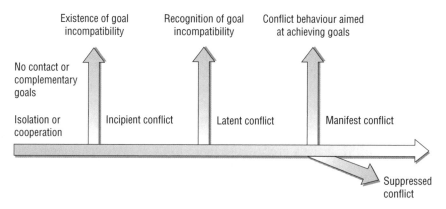

Figure 2.2 Conflict processes. Source: Adapted from Mitchell (1981a: 51).

palliatives. The result may be that the slave feels devotion to her mistress and may, if offered, reject the chance of freedom. Thus, the relationship between the two is cooperative. Both actors conform to agreed rules, and there is little or no conflict over values, interests, goods and so on. For a subjectivist, this situation can only be identified as incipient, latent or suppressed and is thus not, for the most part, the subject matter of the conflict analyst. It is, in other words, 'peace'.

Such a view has considerable implications. If, for instance, the slave perceives that she is in a conflictive situation and acts by effecting some form of conflictive behaviour, then, according to the subjectivist position, she has changed her goals and manifested a conflict. By implication, then, it is her behaviour that is the primary concern of the conflict analyst rather than the role of the mistress or the nature of their relationship. As Anthony de Reuck puts it, 'the first party whose conflict behaviour becomes conscious and deliberate is often labelled the aggressor, whether or not he is the aggrieved party' (1984: 100–1). This is obviously problematic, as it suggests an assumption that conflictive behaviour represents an unwelcome event per se and that it is the role of the analyst to try to find ways of reducing the intensity of this behaviour, rather than to attempt a reconstruction of the conflictive relationship itself.

A further problem with the subjectivist position is that the differences in power that exist between conflict actors are often ignored in favour of the presumption of a shared commitment to 'peace'. As, in order to analyse different aspects of conflictive situations, attitudes and behaviour accurately and ultimately suggest ways of reducing the intensity of that conflict, the researcher must have comparable levels of access to the actors involved, subjectivist models mostly advocate various notions of neutrality; an idea that is supported by the adherence to the idea that the *subjects* themselves must provide the contextual details of the conflict (Burton and Dukes 1990). By and large, then, it is assumed that it is both possible and desirable for the researcher to be positioned equidistantly from each of the conflict actors. Of course, some conflicts, such as the Cold War confrontation between the Warsaw Pact and the West, do involve approximate power parity, and thus may, for researchers from non-aligned states, offer a viable, 'neutral' ground roughly halfway between each. Mostly, though, conflicts are between parties with asymmetrical capabilities.

So, in terms of power, to be equidistant from each actor, the researcher must, as Herman Schmid has observed, actually be closer to the less powerful party in order to be in a mutually neutral space (1968). However, is such a location likely when the powerful are both better equipped to commit resources to the analysis process and more likely to welcome a return to the pre-existent situation? To explain this, Keith Webb offers the example of an industrial dispute in which a conflict analyst is only acceptable to the management if she accepts the basic structure, and inherent inequalities, of capitalist production and exchange. Bringing an end to the dispute can thus only hope 'to restore the status quo, leaving the relationship still asymmetrical' (Webb 1986: 432). So, given such power differentials, Schmid is perhaps correct to assert that the subjectivists' 'claim of political neutrality is hardly satisfied by leaving the evaluations to the decision-makers' (1968: 220).

The concept of a collective dedication to peace is similarly tricky. Even where parties possess broad power parity, as in the bipolar blocs of the Cold War, it is uncommon that a shared commitment to a *positive* future is sufficiently potent to provide a normative basis for a reduction in conflict intensity. Subjectivist analyses of conflict therefore often resort to the 'minimalist' objective of war avoidance – in this case, the universally catastrophic effects of a Superpower nuclear exchange (Rogers and Ramsbotham 1999: 744). The fear of a mutually harmful outcome is thus presented as the primary grounds for the work of the conflict analyst, for the tractability of the conflict itself and for the amenability of the conflict actors. For many, though, the mere absence of overt, behavioural violence does not constitute a satisfactory definition of peace. Adam Curle, for instance, suggests that accepting such a *negative* notion of peace frequently becomes a means for more powerful parties to obscure *objective* goal incompatibilities. He points to the South African government's policy of granting a number of 'Bantustan' settlements some degree of autonomy during apartheid. Although these had, by 1994, been abolished and reabsorbed into the South African state, 'the illusion of a certain degree of independence for the non-whites blunt[ed] perceptions of the deep conflict of interest between black and white South Africans' (Curle 1971: 9).

As a negative peace may not have any actual manifest conflict, a positive peace is not merely an absence of conflictive behaviour, but involves cooperative relations leading to an end to the exploitation of the powerless by the powerful. Curle puts it like this:

> a peaceful relationship would, on a personal scale, mean friendship and understanding sufficiently strong to overcome any differences that might occur. On a larger scale, peaceful relationships would imply active association, planned cooperation, an intelligent effort to forestall or resolve potential conflict.
>
> (1971: 15)

Such a future, does not, for Curle, necessarily imply an idealistic egalitarianism or a vision of future socialism. Positive peace may contain goal incompatibilities born of varying power capabilities and access to material resources. The key difference lies in the management of the difference in power. For Curle's positive peace, the powerless are helped to develop their capabilities by the powerful. An example might be a parent–child relationship or a pluralist society in which latent, incipient and suppressed conflicts do not emerge.

Herman Schmid offers a different perspective. He argues that, first, inequitable structures and institutions, which are broadly accepted by Curle and others, are a fundamental part of any given conflictive situation. Second, he suggests that the way in which these are understood is primarily drawn from 'the wealth of social science theory developed for the control and integration of the national system' and is thus a component of conflictive attitudes (1968: 219). Consequently, conflict studies should not, he continues, simply attempt to analyse conflicts, nor should they seek to make policy recommendations to governments who frequently represent the powerful side of an asymmetrical conflict. The fact that the bulk of this type of research is located in, and frequently directly financed by, the United States and northern Europe – those with the greatest vested interest in maintaining the status quo – adds considerable credence to Schmid's position. The overall result, he suggests, is that conflict analysts have a strong propensity to adopt 'a system perspective and a value orientation which is identical with those of the existing international institutions and lies very close to those of the rich and powerful nations' (Schmid 1968: 221). Given that, throughout history, positive social change has generally occurred through an increase in conflict levels rather than a decline, should, Schmid asks, conflict analysts continue to advocate reductions in conflict intensities?

In conclusion, it is clear that the objectivist critique of subjectivism is both comprehensive and an ongoing feature of the discipline. It has not, however, passed without rebuttal. As Mitchell notes, objectivism's tendency to conflate inequality with conflict contains the real danger that the peculiar importance of conflict analysis is lost within broader discourses on the egregious effects of injustice and imparity – a particular problem for notions of structural violence discussed in Chapter 3 (1981b). Moreover, does differential status and wealth inevitably imply an incompatibility of goals? The elites of the developing world are, for instance, mostly poorer and less powerful than the elites of the West, yet does this mean that there is a conflict between them while both are prospering from the international terms of trade and relations of production? Simply because actors operate within an unequal environment, it does not self-evidently follow that they will wish to redress the inequities of the negative peace in which they operate. To assume that they are blind to the 'objective' truth of their position is, it has been claimed, to give conflict research 'the qualities of an intellectual black hole' (Lawler 1995: 237). Moreover, such a positivist faith in a 'reality' obvious only to the initiated contains the danger that conflict analysts will arrogantly export their vision of equality, peace, etc. without regard for contextual specificity, thereby escalating, or even fomenting, conflictive behaviour – Schmid's ultimate conclusion. As adherents of the objectivist position are neither free from value-driven judgement nor able to predict the outcome of any change in social structures and institutions, they tend to become entrapped by their own critique of subjectivism. In other words, they too attempt to base their analysis on questionably universal notions of a positive future, in this case the value of wholesale systemic change.

Levels of analysis

The following section presents an overview of some of the ways in which these controversies and ideas have been structured by attempts to identify the causes of conflict at various levels of analysis, first put forward by Waltz in 1959. He suggested that the causes of conflict could be found within three different, but interlinked, social strata – the individual, the state and the international system. Since then, commentators have expanded these to include various substate and supranational groupings which, depending on the research question posed, can be employed as taxonomical devices to categorise and compare instances of conflict. Sometimes, these may be discrete and distinct. Assessing macro-changes in the frequency of warfare over the last few centuries would, for example, clearly necessitate studies linked to the level of the system, whereas the reasons for a government choosing certain foreign policy options would tend to lead the analyst towards a concentration upon state-level concerns. It is, however, generally not necessary to include all levels in an analysis and, most often, conflicts are examined as an interaction of a number of different levels. Liberal theories of economic competition, for instance, combine models of global exchange with both state-based processes of expansion and recession and rational actor accounts of individual behaviour (Hayek 1991).

Indeed, as Table 2.2 illustrates, conflicts frequently take different forms at different levels as they proceed. In this case, it would appear that the actors' values are, in Mitchell's terms, going through a process of intensification followed by de-intensification, thereby causing the conflictive situation to escalate, de-escalate and, ultimately, to end in some reparatory interaction. Categorising conflictive behaviour like this offers a fruitful way of considering inter-relations between various parties. Each row represents a particular way in which actors respond to goal incompatibility. Costs and benefits are conferred or withheld, through either action or threat. Each column shows how this behaviour may be manifested at different social levels. The first of these outlines a common pattern of interpersonal conflictive behaviour, while the second and third columns use the example of industrial and international relations respectively.

At both the systemic and the state levels of analysis, a longstanding tension has existed between realist, liberal and socialist traditions. As an approach to foreign policy, the first tends to take states to be the key actors and assumes that they attempt to behave rationally and to advance their security and wealth in an environment which, in the absence of a legitimate source of coercive power (a police force in other words), is perceived to be anarchic and intrinsically threatening (Levy 1996). As wealth is born of trade, which in turn relies on pacific markets, it is thus argued that the primary role of governments operating at the international level should be to ensure their country's own defence through armaments (Sheehan 1996). To do this, assessments of other states' power should proceed on the basis of 'worst-case

Table 2.2 Types of conflict process

	Conflict level		
Conflict behaviour	Individual	Collective	International
Reduce benefits to adversary	Reduce contact with person	Work to rule	Delay aid deliveries
End interaction with adversary	Send to Coventry	Strike	Stop aid, trade and diplomacy
Begin imposing costs on adversary	Insult person	Prosecute union leaders	Confiscate local assets
Intensify cost imposition	Physically assault person	Hire violent strike-breakers	Deploy armed forces
Reduce cost imposition	End aggression outside self-defence	End strikers' sit-in	Reduce conflict intensity
End cost imposition	End all aggression	Stop prosecution	Armistice
Begin benefit-conferring action	Find excuses for adversary's conduct	Limited return to work	Resume diplomacy aid and trade
Intensify benefit-conferring action	Praise adversary	Improve pay and conditions	Increase trade and aid to new levels

Source: Adapted from Mitchell (1981a: 127).

scenario' reasoning. Only then will a state be sufficiently prepared to accomplish goals that are incompatible with others'. Achieving these generally involves the extensive use of threats, brinkmanship and coercion. Conflicts may, therefore, result from a policy preference deliberately pursued, incompetence and failures of rational predictions or, as the notion of the 'security dilemma' (discussed in Chapter 9) suggests, an accidental outcome of a rational strategy of loss avoidance (Cox 1996).

In this sense, conflicts emerge from the absence of generally agreed upon and authoritative regulation. For Waltz, states seek order and stability by attempting to institutionalise a durable balance of power in which equal blocs of alliances maintain peace through a combination of satisfying the security concerns of their members and intimidating potentially recalcitrant non-members (1979). At the level of the international system, these are, as Chapter 10 outlines, particularly stable if there is a clear hierarchical equilibrium within each bloc as well as between blocs. The Cold War is often cited as approaching an example of this, although uncertainty over the alignment of many peripheral countries produced numerous proxy conflicts outside the more fundamental confrontation between the United States and the Soviet Union. When the hierarchical equilibrium of the Warsaw Pact collapsed in 1989, this bipolarity was replaced by a period of considerable instability with an accompanying rise in conflictive behaviour within former client states, which peaked in 1992 (Wallensteen and Sollenberg 2000). If the Eastern bloc had still been a credible balancing force in 1990, for instance, it is unclear whether the Western bloc would have responded to Iraq's invasion of Kuwait with the same wholesale destruction of the Iraqi military, the same merciless siege and the same prolonged occupation of the Gulf.

Particularly dangerous to this notion of a balanced international order is, for Waltz, the emergence of a single hegemon or hegemonic bloc (1979). He argues that this unipolar arrangement threatens all who are outside its goal orientation, leading to a rise in insecurity, an increase in armament purchasing and the creation of new and aggressive alliances. For some, the growth of internationalised conflicts during the 1970s was an indication of the United States' intensifying hegemony (Harbom and Wallensteen 2005). More recently, the French government's cooperation with Germany during the run-up to the 2003 Iraq war to ensure that the United Nations' Security Council did not pass a resolution legalising the forthcoming conflict can, for instance, be seen as an attempt to prevent the further strengthening of American leadership. Furthermore, if unipolarity is stabilised through the establishment of norms that protect the position of the hegemon, it is frequently argued that a large-scale conflict of great severity becomes more likely. As we shall see in Chapter 10, this is because the ability of the hegemon to dominate the international order inevitably declines, prompting either a speculative war from their nearest rival or a pre-emptive war from the hegemon itself (Kugler and Lemke 2000). Both would, of course, have catastrophic results. In all then, realist interpretations at the systemic level of analysis tend to see conflict as a consequence of three inter-related features of the system itself – the inherently uneven and chaotic nature of geopolitics, the constantly shifting relative power of military force and the changing objectives of states.

In contrast, liberal approaches to the international system point to the failure of realism to predict repeated catastrophic conflicts and the inherent danger that such an outlook might provoke these through misperception and error. Instead, conflict analysis should focus on the considerable commonalities between states struggling with the shared uncertainties of the geopolitical arena (Jeong 2000: 297–9). Order should, it is proposed, rest on the twin pillars of democracy and economic cooperaion, which are themselves grounded upon an optimistic view of the human character as non-violent and resistant to imposed authority. As Boutros Boutros-Ghali describes the former, 'there is an obvious connection between democratic practices – such as the rule of law and transparency in decision-making – and the achievement of true peace and security' (1992: 5). Unlike realism, this proposes an association between the character of domestic polities and the external behaviour of the state. Just as individuals within states are, as Chapter 7 explains, less likely to rebel if their needs are meet, it is improbable that states within the international system will behave belligerently if their leaders are accountable for their actions (MacGinty 2006).

The liberal vision of the international level of analysis also reserves an important place for free trade in the creation and maintenance of systemic peace. This was evident in Woodrow Wilson's call for 'the removal, so far as possible, of all economic barriers and the establishment of an equality of trade conditions among all the nations consenting to the peace' that followed the First World War (cited in Kindleberger 1977: 402). Similarly, the 1941 Atlantic Charter, which formulated the basis for Anglo-American cooperation during the Second World War, was grounded upon a need to restore to all states 'access, on equal terms, to the trade and to the raw materials of the world which are needed for their economic prosperity' (cited in Whelan and Donnelly 2006: 4). After both wars, attempts were made to create complex structures of economic interdependence between sovereign states that would minimise the fluxes in relative power which underpin the realist paradigm and, as it is irrational to bomb your own bank (as Swiss neutrality demonstrates), create a disincentive for war. Although the security imperatives of the Cold War frequently meant that the liquidity of foreign capital was obstructed, markets were gradually deregulated and public sectors privatised – especially following the United States' shift towards monetarism during the early 1980s. More recently, President Bush and the White House have reiterated the fundamentals of the liberal peace by explaining that 'across the globe, free markets and trade have helped defeat poverty, and taught men and women the habits of liberty'. They are the 'real freedom, the freedom for a person – or a nation – to make a living' (cited in Jacoby 2005: 226).

In both their realist and their liberal forms, these systemic-level analyses all tend to be restricted by very general assumptions about states' foreign policy objectives. All, for instance, are seen as rationally pursuing their objectives in a value-maximising way, yet, as we shall see in Chapter 9, such a premise may not always offer an accurate assessment of how decisions are made. For this reason, it is difficult for writers using this level of analysis to account for major variations in governmental approaches, a problem that has maintained interest in the state as a discrete level of analysis. A key tenet here is the relationship between domestic forces within states and the leadership of the state itself. For Lenin, this is clear. The state is no more than a committee of the bourgeoisie driven towards conflictive behaviour by the inherent contradictions of capitalism. These, he suggested in his 1916 pamphlet, *Imperialism: The Highest Form of Capitalism*, were to be found in the ever greater concentration of capital in corporate hands. Over 50 per cent of American production was, he suggests, controlled by 1.1 per cent of the country's businesses in 1904. Evidently, such economic might could not be ignored by political decision-makers who, he continues, were guided into the First World War by the exhaustion of domestic markets.

Although they remain influential, these types of Marxist understanding of the state level of analysis have been heavily criticised as excessively deterministic. Political domination cannot, it is argued, be reduced to economic tendencies. To do so would be to ignore historical contingency, non-Western patterns of leadership, the role of fundamentally non-economic lobbies (such as Zionism) and the ideological proclivities of decision-makers (Willoughby 1995). An alternative perspective, perhaps most comprehensively elucidated in Bob Altemeyer's revival of Theodore Adorno's notion of the 'authoritarian personality' (1998), is to emphasise the internal processes of individual actors and the way in which these are modified in relation to their environment. Here, the view that an actor's propensity to engage in conflict is *caused* by 'socially and culturally influenced socialisation and family structure [is] completely discarded' (Duckitt 2000: 91). Instead, actors' tendency to behave in very different ways from each other in quite similar situations is explained by their different values and personalities developed individualistically. However, these can have a measurable impact only if they are implemented with the cooperation, or despite the opposition, of others. Conflicts thus emerge from the way in which personal attributes are mediated through the relationships that surround decision-makers. The focus on how policy is formulated and decisions are reached at this individual level of analysis is, therefore, often grounded on variables such as personal rationality, worldview, prejudice and insularity. An example of how such an approach might analyse the Iran–Iraq War is offered in Table 2.3 (Goldstein 1984; Post 1993).

When compared with the state and international levels of analysis, approaches based on individual preference can, as Jack Levy points out, facilitate 'the construction of richer and more descriptively accurate theories of international conflict' (1996: 16). They are, for instance, less tied to notions

Table 2.3 Iran–Iraq war (individual level of analysis)

Iran	Iraq
Khomeini came from a relatively well-off background	Hussein came from abject poverty
Khomeini came from an eminent family descended from other famous imams	Hussein came from an inconsequential and violently dysfunctional family
Khomeini's ideology was religious and revivalist	Hussein's ideology was *Ba'athism* – a secular blend of socialism and pan-Arab nationalism
Khomeini was a cleric	Hussein was a party official
Khomeini came to power in a hugely popular revolution	Hussein came to power by organising the mass execution of the government
Khomeini was widely loved by Iranians	Hussein was widely feared by Iraqis
Khomeini was a Shia supported by the notion of the *Mahdi* (divinely inspired leader)	Hussein was a Sunni and thus restrained (in theory) by notions of *shura* (popular consent)
Khomeini was a highly educated scholar	Hussein was not well educated
Khomeini was supported by the Soviets against the Shah	Hussein was supported by the West and the Soviets

of unitary action and more conscious of the misperceptions and professional failings, and thus the unpredictability, of individual decision-makers. As we shall see when looking at Allison's account of the Cuban Missile Crisis in Chapter 9, leaders may, for instance, either over- or underestimate opponents' strength. The former error tends to exacerbate their sense of insecurity and provoke an increase in conflict planning. Underestimation, on the other hand, may lower preparation, reduce deterrence and lead either to conflictive behaviour based on the anticipation that the opponent will back down or to the opponent initiating a pre-emptive action. Either error can also produce a false expectation that a third party will intervene on the actor's own side, on the side of the opponent or in an attempt to lower conflict intensities (Jervis 1988). Such complexity does, however, mean that, in general, studies grounded upon the individual level of analysis are 'less elegant or parsimonious, more demanding in terms of the types of data that are necessary to test them, and less powerful in terms of their generalizability across different states in different situations at different times' (Levy 1996: 16). These rigorous requirements are certainly not always met. Assessing individuals' internal mental processes is something of a challenge, to say the least. Even if this is achieved convincingly, there is also a danger of overemphasising individual autonomy, ignoring the structural constraints that surround decision-makers and squeezing characterisations into imprecise and arbitrary typologies (Wayne 1993: 30).

Conclusion

In keeping with the rest of the book, this chapter has covered an eclectic selection of literature dealing with a wide range of debates and problems broadly connected to the difficulty of undertaking conflict research. In particular, it has looked at three aspects of conflict dimensions. The first relates to the existence of fundamental insights that seem to be true of *all* conflicts – an attempt, in other words, to identify essential patterns of similarity between ostensibly very different social phenomena. Iraq's invasion of Kuwait, the Khmer Rouge's activism in Cambodia, the French Revolution and domestic violence may appear to be utterly unlike, yet at their heart lies a basic struggle for status recognition, for resources or, even more broadly, for the realisation of an incompatible set of goals. To make sense of this, Mitchell's triangular model of situation, behaviour and attitudes is, this chapter has suggested, an efficacious means of understanding both the various elements that make up an analysis of a conflict and the ways in which these change over time.

The second section above highlighted some of the implications of analysing the components and dynamics of conflictive behaviour, attitudes and situations. Here, a fundamental divide was noted and explained. On the one side, the need to empower protagonists to respond to their own social environment underpins a tendency to define a conflictive situation as existent only at the point of actor perception; when, in other words, conflictive behaviour manifests itself. By and large, this approach focuses on the demonstrable actions of *subjects*, thereby maintaining an interest in the 'minimal' objective of reducing conflict intensities and scope as the foremost priority of the parties involved. Objectivism, by contrast, tends to concentrate on the conflict as a definitional unit commonly independent of parties' perceptions and often identifiable only by a third party. Conflictive situations can, therefore, be latent, hidden from view or endemic to the 'normal' functioning of society. Such ideas are frequently found in notions of 'false consciousness' as well as other 'universalisms', such as inalienable human rights, and are thus associated with a more 'maximalist' agenda for social change, revolution and peace.

Third, this chapter also considered the levels of analysis debate. This was initiated by Kenneth Waltz, who suggested that the causes of collective violence could be found in three interlinked strata: (1) individual belief systems, instincts, personalities and psychological processes; (2) societal factors such as government, economic exchange and national ideology; and (3) an international system structured by power differentials, alliances and trade. Other writers have augmented these by disaggregating intrastate groups and by emphasising the independent role of suprastate formations within the global system. In some ways, concentrating on one particular level of analysis reinforces disciplinary boundaries; states and systems constitute the basis of international relations, while the individual level informs much of social psychology's contribution to conflict studies. Introducing them together does, however, help to highlight their comparative strengths, and placing them within the context of this chapter's overall focus on generality and definition also serves to mark out the parameters of conflict studies and to frame the context of the rest of the book. In the next chapter, for instance, we will look at the notion of the structure at various levels of analysis. Particularly focused upon will be objectivist visions of how the causes of violence might be understood and measured across the international system, inside states and within families once the need to define them through subjective perception and direct, interpersonal agency is abandoned.

3 Structure

Building on the previous chapter's focus on levels of analysis, notions of peace and issues of defining conflict and violence, this chapter traces the turn towards structural explanations of social phenomena, which attempt to get beyond a reliance on individual agency during the 1960s. The emergence of concerns over the structural, rather than the behavioural, character of violent conflict coincided with, and was influenced by, a broader rise in Marxist understandings of global political economy. Social dissent in Europe and the United States, the rigidity of the Cold War and the failure of the South to convert growth into development informed a radicalisation of the social sciences and a move away from traditional methods of conflict and peace research. A growing awareness of the violent consequences of the world's inequities led many to question subjectivism's tendency to endorse a negative peace (discussed in the previous chapter), a concern still prevalent today. This chapter looks initially at the challenge of objectivist definitions of the conflictive situation. It locates this radical critique within the social and academic debates of the day. It then goes on to outline the main contours of Johan Galtung's original characterisation of structural violence before dealing with some of the critical attention it has received. In particular, it looks at some of the conceptual difficulties Galtung faces in trying to present the notion of structural violence as both a response to ascendant radicalism and an attempt to reconcile its iconoclasm with the established order of peace and conflict research. Finally, the chapter examines some of the ways in which Galtung's model has been adapted and applied. Cases employing his, and other, notions of structural violence are drawn from the systemic, state and substate levels of analysis.

Radical peace research

The notion of structural violence was first articulated by Johan Galtung in 1969. In many ways, it was a response to dissatisfaction with social science in general and peace and conflict studies in particular – frustrations that had been increasing throughout the 1960s. Previously dominant notions of evolutionary social change came under increasing pressure. These had tended to offer functionalist and linear accounts of industrialisation, population growth, urbanisation, education and the increased role of the nation-state in the bureaucratic management of everyday social interactions. Writers such as Talcott Parsons (1951) and Walt Rostow (1953) had become prominent during the late 1950s and early 1960s by offering accounts of the societal factors that promote or inhibit the development of these features in order to understand why some countries adopted them while others did not. They noted a shift from being 'traditional' to being 'modern' (from being segmented, contained communities to more complex societies in which there was greater interdependency and an increasingly complex division of labour) with the overall aim of bringing newly decolonised nations under the Western bloc's influence. Encouraged by the Marshall Plan's role in Europe's restitution, it was widely believed that

> helping the free underdeveloped countries to create the conditions for self-sustaining economic growth can, in the short run, materially reduce the danger of conflict triggered by aggressive minor powers, and can, in say 2 to 3 decades, result in an overwhelming preponderance of stable, effective and democratic societies . . . giv[ing] the best promise of a favorable settlement of the Cold War.
>
> (Millikan and Rostow cited in Ohlin 1966: 17)

By the late 1960s, however, the conflict between the West and the Warsaw Pact, along with associated weapons transfers and highly destructive proxy wars, combined to define developing countries' domestic policy and nullify much of the possible benefits of economic assistance. A growing awareness that, despite considerable economic growth over the postwar period as a whole, the divide between rich and developing countries was widening led former Canadian Prime Minister, Lester Pearson, to conclude, in 1969, that attempts to bring stability and prosperity to the developing world were 'heavy with disillusion and distrust' (quoted in UNICEF 1986: 308; Singh 2002: 297). This combined with vociferous social forces in the West, such as the radicalisation of black consciousness, the anti-Vietnam movement, student protests and industrial unrest, to produce a sharp rise in civil dissent in what Jürgen Habermas called 'the first bourgeois revolt against the principles of a bourgeois society' (1971: 28).

The sense that Western capitalism was facing a crisis of legitimation also influenced the social sciences (Bendix 1967). Within conflict studies, the discipline's apparently close relationship with Western interests came in for particular attention. For much of the postwar period, analyses of conflict had focused disproportionately on the study of Superpower politics and the nuclear threat (Dunn 1978). Predominant was the view that international tension could be best reduced through the establishment of a powerful multilateral authority. For the most part, issues of domestic civil disorder, revolutionary irredentism and protest movements were either ignored or reduced to a problem of counterinsurgency. The use of force by Western states therefore remained undertheorised, leading to a commonplace assumption of legitimacy, public authorisation and, as the 1960s progressed, a sense that a normative emphasis upon the universal value of pacifism was becoming increasingly irrelevant (Garver 1968).

Dependency theories, which first appeared within networks of South American writers, led to a greater focus on the extent to which policies pursued by rich countries actively prevent poorer countries from developing (Valenzuela and Valenzuela 1978). In general, these owed much to Lenin's work on the economic causes of imperialism and Marx's theory of colonialism. They refuted modernisation theories' emphasis on the internal characteristics of developing countries in favour of a structural, internationalised analysis in which global inequality, as the stimulus of much of the world's conflict, is perpetuated by the normal operation of the economic system and its trading structures – thereby ensuring that developing countries remain dependent on Western power (Smith 1979). The protection of European agriculture, for instance, excludes competition from the South and ensures that most added value is located in the West and its manufacturing sector (cocoa is grown in Ghana, sold to the West at raw material prices, processed and distributed to Western consumers at high prices, while locally produced chocolate is denied access to Western markets by exorbitant tariffs) (Griffin and Gurley 1985).

This is, it was suggested, backed up the West's policy of aggressively exporting its culture to stimulate sales of its consumer goods (which are often manufactured in the developing world to undercut local competition and institutionalise further exogenous control of developing markets). Furthermore, dependency is enhanced by the international legal regime and its capacity to facilitate penetration of developing economies through land purchases, military bases, World Trade Organization rulings, United Nations missions and so on. These are, it was argued, frequently supported by the arming of internal dissenters, exerting diplomatic or economic pressure, invading, bombing, forming hostile alliances with unfriendly neighbours or demonising local cultures and leaders through Western media outlets. Finally, *dependencia* theorists argued that the development industry itself serves to maintain Western supremacy. As aid now props up many of the poorest countries, this too can be used to exert enormous influence. Development agencies can thus become states within states or, in the longer term, undermine developing economies by distorting the labour market and suppressing the emergence of domestic skills (Dos Santos 1970).

Within the West of the late 1960s, the influence of the dependency school was discernible in a growing tendency to question the 'senseless reproduction of [the] now superfluous virtues' of liberal capitalism and an acknowledgement of the 'untruth of [its] prevailing legitimations' (Habermas 1971: 25). Mainstream sociological trends were, as Peter Lawler notes, 'increasingly cast as an uncritical, technological and scientistic [sic] rationalization of the status quo' (1995: 68). This was most strongly felt in Europe where the postwar emphasis on positivism had not taken hold with the same potency as in the United States. There, the purportedly 'value-neutral standpoint of an impartial observer [began to] give way to the subjectively open, value-committed attitude of an interlocutor in a shared practice' (Ingram 1987: 4). This permeated the lower echelons of the main conflict research centres – the Peace Research Institute in Oslo (the forerunner of which was founded in 1959), the Polemological Institute and the International Peace Research Association (both established in Groningen in 1961 and 1963 respectively), the Peace Research Society (International) (convened in Malmö in 1963) and the Stockholm International Peace Research Institute (formed in 1966).

Within these organisations, there emerged a pronounced sense of dissatisfaction with what Lars Dencik (one of the leading writers of the new movement) called (in a paper written in 1969) 'conventional or conservative peace research' (1982: 177). Strongly influenced by dependency theory, this group of mainly young European academics and activists accused fellow academics of being 'an unwitting tool of American policy' and 'in the service of capitalist and neocolonial interests and purposes' (Dencik 1982: 195). Following a Peace Research Society (International) conference in 1967 on the war in Vietnam, at which papers were presented predominantly focused on game theories and security studies (thereby bypassing a more fundamental evaluation of American involvement in the conflict), they concluded that, in general, conflict analysis 'has a adopted a system perspective and a value orientation which is identical with those of the existing international institutions and lies very close to those of the rich and powerful nations' (Schmid 1968: 221). At a subsequent meeting of the organisation in Copenhagen in 1969, discontent took the form of a strongly worded petition signed by a large number of delegates. It proclaimed that 'conferences like the one on Vietnam will only serve to discredit peace research', which should, instead, seek to offer 'active solidarity with the peoples struggling against imperialism and super-power supremacy' (cited in Dencik 1982: 194–5).

The impact of such vociferousness was considerable. In a remarkable tirade first published in 1970, Kenneth Boulding, President of the International Peace Research Association, characterised the 'radical school' thus:

They tend to wear beards and have a fancy for what might be called academic guerrilla theatre. They are not inhibited by the customs of personal courtesy which tended to characterize the older generation and they have moral feelings which are so strong that morals are regarded as a substitute for manners . . . . They regard the older generation of peace researchers as obsessed by the cold war and by the necessity for resolving conflicts, as they regard this conflict essentially as no longer crucial and the thing that interests them is how to increase conflict which is 'objective' but of which people are not aware.

(1982: 82–3)

Unsurprisingly, perhaps, such a divergence proved irreconcilable and a split appeared between a 'narrow' group of predominantly American-based researchers and a 'radical', mostly European, network of theorists influenced by ideas of dependency. The former continued to maintain a commitment to behavioural scientism (the Peace Research Society (International) was renamed the Peace Science Society (International) in 1973 and moved to Cornell University) and to reject 'political action or polemical discussion' (Boulding 1977: 76). For the latter, on the other hand 'pacifism . . . [was] replaced by Marxism, conflict resolution by class-struggle, peace by revolution and if necessary bloody revolution' (Goldmann quoted in Dencik 1982: 177).

Despite the animosity with which the two factions communicated their point of view and the polarisation that resulted, the influence of the radical newcomers could not be fully resisted. For instance, *The Journal of Conflict Resolution*, which had emerged from Boulding's Centre for Advanced Studies in the Behavioural Sciences, announced in 1973 that, along with deterrence and disarmament studies, 'the journal must also attend to international conflict over justice, equality, and human dignity' (quoted in Rogers and Ramsbotham 1999: 745). It also prompted a reconsideration of 'violence' as a concealed and structural, rather than overt and relational, phenomenon. The notion of 'peace' was also extended to be understood as a discrete concept, a pursuant set of policies and an ideal. Adam Curle's explication of negative and positive peace, published in 1971 and discussed in the previous chapter, was seen as an example of such a more nuanced understanding. The overall result of the radical challenge was that conflict analysis began to include

> a view of social science as containing implicit justifications for particular policies as well as explanations of social phenomena, an effort to 'unmask' the pretensions to scientific objectivity and political neutrality, and finally the attempt to suggest an alternative approach to theory which would . . . provide the foundations for a more defensible public policy.
> (Nardin 1980: 468)

The contours of structural violence

In many ways, Johan Galtung's response to the radical challenge was an attempt to do just this – to provide the foundations for a more defensible public policy by salvaging the pacifism which, as Chapter 1 highlighted, had been so influential in conflict studies' evolution. From an elite Norwegian family and thus, perhaps, with a vested interest in a harmonious social order, Galtung had, by the late 1960s, developed a formidable reputation as a Ghandian philosopher, prolific writer and peace activist. Having spent six months in jail (where he completed a book on Indian political ethics) for resisting the Norwegian draft, he was appointed to the Sociology Faculty at Columbia University in 1958. Two years later, he returned to help found the

Peace Research Institute in Oslo, establishing himself as its leading thinker by means of a prodigious publication record and through the editorship of its flagship periodical, *Journal of Peace Research*. Soon after, he took up a UNESCO-funded position in Chile, where he came into contact with *dependencia* ideas of political economy. So, as a senior European theorist with both strong transatlantic and Southern links, as well as an implacable commitment to reducing violent conflict, Galtung represented something of a crossover between the narrow and radical schools.

His seminal paper, 'Violence, Peace, and Peace Research', published in the *Journal of Peace Research* in 1969, needs to be read in this context (Lawler 1995: 77–80). In it and in a series of related papers over the following three decades, Galtung seeks both to moderate the limited scientism of the narrow school and to rebuff the notion that peace research is, in seeking to reduce violence, inherently supportive of the powerful. It is not, he argues, the efficacy of non-violence that needs to be reconsidered (this is retained as a self-evident good), but the way in which violence is understood. He rejects the idea, implicit in the objectivist work of Schmid and Dencik, that violence may need to be intensified in order to bring about a more peaceful outcome, yet he accepts much of dependency theory's global analysis. Furthermore, he concedes that peace research must go beyond a subjectivist concern with manifest conflicts and establish a broader understanding of violence than the behavioural model favoured by the empiricism of the narrow school. Rather than being limited to a particularly intense manifestation of goal incompatibility, violence is also structural and more fruitfully conceived as 'the cause of the difference between the potential and the actual' (Galtung 1969: 168).

This difference (or the conflictive situation to Mitchell) may be defined by third parties or the subjects themselves, but it should only be regarded as indicative of violence if this gap is known to be avoidable. For example, a premature death from tuberculosis 200 years ago cannot be regarded as violence as the potential to survive (the medicine) was not present but, should this happen today, it must be regarded as resulting from the inequitable distribution of the world's resources. A conflictive situation might then be more clearly understood as circumstances in which 'damage that occurs to individuals or groups due to differential access to social resources and which is due to the normal operation of the social system' (Webb 1986: 431). It is, in other words, structural as well as agential. A ubiquitous manifestation of violence is, therefore, the commonplace denial of rights and needs such as economic well-being, dignity, equality, education and so on which, scarcely reported or even acknowledged, emerges from everyday activities and from the actions of people who are rarely, if ever, directly violent.

Structural violence is thus both conceptually and empirically separable from behavioural violence in six ways (Galtung 1969). First, violence can be psychological as well as physical. It may work on the body and the soul. The latter may include indoctrination, threats and the unequal distribution of transportation resources (thereby increasing individual isolation and loneliness). In this sense, the violence of containing a person's potential can be done mentally and institutionally as well as affecting them bodily. Second, violence may be contained within rewards and not simply punishments. Immoderate expenditure, for instance, is readily rewarded under capitalism – 'buy three, get one free' reduces the per-unit cost for those with capital and militates against those without the disposable resources to consume excessively. Here, it is important to note that conflictive behaviour in general, and violence in particular, can be seen in the narrowing of the range of options that individuals have available to pursue their objectives and fulfil their potential. Third, violence exists even though someone is not hurt. Conflictive behaviour such as the issuing of credible threats to others' interests and values, the destruction of property and forced displacement can dissuade people from acting volitionally, obstruct a realisation of potential and therefore do violence.

Fourth, violence is present even when there is no subject-to-object relationship – no overt and distinguishable goal incompatibility in other words. There is, for instance, a growing acknowledgement that institutional racism within many large organisations limits the potential of individuals from minority backgrounds. Its anonymous and impersonal character makes it difficult for people to perceive, and the subject-to-object emphasis of most languages inhibits its articulation. Fifth, violence emerges from non-violent intentions and is therefore included in conflictive attitudes despite the absence of a self-proclaimed intention to harm. Criminal law derived from Greco-Roman tradition is based largely on purpose rather than consequence (causing death by careless driving is, for instance, not subject to such severe penalties as less consequential actions carried out with criminal intent). So the West's taste for cheap agricultural products from the developing world is not generally regarded as violence as there is no intent to harm at the point of purchase although the international trading structures that govern North–South exchange clearly help to maintain rural poverty, thereby limiting individual potential (most obviously life expectancy – to be discussed in more detail shortly). Sixth, violence is latent as well as manifest. Increases in the latent potential for violence, such as highly tense situations without the presence of behavioural violence, can still inhibit potential and reduce individuals' capacity to pursue their objectives. As Chapter 2 explained, this is acknowledged by many subjectivist definitions of conflictive situations, but is not categorised as an instance of violence and is thus neither theorised nor operationalised.

Essentially then, Galtung's construction of structural violence offers a way of understanding conflict causality both freed from the constraints of behavioural evidence and as a possible instigator of overt goal incompatibility. In other words, structural violence is, simultaneously, a cause of instrumental violence and a conflictive result of less perceptible global processes – identified by Galtung as 'exploitation'. This owes much to the dependency school and has four facets (Galtung 1990: 294). The first, penetration, involves the implantation of agents of the powerful within the collective underdog, which creates a harmony of interests between the global centre and the comprador bridgehead within the periphery (Galtung 1971). The second, segmentation, acts to obscure the true nature of the relationship between strong and weak, while the third and fourth facets, marginalisation and fragmentation, exclude the peripheral agents from the centre and from each other. Together, these serve to create greater levels of disharmony within the periphery than within the centre, while simultaneously preventing the interests of the exploited within the periphery from coinciding with the exploited within the centre.

For Galtung, these features of structural violence are accompanied by cultural violence, which makes structures of exploitation 'look, even feel, right – or at least not wrong' and, as such, prevents its subjects from developing an awareness of the conflictive situation in which they are embedded and from accurately perceiving their interests (1990: 291). He gives six examples of violent 'cultural domains'. First, organised transcendental religion, he suggests, tends to establish exclusionary categories of 'chosen' and 'lost', thereby legitimising the exploitation of the latter through the perpetuation of a kind of ordained inevitability. Second, secular ideologies construct comparable dichotomies of the collective 'self' and 'other'. A failure to accept the group's articles of faith, such as the inconvertible value of national allegiance, capitalism, racial identity, technological advance, development, achievement and other apodictic features of modernity, can lead to a curtailment of individual potential. Third, Galtung points to the exclusionary use of verbal and written communication by identifying the tendency of those languages with Latin origins 'to make women invisible by using the same word for the male gender as for the entire human species', thereby helping to conceal the gendered character of structural violence (1990: 299).

Fourth, Galtung argues that 'art', within which he appears to subsume historiography, can be a significant vehicle of cultural violence. Medieval European constructions of the oriental 'other' are, for instance, deeply rooted in Western representations of its borderlands. As we shall see in Chapter 5, this finds expression at all levels of society – British pub names (The Turk's Head), French cuisine (the croissant), Italian literature (Dante), Serbian poetry (the martyrdom of Prince Lazar), European Union (EU) accession (a myth of a European 'culture'), the despotism of the Asian mode of production and many others – and combines to inform a vision of the East as lascivious, tyrannical and stagnant. Violence, as the containment of potential, is thus exerted upon individuals both within the global periphery and, via diasporic communities, within the periphery of the centre. Galtung's fifth and six aspects of cultural violence concern 'empirical' and 'formal' science respectively. The former is, he suggests, exemplified by the current omnipotence of neoclassical economics (Galtung 1980). The conventional wisdom of comparative advantage, which has emerged over the last 25 years, has, for Galtung, both helped to create an order based on inherently unequal production factors – thereby reinforcing centre–periphery divisions – and served to obscure alternative options for structuring the international terms of trade. Such dichotomies are, Galtung argues, reinforced by the bivalent logic of formal science, which tends to 'discipline us into a particular mode of thought highly compatible with black–white thinking and polarization in personal, social and world spaces' (1990: 301).

Clearly, then, in rejecting both positivist empiricism and the economistic historicism of Marxism, Galtung seeks to locate his model of violence somewhere between the scientism of the narrow school and the dialectic materialism of the radicals. As a result, it has attracted a body of critical comment from both. Unsurprisingly, perhaps, a prominent theme within the former critique has been the charge that Galtung's elucidation of structural violence lacks precision. For Kenneth Boulding, this fatally undermines his premise 'that some people are rich and some people are poor because of the structures of property and power' (1977: 81). Such an alleged relationship is, he continues, likely to be highly complex, and it must, therefore, be specified in detail rather than simply asserted. This failure to establish, let alone explain, the points at which the centre touches the periphery means that the locus of exploitation is left undertheorised, raising, but not accounting for, a number of important anomalies. If, for instance, structural violence is, at the level of society, gendered, why is it that female life expectancy is frequently significantly higher than that of men? Moreover, how, at the international level of analysis, can indicators of structural violence be explained inside states that have little contact with the global centre (such as Bhutan, Burma and North Korea)?

Evidently, quantifying violence depends greatly on the comparative units selected, underlining further the need for an explicit specification of the structure's relational features (Webb 1986: 432). This is important not only in order to comprehend its hierarchical form, but also to imagine how a remedied world order might balance the imposition of greater equality with the protection of individual liberty. Without an account of such change, the presence of structural violence appears to be static. It is used to specify an intolerable present and a desirable future, but offers no explanatory account of how the space between these two fixed poles might be traversed – how, in other words, the disingenuous effects of cultural violence might be reduced to reveal the exploitative nature of the modern world and how such exploitation might be ameliorated. This is, for Godfried van Benthem van den Bergh, particularly debilitating as, despite the obvious historical antecedents of the centre–periphery duality, it precludes an understanding of violence as a structured *process* (1972: 78).

Similar concerns have been voiced by writers influenced by Marx. Chris Brown, for instance, notes that Galtung's 'notion of structure allows him to determine that change . . . has occurred, but it cannot account for the change itself'. This, he continues, stands in contrast to most Marxist approaches which are 'based on both a sense of structure *and* a sense of history' (1981:

226). Indeed, in presenting a less mutable version of the generalist world systems perspectives of Emmanuel Arrighi (1972) and Immanuel Wallerstein (1974a), Galtung seeks to distance his work from orthodox Marxist approaches. For example, he abandons their commitment to concrete historical dynamics 'motivated by the need for expanding markets' in favour of a holistic, yet rudderless, abstract structuralism (Galtung 1971: 81). So, rather than a necessary and teleological step away from feudal idiocy and towards a socialist future brought about by collective agency, the structural violence of global capitalism is, for Galtung, a self-recreating and mostly imperceptible evil. The international system is thus

> structural in the sense that no specific actors are indicated, and in the sense that for the concrete actors that happen to be performing roles in that structure no specific motivation is necessary. [Once the structure] . . . has started operating it is not necessary for those who are acting within it to will all the consequences.
>
> (Galtung 1980: 183)

This 'seems to suggest an initial creation of structure after which the relationship between structure and action is one-way only' (Brown 1981: 223). Such a rejection of agential utility serves to distance Galtung's model of structural violence from the Marxist emphasis on revolutionary action stressed by more radical conflict analysts. In particular, it avoids the difficult proposition that behavioural violence might be a way of bringing about a reduction in structural violence. Indeed, given that, in one calculation, structural violence kills over 1,000 times more people than behavioural violence each year, there is, perhaps, some credibility to the argument that 'revolutionary violence against structural violence aimed at reducing the sum-total of violence in the world should also be fairly evaluated in relation to reactionary violence which is aimed at maintaining or increasing structural violence' (Eckhardt and Young 1974: 93). For Galtung, though, 'the elimination of the members of an oppressive elite would not necessarily end structural violence if new forms of it were latent within the ideological perspective of the new holders of power' (Lawler 1995: 82). Beyond a normative commitment to pacifism and its moral posture of refusal, then, Galtung offers no positive philosophy of agential action. This leaves the peace analyst to define a priori the difference between the potential and the actual and the means to reconcile the two – a sense of vagueness potentially efficacious to both liberal notions of redistribution and Marxist accounts of structural transformation.

Indeed, the elasticity of Galtung's terminology and taxonomy has proved an advantage as well as a limitation, doubtless contributing to the wide number of applications that his work has attracted. Unsurprisingly, given Galtung's concern with global exploitation, a number of subsequent studies have focused on the level of the international system and its structural violence between the developed and the developing world (Farmer 2003;

McGregor 2003). Accompanying these has been a more recent body of work looking at structural violence at the level of states (Jacobs and O'Brien 1998; Mazurana and McKay 2001; Preti 2002), as well as numerous studies concerned with substate issues such as individual rights and the protection of children (Farmer 1996; Kent 1999; Kostelny and Garbarino 2001). Within each analytical framework, gender, ethnic and class axes are common structural determinants of violence. The following section will outline some examples of the ways in which various conceptions of structural violence have informed case studies at different levels of analysis.

The axes of structural violence

The starting point for many analyses of structural violence at the level of the international system is a focus on its less immediately perceptible features. There has been a growing acknowledgement that the suffering of those who are remote, in terms of both geography and culture, is frequently overlooked in favour of more proximate concerns (Chopp 1986). Perhaps influenced by Galtung's residual scientism, there has been a particular concern to quantify this suffering and to compare it with the destructive effects of behavioural violence. Most commonly, calculations of mortality, as an indicator of structural violence, have made up the focus of such studies. This is hardly surprising given

> (1) the intrinsic importance we attach – and have reason to attach – to living, (2) the fact that many other capabilities that we value are contingent on our being alive, and (3) the further fact that data on age-specific mortality can, to some extent, serve as a proxy for associated failures and achievements to which we may attach importance.
>
> (Sen 1998: 5)

Soon after the split in the peace research community, Galtung, in keeping with his commitment to empiricism, sought to enumerate structural violence in an arithmetical essay (co-authored with Tord Høivik) published in 1971. Later, Høivik (1977) and other writers, such as William Eckhardt and Christopher Young (1974), attempted to operationalise more complex quantifications of those whose lives have been shortened by inadequate access to a range of otherwise available resources. Working on the assumption that there is no innate deficiency within the physiology of the poor and thus no reason why they cannot achieve the same lifespan as the world's wealthiest societies, analysts compared the violence of structures with the violence of behaviour – an idea illustrated in Table 3.1. In what is arguably the best articulated study of its kind, Gernot Köhler and Norman Alcock used two methods to 'present some estimates of the fatal consequences of structural violence in global society' (1976: 343). First, in the Swedish model, they took the country with the highest life expectancy as a benchmark for the age

Table 3.1 Indicators of violence

	Violent input	Violent output
Direct violence	Deployment of armed men, shelling, bombing, etc.	People killed by war
Structural violence	Malnutrition, lack of shelter, health care, etc.	People killed by a lack of necessities

Source: Adapted from Köhler and Alcock (1976: 343).

(or potential) that people could achieve. This was fixed at Sweden's 1965 average of 74.7 years (E_s). They then took the country with the lowest life expectancy (again using data from 1965). This was Guinea's average of 27 years. To calculate Guinea's level of structural violence, they divided the country's overall population (3.5 million) by 27 to give the number of Guineans who actually died in 1965 (129,630) and by 74.7 to give the number of Guineans who would have died in 1965 had they enjoyed the same life expectancy as Swedes (46,854) – the difference is the number of people who died as a result of structural violence in 1965 (129,630 – 46,854 = 82,766).

Second, in the egalitarian model, Köhler and Alcock estimated the effects of a complete and equal redistribution of the world's resources. To do this, they plotted every country's gross national product (GNP) on a scatter-gram (Figure 3.1), before adding each of these together to give 1965's gross global product (the entire world's economic product) which, once divided by the population of the planet, could be used to calculate a per capita figure of $651 (g*), equating to a life expectancy of 68.3 years (c*). Using this figure, the number of deaths due to structural violence in Guinea came out at 78,385. As it produces slightly lower results, the egalitarian model was then run throughout the world giving a total of those killed due to structural violence for 1965 of 14 million – the figure for the Swedish model was 18 million – amounting to a shortfall of over 300 million life–years. Of this, 480,000 lives (or 3.42 per cent) were lost in the global North compared with over 96 per cent in developing countries. Both figures far outweighed the numbers of people killed as a result of warfare for 1965 – 2,207 in the North and 113,000 in the South.

An important aspect of the Köhler and Alcock egalitarian model is the position of its predicted life expectancy – 68.3 – in relation to existing mortality ranges. While it is more than 40 years higher than in Guinea, it is less than six years lower than in Sweden. This leads the authors to conclude that 'under conditions of complete global equality, the rich countries would lose only minor amounts of life expectancy, whereas the poor would gain tremendously' (1976: 355). So, for global equality to come about, life expectancy in the North would have to drop only by just over five years. Furthermore, Figure 3.1 reveals that, for the North, economic growth is associated with only a limited increase in life expectancy, whereas for countries in the $40–600

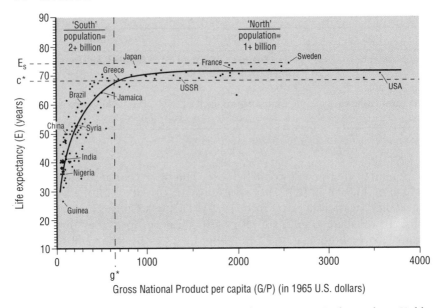

Figure 3.1   An empirical table of structural violence. Source: Redrawn from Köhler and Alcock (1976: 353).

per capita range, an increase of 7.68 per cent in GNP correlates to a rise in life expectancy of one year. 'In other words, wealth cannot only buy a higher *standard of living*, it also buys *life* itself' (Köhler and Alcock 1976: 355).

Although similar types of approach based on the value of economic growth were often hailed as potential ways of measuring social development empirically (Galtung *et al.* 1975), more differentiated methods began to emerge during the 1980s and 1990s (summarised in Alkire 2002). As it became increasing clear that rises in GNP were not being converted into quantifiable forms of social development, per capita measures of economic wealth came to be regarded as especially crude. By 1992, for instance, life expectancy in Sri Lanka had reached 72 years on the basis of a per capita income of only $540 per annum, while Gabon's yearly per capita income of $4,450 was producing an average life expectancy of only 54 years (Sen 1998: 10). It therefore became common for studies to emphasis intrastate factors in examining development in general and conflict variables in particular. This was, not least, due to the growing cost of warfare to civilian populations and its accompanying media attention. Since the Second World War, for instance, over 170 million people have been killed by their own governments and, of these, non-combatants have, as Chapter 1 outlined, absorbed ever increasing proportions (Sivard 1993: 20; Rummel 1994).

Consequently, academic interest began to focus on axes of structural violence within states. It was argued that certain groups could be structurally repressed, yet individuals from those groups could still be immensely powerful. An example of this might be the gendered nature of structural violence in Pakistan where poor health care and other social factors have combined to reduce the country's overall female population by almost 1 per cent (1993 data) at a time when Benazir Bhutto was beginning her second term as prime minister. Similarly, the Afro-American community, who have a mortality rate almost double that of the white majority, is often regarded as being subject to extensive structural violence despite recently supplying two of the state's most powerful leaders, Condoleezza Rice and Colin Powell (Sen 1998: 10–17). These prominent exceptions combine with the banality of social exclusion to make such structures hard to recognise (although they are rarely hidden – rather, they are 'right before our eyes and therefore simply taken for granted' (Scheper-Hughes 1996: 889)). Such habituation is grounded upon the capacities of ideologies, languages, arts and sciences – the aspects of what Galtung identified as 'cultural violence' – to make exploitation look and feel right (1990: 291). For instance, the structural violence of being forced to swear allegiance to the monarch in order to take up a seat in the British parliament or to apply for UK citizenship is sufficiently obscured by ritual and tradition to appear superficially innocuous, yet it has, for many years, served both to exclude Irish republican parliamentarians and to present a considerable obstacle to religiously observant Muslims.

The ordinariness of structural violence is well illustrated by Peter Uvin's study of Rwanda (1998: 103–60). Reviewing a series of World Bank reports during the run-up to the 1994 genocide, he finds that, by relying on official data and the stated aims of legislation rather than academic research and actual policy implementations, they were able to reach the mistaken conclusion that 'land is less unequally divided than elsewhere, . . . household expenditure is relatively evenly distributed in Rwanda, and . . . government expenditure and tax policies are income neutral' (cited in Uvin 1998: 110–11). In reality, 'the privileged of the regime' had been able to garner aid rents of enormous proportions leading to 'the constitution of large pastoral domains' under their clients' control and landlessness as high as 75 per cent in some regions (International Fund for Agricultural Development 1992: 8; Pierre Erny cited in Uvin 1998: 114). The patrimonial nature of urban politics produced comparable disparities in income levels with the wealthiest decile in Rwanda increasing their share of the country's income from 22 per cent in 1982 to 52 per cent in 1994 (Jeff Maton cited in Uvin 1998: 115).

Despite the fact that the great majority of those benefiting in this way were Hutus and that much of the resources that the Hutu political elite (a third of whom were drawn from the President's own province of Gisenyi) were distributing came from international aid donors, spending patterns continued to favour 'the smallest groups in society, that is, the richest 1 per cent or so, composed of technical assistants and their "homologues", plus merchants and high-level government officials' (Uvin 1998: 143). In many ways, this is closely in keeping with Galtung's notion of 'exploitation' as the causal mechanism behind his propositions of structural violence. According to Uvin's analysis, much of the international development effort in Rwanda worked with domestic political elites to institutionalise Western 'penetration' (defined by Galtung as 'implanting the top dog inside the underdog'), 'segmentation' ('giving the underdog only a very partial view of what goes on'), 'marginalisation' ('keeping the underdogs on the outside') and 'fragmentation' ('keeping the underdogs away from each other' (1990: 294)). So, while donors were insulated by a moralising afflatus of philanthropy in which power relations were comprehensively ignored and their response to 'ordinary' communal violence in Rwanda was simply an apolitical 'mirror image of need' (Duffield 1999: 32), the actual effect of development policy was a growth in domestic exploitation and structural violence.

Here, then, structural violence may be a facilitative or a linear causative element in behavioural violence. Studies that focus on the latter tend to consider behavioural violence to be a response to the inequalities and exploitation that underpin structural violence. As we shall see in Chapter 7, these frequently build on theories of human needs (particularly in terms of the frustration of material wants, civil rights and the deprivation of higher social requirements) to suggest that structural violence contains the intrinsic capacity to provoke behavioural violence from the deprived group (Khan 1978: 836). In terms of the former, the potential of structural violence to lead on to direct bloodshed is, in contrast, contained within its capacity to create an atmosphere of ordinariness through which elites can both mobilise their clients and prosper politically – a capability related to both diversionary theories of rule (dealt with in Chapter 4) and the construction of social identity (the topic of Chapter 6). Uvin argues that the subjugation of non-Hutus, for example, lowered social barriers to greater tyranny, thereby preparing the ground for behavioural violence on a grand scale. He concludes that

> as the norms of society lose legitimacy, as people's knowledge base is reduce to slogans, as progress becomes a meaningless concept, as communities are riveted by conflict and jealousy [and] as people's sense of self-respect is reduced, . . . people become increasingly unhampered by constraints on the use of violence to deal with problems.
>
> (1998: 138)

Structural violence need not be so consciously organised though. It does not need to have a clear relationship with behavioural violence (as either an action or a reaction), nor is it restricted to relationships with, or between, those in the developing world. Structural violence against children, for instance, is rarely organised at the level of states, it cannot be easily associated with levels of physical abuse, and it is not a phenomenon limited to the South. As Peter Gottschalk and Timothy Smeeding point out, structural inequalities between American families are among the most acute in the industrial world (2000). Milton Schwebel and Daniel Christie identify three ways in which this affects American children (2001: 122–5). First, in psychosocial terms, material poverty increases the likelihood of maternal complications, but reduces the probability that expectant mothers will re-ceive medical attention. It also heightens the incidence of low birthweight, prematurity, learning difficulties and physical disability (Crooks 1995).

Second, the structural violence inherent in the capitalist cycle of boom and recession similarly affects children's well-being. A rise in unemploy-ment of 1 per cent, for example, has been found to increase homicides by 5.7 per cent and suicides by 4.1 per cent – many of which involve par-ents – while a rapid enlargement of over 200 per cent in the number of temporary workers employed in the American economy during the early 1990s has 'exacerbate[d] feelings of insecurity, undermine[d] self-esteem, and increase[d] stress in spousal and parental relationships' (Schwebel 1997: 339–40; Brenner cited in Schwebel and Christie 2001: 122). Indeed, a wide range of research carried out over the last three decades has demonstrated ex-tensive links between poverty and weak levels of attachment between infants and their carers (Ainsworth *et al.* 1978; Bee 1997). This is demonstrated in a lack of contingent responses, such as warmth, guidance and authoritative instruction, and has been found to be particularly common among parents and carers who experience inadequate housing, health care, education and day-care facilities and are, therefore, repeatedly and unpredictably anxious. Resultant outcomes in children include aggression, a lack of self-reliance and low levels of self-esteem (McLoyd and Wilson 1991). Third, high levels of structural violence are correlated with weak school performance. Poor children are more likely not to attend school, to attain inferior marks and fail courses, to be assigned special education measures, to experience emo-tional and behavioural difficulties in school, to lose academic ground during holidays and not to graduate (Kellaghan 1994).

Conclusion

The notion of structural violence emerged during the late 1960s largely as a response to a perceived failure of academia to take up a position critical of contemporary Great Power policy – a situation perhaps similar, as Chapter 1 suggested, to that of today. It sought to expand definitions of conflict be-yond apolitical and scientist studies which tended to avoid moral concerns and thus, in the view of some, served to endorse the subjectivist preferences of the powerful. Violence may thus be psychological as well as physical, it may be contained within rewards and not simply punishments, and it may be present even though someone is not hurt and there is no subject-to-object relationship. It may also emerge from non-violent intentions, be latent as well as manifest and include many of the results of the international system's normal operation. Exerted at the level of the structure and not simply the individual behaviour of aggression and warfare, violence may be regarded as present whenever damage is done to a person's potential.

Structural violence thus represents one of the key conceptual advances in the study of conflict. It has influenced, and continues to influence, a considerable amount of important analysis with a wide range of concerns and approaches. Its opposition to the staid empiricism and uncritical pacifism so often found within the canonical establishment of peace studies remains a pertinent and powerful challenge today. Yet, in many ways, it has succeeded in straddling both methodological and ideological divides. Its elasticity clearly appeals to proponents of reasonably conservative policies of redistribution as well as to those who espouse more radical transformative agenda. This is evident in its antecedents, in its theoretical focus, in the critical responses it has attracted and absorbed and in the various applications it has provoked or informed. These include studies at the global, national and individual levels of analysis. The first reveals mortality differentials resulting from low life expectancies in developing countries and quantifies what might be required to redress such a massive loss of human potential, the second casts light on the way in which the ground might be prepared for behavioural violence (including incidents of an unprecedented scale), and the third helps to increase our understanding of the impact of socio-economic stratification on the lives of children. Structural violence is thus an arithmetic tool, a conceptual framework and a concrete social phenomenon. It offers a way of quantifying exploitation and inequality at various analytical levels. Conceptually, it can be understood as a result of latent conflict and, in its capacity both to facilitate and to provoke conflict, as a cause of behavioural violence. As an issue for modern society, it has helped to maintain attention on discriminatory axes of class, gender, race, age and culture.

4   Functions

In the preceding chapter, we looked at the structural aspects of conflict and violence at various levels of analysis. Although explicit in this is a distinction between those who prosper from the normal operation of the world's social structures and those who do not, the emphasis of the objectivist challenge to conflict analysis (and therefore the last chapter) was predominantly upon violence's capacity to limit human potential – the losers in other words. We did not explore how conflicts, including violence, may be beneficial or functional. To do this, the following chapter considers, first, the different ways in which the social impact of conflictive behaviour, both violent and non-violent, has been evaluated. Here, it is important to note that analyses have moved away from both the traditional idea that conflict is, in itself, a negative feature of human interaction and the belief that it can be classified as *either* functional *or* dysfunctional. The second is the peculiarly integrative functions of social conflict. These are considered as a means of cohering groups and demarcating their boundaries from others. Approaches emphasising conflict's integrative function can be applied to substate groups, to state behaviour in relation to their domestic environment and to international alliance structures. The third focus of this chapter is the body of literature concentrating on what are known as 'diversionary' theories of conflict instigation. Such models are grounded on the assumption that the management of conflicts *within* countries influences the conflictive behaviour of states in the international arena. In each of these sections, emphasis will be placed both on tracing the different forms that these approaches have taken over the years and on highlighting some of their more significant issues and responses.

Evaluating conflict

During the 1950s, writers began to question the generally held view that conflict (in both its violent and non-violent forms) was a universally destructive feature of human life and one to be avoided or minimised. Writers such as Rolf Dahrendorf offered a challenge to the predominant view of society as structured by a tendency towards equilibrium which, as Table 4.1 illustrates, tended to see conflict as an aberration or temporary pathology (1959: 159–61). Indeed, 'the equilibrium model, by stressing integration and consensus, leads directly to the position that conflict, which is a threat to stability, must be curtailed in order for the integration of the social structure to be maintained' (Stohl 1976: 7–8). As it is the state that is responsible for the maintenance of order in society, such a position is inherently conservative. Dahrendorf's alternative model, in contrast, tends to view equilibrium or passivity as abnormal and born of repression. Here, conflict is regarded as a vital part of societal change.

So, with this in mind, the primary question becomes how to *measure* the effect of conflict on society rather than simply how to *reduce* its impact. Writers started to classify conflicts as 'functional' if their benefits outweighed their costs and 'dysfunctional' if their costs outweighed their benefits. Typically, four groups have been identified (Mitchell 1980: 71–2). The first are those who gain from the existing distribution of values and resources. These may, for instance, be large landowners in South America who have an interest in preventing certain types of conflict. Their interest is in the status quo. In order to protect this, they may engage in a variety of conflictive behaviour including coercion, threats and compromise. The second are those who lose from the existing distribution of values and resources. To continue the previous example, agricultural workers in South America who wish to amend their position may also engage in conflictive behaviour in order to effect this change. A third group consists of those who do, or will, derive benefits from a conflictive situation. This may include a range of actors, from glaziers in Northern Ireland prospering from bomb damage to organised crime syndicates in south-east Turkey who use Kurdish activism to traffic narcotics. A fourth group are those who are directly, or indirectly, harmed by a conflictive situation. This might be the deceased and bereaved or (often utterly unrelated) actors such as employees in the Turkish tourist industry whose livelihoods were damaged by the conflicts in Iraq.

Using these categories to evaluate conflictive behaviour is, however, problematic. The fact that they are not mutually exclusive – actors are likely to

Table 4.1 Contrasting models of society and conflict

Equilibrium model	*Conflict model*
Societal elements seen as relatively persistent and constant	Society seen as subject to constant change and flux
Society tends to be well integrated	Society is an attempt to manage disagreement
Societal elements contribute to the functioning of the system	Societal elements tend to disaggregate and pursue their own objectives
Functioning social systems aim to reach a consensus over the values of its members	Society is based on the coercion of some of its members by others

fall into different groups at different locations and at different points during conflictive processes – makes it difficult to categorise conflicts as clearly functional or dysfunctional. Much depends on when the assessment is made, whom the assessment is made of and who makes the assessment. One person's cost is another's benefit. Moreover, as conflicts are likely to change rapidly, the same process of interaction may be functional and dysfunctional at different points. They may, for instance, often involve 'deferred' cost. The use of depleted and non-depleted uranium ordnance in the Balkans, Afghanistan and Iraq has produced a number of, as yet not fully understood, health implications for both combatants and civilians (Durakovic 2003). Conflicts may also involve deferred benefits. The costs of the Allied operation to destroy Hitler's heavy water factory in Telemark in 1942 were, for example, accepted on the grounds that considerable benefits would accrue in the future from Nazi Germany not acquiring a nuclear capability. Much depends, therefore, on the social and temporal subjectivity of the agent making functionality assessments. Perhaps a more useful way to approach the issue is to return to the levels of analysis discussed in Chapter 2. In this way, the impact of conflict may relate to individuals, groups involved in the conflict and for the society or system as a whole. As such, any qualitative evaluation would tend to combine *both* functional and dysfunctional dimensions. Table 4.2 illustrates how this might appear.

At the individual level of analysis, it is clear that numerous benefits accrue from participating in conflictive behaviour. These may take three forms (Mitchell 1980: 65–6). First, material rewards may include personal enrichment through looting, extortion and conflict-related trade. The former Liberian leader Charles Taylor, for example, is said to have made millions of dollars from the conflict there and in Sierra Leone. It may also involve financial incentives for organisational employees, particularly those whose accomplishments are assessed by the amount of money they are able to spend rather than how much they can produce. As the Corporate Engagement Project notes of community participation initiatives in conflict-affected contexts, 'when salary levels are linked to the level of financial responsibility[,] staff members . . . stand to benefit from perpetuating problems, in order to increase their budgets' (2003: 3–4). Second, political rewards may emerge for leaders in the form of greater in-group support, a reduction in

Table 4.2 Calculating the functionality of conflict

	Benefits from:		Costs of:	
	Engagement	Outcome	Engagement	Outcome
To individuals				
To groups				
To society				

Source: Adapted from Mitchell (1980: 71).

constituent dissent or, as in the case of colonial troops' involvement in the Second World War, a greater awareness of goal incompatibility – in this instance, growing support for decolonisation. This will be discussed in more detail in the final section of this chapter. Third, psychological benefits may be accumulated by individuals engaged in conflictive behaviour. As well as the 'dysfunctional' attitudinal responses outlined by Mitchell and considered in Chapter 2, individuals' self-esteem and empathy with others may be raised by the feeling that something is being done about a perceived goal incompatibility. So, while resentment and suspicion are common, as are cognitive processes such as stereotyping and selective attitudes to information, these are frequently accompanied and mitigated by a sense of cathartic release and perceptions of enhanced status – feelings recorded by Birrell in his study of Republican activists in deprived urban areas of Northern Ireland (1972).

Conflictive behaviour may also contain benefits for society. Obviously, as an aggregation of individuals, societies profit from many of the rewards discussed above. In addition, however, there is the notion that conflict, if properly managed, 'prevents stagnation, it stimulates interest and curiosity [and] it is the medium through which problems are aired and solutions are arrived at' (Deutsch 1969: 19). So, in this light, societies that permit controlled levels of conflict are, in contrast to the closed polities of authoritarian states, often regarded as more durable and functional. Conflicts over matters that do not call into question the basis of society itself – in other words, conflicts over interest rather than value – help to stabilise societies and produce a type of equilibrium born not of passivity but of active dissent. As Coser puts it,

> by permitting immediate and direct expression of rival claims, such social systems are able to readjust their structures by eliminating the sources of dissatisfaction. The multiple conflicts which they experience serve to eliminate the causes for dissociation and to re-establish unity.
>
> (1956: 154)

Subscribing to this view, Mitchell puts forward four ways in which interest conflicts may benefit society as a whole (1980: 64–5). The first is that they establish numerous patterns of crosscutting antagonisms and coalitions. These tend to prevent the emergence of fewer, more acute divisions grounded upon overlapping value-based differences. The second is that the presence of interest conflicts helps to offer members of society a 'safety valve' through which grievances can be legitimately channelled without disrupting the normal operating patterns of the system itself. Third, conflicts can establish or promote mechanisms for managing grievances and disquiet. This may be either through the creation of new institutions and measures, such as the appointment of a commission of inquiry, or by emphasising existent norms such as campaigns to improve road safety, food standards or public accountability. Fourth, conflicts may create relationships, or improve awareness, between previously disassociated groups. Although this may involve some initial costs, benefits in the form of enhanced interaction may outlast the conflict by many years. For instance, periodical race riots in British cities have helped to highlight the institutionalised prejudices that exist within sections of the United Kingdom's police force and have arguably led to an improved relationship between minority groups and the constabulary's senior management.

Conflicts of value may also be regarded as containing functional facets if a quantifiably 'better' future can be expected to ensue. Such ideas can be broadly separated into three categories. First, from a liberal internationalist perspective, many people would argue that the devastating conflict with fascism in the 1930s and 1940s was necessary and, therefore, broadly functional as it led to an international system in which fascism is no longer a major part. In addition, it could be said to conform with Mitchell's first and third points above, in the sense that the new world order that emerged from the Second World War replaced the polarisation of the interwar period with numerous crosscutting relations and helped to establish multilateral regimes such as the United Nations, the EU and normative conventions concerning human rights, refugee protection and so on.

Second, conflicts of values can be seen to underpin dialectical visions of society and the ways in which different systems and structures have emerged over time. Both Hegel and Marx regarded conflict as a functional way for societies to attain greater sophistication and development through trial and error. Each saw conflict between different theses, or classes, as important in perceiving the 'real' nature of modernity and in moving towards a superior synthesis in which existent inequities and stratifications are absent. Third, writers from a socio-biological perspective have suggested that conflict is an effective means of reducing demographic pressures. This is derived from the economist Thomas Malthus (1766–1834), who argued that exponential increases in human populations born of the improvements in public health provided for in the industrial society could be offset (though not entirely thwarted) by the 'positive checks' of pestilence, famine and warfare. Here, collective violent conflict has replaced the predation threat of large carnivores. Although all human beings belong to a single species, non-biological differentiations such as religions, languages, cultures, national identities and so on are, as Chapter 5 will show, held to constitute 'quasi-species'. In killing each others' members in war, these are deemed to self-limit human impact on the ecosystem (Hutchinson 1965).

Indeed, it is perhaps at this level of the substate group that most attention has been focused upon the functions of conflict. Five basic ideas predominate – all of which may be considered alongside Mitchell's triangular model of mutually interactive conflictive attitudes, behaviour and situations looked at in Chapter 2. First, participating in conflictive behaviour may, as Raymond Mack has noted, help to coalesce groups by making individuals aware of their shared goals and mutual interests (1965: 335). Afro-Americans' resistance to racism has, for instance, helped to extend notions of black identity across the United States. Second, engaging in conflictive behaviour can in-crease the critical focus on views that are held within the group, thereby bringing problems to the surface. In this way, group structures can become more egalitarian through a shared commitment to a cause. Examples of this include the enhanced capacity of female insurgents in Guatemala and Turkey to challenge traditional patriarchal hierarchies and the enfranchisement of British women following the boost that the First World War gave to the suffrage movement. Third, conflicts may increase motivation levels within groups, which may then stimulate industry, solve technological problems and lead to innovative thinking. The Second World War was, for example, a period of both scientific advance and very high per capita outputs. Fourth, the experience of conflict may oblige parties to establish contact with oppos-ing groups, to modify previously unobtainable goals or to assess and gain a greater understanding of their, and others', goals – thereby ending a stalled relationship (Mitchell 1980: 62–3).

The integrative function of conflict

The fifth type of substate focus is the idea that conflicts may also assist in demarcating boundaries between groups and solidifying in-group cohesion (Coser 1956: 38). The origins of such an emphasis on the 'integrative' func-tions of conflictive behaviour lie in Darwin's social premise that there is an innate human proclivity to direct sympathy 'solely towards members of the same community, and therefore towards known, and more or less loved, members but not to all the members of the same species' (1871: 163). In oth-er words, humankind has, as a general pattern of social interaction, sought to establish 'in' or 'we' groups in opposition to 'out' or 'other' groups. Build-ing on the work of Darwin, writers such as William Sumner have argued that 'the relation of comradeship and peace in the we-group and that of hostility and war towards other-groups are correlative to each other. The exigencies of war with outsiders are what make peace inside' (1906: 12). Such a view remains current today. The idea that conflict-induced cohesion evolved as a means of protecting vulnerable females and young from external threats is, as Chapter 5 will outline in more detail, still frequently offered as an expla-nation for ethnocentrism and nationalism (Somit and Peterson 1997).

Indeed, a number of anthropological investigations would seem to provide some support for these views. Studies of feuding groups in rural Morocco and Brazil, for instance, found that each enjoyed much greater solidarity when involved in periods of violent conflict (Lewis 1961). Indeed, the correlation was so strong in the latter case that some writers went on to allege that the need to maintain internal order led groups to seek conflict with others – a claim that will be discussed further in the following section (Murphy 1957: 1032). Subsequent research by Keith Otterbein modified these findings by looking at a wide range of small communities involved in collective conflict (1994). His conclusions included the caveat that the integrative effects of conflict participation were a feature only of groups that possessed pre-existent structures of centralised power. These effects could not, in other words, transform an aggregation of individuals into a cohesive group, nor could they meld groups into larger collectives if they lacked prior experience of operating together. As such, individual reactions, including panic, resignation and initiating violent attacks upon other group members, are predicted to be more common among people grouped together by an acute, collectively experienced threat (Foreman 1963). In some instances, however, the imminent presence of danger has exerted a demonstrably cohering effect upon previously unconnected, even antagonistic, individuals. White seamen from areas of the southern United States where racial tensions were prevalent who served with Afro-American colleagues during the Second World War were, for example, found to demonstrate decreasing levels of racial prejudice the longer they spent at sea (Brophy 1945).

In order for integration to result from the shared experience of risk, Arthur Stein suggests that three conditions need to be met:

> First, the threat and danger come from outside and the causes can clearly be seen and specified. Second, the immediate needs are clearly recognizable, and direct action can be undertaken with discernible results. Third, all are affected indiscriminately and thus the danger and suffering become public phenomena equally shared. The resultant solidarity eliminates even social distinctions.
>
> (1976: 151)

For Stein, the elimination of social distinctions does not imply the presence of the kind of societal equilibrium discussed at the start of this chapter. If we take Ernst Haas' definition of cohesion as 'the likelihood of internal peaceful change in a setting of groups with mutually antagonistic claims', then a group subject to the integrative effects of conflict engagement would remain fundamentally conflictive (1961: 367). In assessing this situation, it is useful to distinguish between attitudes and behaviour by returning to Mitchell's triangular schema presented in Chapter 2. His model suggests that a conflictive situation can lead to a change in attitude whereby individuals, first, seek security and prestige in identifying with groups and, second, tend to experience personal challenges as a threat to the values of the group as a whole. This cohering effect is thus likely to impact upon conflictive behaviour within the group. Of the three types of conflictive behaviour that he identifies – coercion, persuasion and compromise – group members are thus more likely to select a combination of the last two during periods of external conflict. Bearing in mind Schmid's point, elaborated in Chapter 3, that persuasion and compromise tend to be strategies preferred by those seeking a return to a favourable status quo, such an effect clearly has a number of potential benefits for leaders wishing to institutionalise a pacific domestic environment. Indeed, in order to ensure in-group integration, leaders may 'actually search for enemies with the deliberate purpose, or the unwitting result, of maintaining unity and internal cohesion' (Coser 1956: 104). As James Madison told Thomas Jefferson in 1798, it is, perhaps, 'a universal truth that the loss of liberty at home is to be charged to provisions against danger, real or pretended, from abroad' (quoted in Smith 1995: 1048).

For the philosopher Leo Strauss (1899–1973), whose students included the architects of the recent invasion of Iraq, Paul Wolfowitz and Abram Shulsky (*The New Yorker* 5 May 2003), liberalism required politicians to iterate 'noble lies' in order to give people moral certainty in a system which, in elevating individual liberty to the zenith of human achievement, contained an intrinsic tendency towards relativism. In a reworking of Nietzsche's 'deadly truths', he argued that leaders – those able to comprehend the deeper meaning in philosophers' deliberately esoteric erudition – had a responsibility to inculcate group identities in their followers in order to prevent a liberal society from descending into Huxleyan vacuousness and chaos. In fact, he went further and questioned the distinction between values and facts that underpins post-Enlightenment rationalism, thereby implying that all claims of objective truth are self-delusional and dangerous (1965). Such a vision of political leadership has proved to be highly influential not only for constructivists and post-modernists who, as Chapter 6 notes, have elaborated accounts of how the manufacture of conflictive environments takes place, but also for a generation of American neo-conservatives, such as William Kristol (the former chief of staff to Secretary of Education William Bennett and Vice President Dan Quayle), and the present Deputy National Security Advisor, Elliot Abrams, both of whom studied under Strauss's protégé, Harvey Mansfield, at Harvard.

The influence of Strauss can be seen in Mary Kaldor's study of what she calls the 'imaginary' Cold War (1990). Here, the leaders of the two blocs of 'Stalinism' and 'Atlanticism' used their huge conventional and nuclear arsenals to control domestic political life and marshal economic resources in ways that would not have been tolerated without a war mentality. It was born, she argues, of the need for a new unifying principle of action following the Second World War. The Soviet threat helped Western leaders to discredit isolationism as well as to repress domestic leftism. The maintenance, design and deployment of both sides' weaponry also stimulated economic growth and secured party loyalties. Kaldor's claims have, more recently, received support from the partly autobiographical accounts of President Carter's National Security Adviser, Zbigniew Brzezinski (1997), and former United States Ambassador to the Soviet Union, George Kennan (1996).

An associated body of work puts forward the idea that external conflict increases the internal coherence of alliance structures – one of the key focuses of Chapter 9. George Liska, for instance, notes that 'reciprocal pressures between roughly equal alliance systems tend to consolidate both' (1962: 26). Terry Hopmann builds on this work by hypothesising that 'the greater the East–West tension, the greater the degree of cohesion within the Communist system'. He concludes that, during the premiership of Joseph Stalin, the eight core countries of the Soviet-led bloc (China, Albania, East Germany, Poland, Hungary, Rumania, Bulgaria and Czechoslovakia) were relatively well integrated behind a structure of Politburo control based upon perceptions of an acute American threat. Following Stalin's death in 1953 and the Geneva Conference in 1955, however, a greater degree of diversity within the alliance's view of the United States emerged. He suggests that a possible way to view Moscow's decision to intervene in Hungary and Poland in 1956 is as a means of solidifying intra-alliance unity through the heightening of East–West tensions. Indeed, strains placed on the Sino-Soviet relationship following the latter's signature of the 1963 Test-Ban Treaty did appear to be considerably alleviated by the United States' decision to begin bombing North Vietnam in February 1965 (1967: 216).

Diversionary theories of conflict

Debates over the political impact of in-group/out-group divisions have co-alesced into a body of literature generally referred to as 'scapegoat' or 'diversionary' theories of international conflict. Broadly, these concern 'the idea that political elites often embark on adventurous foreign policies or even resort to war in order to distract popular attention away from internal social and economic problems and consolidate their own domestic political support' (Levy 1993: 259). Such an understanding of the expediencies of rule is far from new. William Shakespeare's Henry IV, for example, said to his son, the future King, 'be it thy course to busy giddy minds with foreign quarrels; that action, hence borne out, may waste the memory of the former days' (*Henry IV*, Part 2, act IV, scene v). More recently, interest in diversionary tactics has emerged as part of a challenge to the state-centric approach of the realist paradigm embodied in Waltz's view that 'the necessities of policy arise from the unregulated competition of states [and that] calculation based on these necessities can discover the policies that will best serve a state's interest' (1979: 117).

For instance, the dual rise of Marxist emphases on substate class competition and liberal visions of civil-internationalist connections, highlighted in Chapter 2, has led to a growth in theories aimed at combining domestic political factors with state behaviour. Both approaches are, for instance, commonplace among analyses of the German entry into the First World War. These generally seek to explain Reichstag policy in terms of 'dissipating social tensions at home by campaigns abroad' (Fischer in Wehler 1985: 196). More recently, a commonly cited example of the diversionary war is British policy preceding the Falklands/Malvinas crisis of March 1982. Studies of this concentrate, for the most part, on Prime Minister Thatcher's failure to respond to the growing threat from Buenos Aires. Having spent 14 years negotiating with the United Kingdom over the future of the islands, the Argentines had been encouraged by the British decision to withdraw the HMS

Endurance from the region in June 1981, but, by early 1982, they had become frustrated by continued British trammelling. On 2 March 1982, their delegation withdrew from further talks and announced that they reserved the 'right to seek other means' of settling the dispute. The following day, Buenos Aires announced that they were considering unspecified unilateral action. Three weeks later, Argentine warships arrived off the islands. By 28 March, a substantial support fleet had left port and, on 2 April, a full-scale land invasion took place (Norpoth 1987a: 6–7). Having broken the Argentine diplomatic code, the British government was, throughout this period, inundated with intelligence reports predicting such a result, yet no cabinet meeting was convened to discuss the crisis until 28 March – four days before the invasion. Although a substantial British fleet was subsequently dispatched (retaking the islands on 14 June), numerous questions remained over the government's failure to react earlier. Of course this could be seen as simply bureaucratic inertia and incompetence, but it might be argued that the crisis was deliberately allowed to escalate in order, first, to divert domestic attention away from the parlous condition of the British economy and, second, to seek a boost in popularity that posturing, or outright war, with Argentina might be expected to provide.

Either way, two things appear certain. The first is that British signals, intentionally or otherwise, indicated to the Argentine government 'that the annexation of the islands would be cheap and easy' (Gelpi 1997: 278). The second is that the war did, as Figure 4.1 illustrates, coincide with a sharp increase in government popularity, despite unemployment moving from under half a million in 1979 to almost three million by the beginning of 1982 (Norpoth 1987b: 953). Alternative causes of such a sharp rise are hard to sustain. More general international issues do not appear to have played a part, with President Reagan and Chancellor Schmidt's popularity declin-

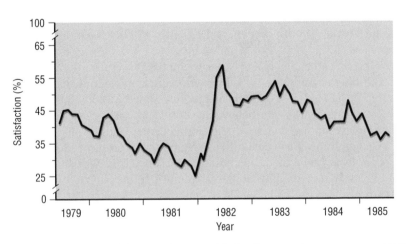

Figure 4.1 The British public's satisfaction with the Conservative government 1979–85. Source: Redrawn from Norpoth (1987b: 953).

ing from 47 to 44 per cent and from 39 to 38 per cent, respectively, and President Mitterrand enjoying a modest rise of one point from 58 to 59 per cent during this period. In the United Kingdom, on the other hand, 61 per cent of those questioned named the Falklands crisis as 'the most important problem facing Britain today' with only 25 per cent citing unemployment (*The Economist* 8 May 1982). By 26 June, over 250 British troops were dead and more than one billion pounds had been spent, yet the same survey found that 76 per cent of the British public remained in agreement with government policy over the issue. While this does not, of course, prove that involvement in the war *caused* the rise in positive public opinion, nor that the British government undertook this conflict *in order* to gain popularity or to divert attention from the miserable economic climate, numerous writers have concluded that the conflict helped to secure a Conservative victory in the 1983 elections and that, in the eyes of many, Mrs Thatcher 'emerged as a remarkable war leader' (Hastings and Jenkins 1984: 355–6). As such, the result of the Falklands/Malvinas crisis offers some support for the general comment that 'a fully specified theory of the causes of international conflict will require an understanding of the role domestic politics plays in foreign policy decisions' (Morgan and Bickers 1992: 26).

Constructing such a general theory has, however, proved extremely difficult. Successive quantitative studies have failed to establish a systematic link between internal political problems and the external use of force. An analysis of nine indicators of domestic strife and of 13 indicators of external conflict undertaken by Rudolph Rummel during the early 1960s, for instance, concluded that 'foreign conflict behaviour is generally and completely unrelated to domestic conflict behaviour' (1963: 24). Similar results were arrived at using various methodologies over the next ten years or so (Tanter 1966; Wilkenfeld 1972). More recently, though, these studies have been brought into question. Clifton Morgan and Christopher Anderson, for instance, note that, in many cases, their findings were based on an inability to establish a clear linear relationship. As the previous section outlines, however, group cohesion cannot be simplistically related to participation in external conflict, and thus the search for such a strong association is, almost inevitably, futile. If, for instance, the integrative effects of conflict are believed to vary across different groups and group constituents, one might expect leaders not to engage in external uses of force if internal cohesion is very weak. Furthermore, if it is assumed that already well-integrated groups would not be significantly affected by conflict participation then, again, leaders would not be expected to deploy such a strategy. The external use of force may therefore be more likely to occur when internal dissent is moderate, producing a curvilinear, inverted 'U' relationship rather than a linear correlation (1999: 801).

Consequently, many writers have argued that leaders' propensity to choose to distract dissatisfied groups by using force externally on another party, as opposed to using the more obvious methods of compromise or repression, is heavily reliant on the type of regime in which they operate (Bueno de

Mesquita and Siverson 1995). The greater autonomy of authoritarian leaders, plus the absence of significant reform pressures may, for instance, make diversionary conflict easier to instigate. Equally, the institutional restraints on democratically elected leaders may mean that the state elite is more likely to acquiesce to the demands of dissenters. Alternatively, it is frequently argued that both types of leadership structure rely on support coalitions, a stable economy and a pacific workforce for survival and thus have a comparable incentive for diversionary conflict (Downs and Rocke 1995). In contrast, other writers, such as Christopher Gelpi, suggest that the relative ease with which authoritarian leaders can repress internal dissent, coupled with the less extensive need for a 'rally-around-the-flag' effect, means that democratically elected leaders will be more likely to use diversionary tactics (1997: 260–1). This is especially so after internal dissent has become sufficiently acute for democratic leaders to regard the granting of concessions as a possible incentive for others.

It has also been noted that the decision to embark on a diversionary conflict rests, first, on the degree to which leaders can be certain that such a course of action will lead to the clear identification of an internal enemy among the public. As some dissenting factions within states may regard an external foe as an ally in their struggle, this policy will only be effective 'if domestic actors view the foreigners as worse than their domestic antagonists' (Morgan and Anderson 1999: 803). Second, leaders must believe that the identification of an internal enemy will solidify their own position in relation to their constituents. As the allegiance of the entire polity is neither possible nor necessary, however, this rests on the perceived relative importance of the leadership's allies. A leader with a large parliamentary majority may not, for instance, be overly anxious at the dismay of opposition parties, but would probably view Cabinet fractures over their choice of external enemy with more concern. Thus, a diversionary strategy becomes especially likely if the leadership support base is perceived to be under threat. Third, leaders will not embark upon *any* hostile act simply because it offers the potential to divert. The expected utility of an external conflict is a vital consideration. It must, for instance, be eminently winnable without the danger of a potentially costly or prolonged engagement. Conversely, though, it must be sufficiently high profile to have an impact on the target dissenters within the leadership's support base.

The diverse nature of leaders' internal constituencies brings us to another problem with much of the statistical literature – its failure to acknowledge that approval for war leaders tends to be short lived (Cotton 1986). The state's extraction of soldiers and taxes is frequently resisted by elites and unpopular with the masses. Furthermore, a focus on external conflict may reduce a government's capacity to repress its opponents, leading to greater internal conflict and instability – particularly when coupled with the de-mobilisation of large numbers of combatants commonly troubled by feelings of social dislocation. In many cases, these factors have led to the downfall of governments. It is not without reason that warfare is often called the midwife of revolution. The disastrous involvement of American forces in Vietnam, for instance, is reckoned to have cost President Johnson over 20 percentage points (Mueller 1973: 196). Indeed, in the case of the Falklands War, it is quite clear that

> had the Thatcher government disappointed its public by either losing the war or being unable to bring it to a swift conclusion, public reaction might have been quite different from what was found. . . . [Indeed] even with a rather quick victory, the Falklands gain in government popularity did not prove permanent.
>
> (Norpoth 1987a: 12)

Perhaps, then, 'we should expect diversionary uses of force to consist of actions short of war' (as the British leadership conceivably intended) rather than the occurrence of large-scale collective violence measured by Rummel and others (Richards *et al.* 1993: 508–9). After all, it may be that brinkmanship with accompanying scapegoating (i.e. the process of mobilisation) is equally effective as, or more effective than, the outcome of the conflict itself. Ned Lebow, for instance, found that, in the case of 13 'brinkmanship crises', only five could be explained using realist models of deterrence (in other words, the adversaries' perceived defence capacity, their credibility and their ability to communicate their threat to others) (1981). Rather, the other eight crises were, he concludes, both initiated and deliberately escalated by political leaders in order to buttress their domestic support.

Perhaps the best known example of a study of this type is Charles Ostrom and Brian Job's analysis of United States foreign policy between 1946 and 1978 (1986). They use Barry Blechman and Stephen Kaplan's dataset of American involvement in overseas conflict as well as their definition of the 'political use of major force' as physical actions

> taken by one or more components of the uniformed armed military services as part of a deliberate attempt by the national authorities to influence, or be prepared to influence, specific behaviour or individuals in another nation without engaging in a continuing contest of violence.
>
> (1978: 12)

They then proceed on the basis of seven presidential decision premises derived from the domestic political environment. These are outlined in column one of Table 4.3. Column two sets out Ostrom and Job's prediction of each premise's impact on the executive's decision-making processes. Correlating these to the 226 occasions on which the United States has deployed the 'political use of major force' overseas, Ostrom and Job find support for the first premise, concluding that public perceptions of international tension are 'negatively related to the probability of a political use of force' (1986: 557).

Table 4.3 American presidential decision-making over the political use of force

Decision premise	Expected impact on presidential decision-making processes
Public attitudes to international tension	Public concern over international tension will lower the president's propensity to use force
Public attitudes to the strategic balance	Public perceptions that the United States is becoming disadvantaged by changes in the strategic balance will act as an incentive for the president to use force
Public aversion to warfare	The president is unlikely to use force following American involvement in warfare
The condition of the domestic economy	Deteriorations in the domestic economy will encourage the president to use force as a diversionary measure
The perceived level of public support	The president will be more likely to use force if he perceives himself to have a buffer of support
Past political success	A decline in presidential success will make him more risk acceptant and thus more likely to use force
The current position in the electoral calendar	The propensity to use force during important periods in the electoral calendar

In terms of the second premise, no relationship was found between the strategic balance and political uses of force. Both the third and fourth premises did, however, find support, leading Ostrom and Job to note that war weariness and periods of economic prosperity acted as inhibitors on presidents' use of major political force between 1946 and 1978 – matters that we shall return to in Chapter 9.

Most significant in their statistical analysis were the fifth and sixth premises. While declines in presidential backing almost always occur during an incumbent's time in office, the use of force was found to transpire most commonly when popularity levels were waning, yet a buffer of support remained. Taken together, however, 'the more negative the president's overall record in office (as represented by declining popular support), the more likely he is to act in the absence of a popularity buffer' (Ostrom and Job 1986: 557–8). The final premise was supported, in that the overseas use of major political force was more likely to occur in the final quarter before an election than in any other quarter of the electoral year. These findings are important as they offer a direct challenge to the realist understanding of state behaviour as primarily grounded on the pressure of international relations as determinants of domestic politics. As Patrick James and John Oneal point out, if 'the desire to divert attention from a troubled economy is a greater influence on the decision to use force than the level of international tension, assumptions regarding the national interest are clearly undermined' (1991: 308).

Question marks do, however, remain over the transferability of these results. Bruce Russett has, for instance, noted that, as the success of diversionary measures relies on a rapid victory, more powerful states are more likely to engage in such actions than those with weaker military capabilities

(1989). Extrapolating from Ostrom and Job's state-level study to the level of the international system without controlling for this would introduce a serious bias into the analysis (Levy 1993: 277). Moreover, their finding that a buffer of support during periods of declining popularity encourages the presidential use of force has been countered by realists. Hans Morgenthau and Kenneth Thompson have argued that this is not a domestic variable at all (1985: 158). They suggest that national support is primarily an indication of leaders' capacity to act internationally. Here, then, internal support is construed as a means of strengthening national security and the 'search for policies which will maintain the leader in power against domestic opposition' (Bueno de Mesquita and Siverson 1995: 853). Such a concession does, however, confirm the broadly non-realist notion that 'decisions regarding international conflict are, as with any policy decisions, affected by the pushing and pulling of competing domestic interests' (Morgan and Bickers 1992: 26).

Conclusion

This chapter looked first at issues related to the evaluation of conflict. In the first section, it traced the various means through which these have been approached over the years and how different methods have informed the way that the impact of conflictive behaviour on group formation, structure and dynamics has been assessed. It contrasted these approaches with the equilibrium model and with simplistic categorisations of conflictive behaviour as either functional or dysfunctional, suggesting that, instead, engaging in conflict may involve both types of outcome depending on who is analysed, when and by whom. Apart from the obvious costs of conflictive behaviour, various material, political and psychological benefits have been identified. These may be at the level of the system (in terms of driving forward change and reducing population pressures), the state (through the consolidation of alliance structures), the group (as a means of cohering hitherto disparately organised elements) and, in providing both an emotional catharsis and a way of responding rationally to duress, the individual.

In the second section, one of these functions – the idea that conflict participation can cohere or integrate social groups and systems – was taken forward and explored in more detail. Evidence from evolutionary science was discussed in the light of an assortment of well-known anthropological studies with the aim of developing a nuanced comprehension of this proposition. It was argued that existent structures, previous experiences and socio-historical trajectories are important in understanding the changes in behaviour that commonly result from, or coincide with, the impact of conflict engagement upon groups, alliances and systems. Here, the presence of structural violence can, as Uvin's study of Rwanda examined in Chapter 3 illustrates, provide a facilitative environment for social differentiation to occur. Galtung's model of cultural violence is particularly apposite here, as a means of revealing the banality of scapegoating 'others' so that groups may feel more 'self'. As we saw in Chapter 3, the intensification of group delimitations can rely on the exclusionary organisation of religious, gender, class, racial or political identities and can be underpinned by the, frequently subliminal, use of discriminatory communication media. Here, the capitalist mode of production and its emphasis on value maximisation, competitiveness and the 'naturalness' of unequal production factors may help to normalise the 'noble lies' identified by Strauss (1965). A similar function might be ascribed to the production of knowledge through science and its power to confer legitimacy upon those elites for whom conflict and violence is efficacious.

The third section focused on the idea that conflictive behaviour stems from political elites' need to divert attention from the domestic arena by pursuing aggressive foreign policy objectives. At its broadest, this body of work merely seeks to establish a connection between domestic and international state actions as a challenge to realist notions of international primacy. In some formulations, however, direct causal linkages are deemed to exist between government unpopularity or internal dissent and the deliberate pursuit of crises or even warfare abroad. A widely cited example of this is the British administration's handling of the Falklands/Malvinas crisis in 1982 and its failure to prevent the dispute from escalating to war. Much clearly depends on the type of regime in which leaders operate. In many cases, brinkmanship might serve a similar purpose to military engagement and may thus be preferred. Yet, the notion that elites are prepared to provoke conflicts in an attempt to obfuscate and cause their citizens to rally around the flag remains an intuitively appealing and important area of research.

5 Innate

A key element in both the creation of enhanced in-group coherence and the legitimisation of aggressive foreign policies considered in the previous chapter is the idea that there is a scientific basis to ethnic or national solidarity born of the immutably conflictive nature of the human condition. This chapter argues that, within the current landscape of conflict analysis, there are two basic facets that build on these premises – constituting the two sections to follow. The first is a focus on the biology of the human body, its evolutionary origins as well as its neurological, psychological and hormonal functions. With its origins in nineteenth-century scientism and the development of the experimental method, this corpus of work is often associated with studies of animal behaviour, physiology and psychiatry and tends to focus on human phenomena as a branch of sensate life. The second set of ideas promulgating the immutable nature of the human propensity for violent conflict is grounded upon the premise that deeply rooted aspects of human experience – namely culture, history and religion – are relatively constant determinants of human behaviour. It has been particularly deployed to cast light on very long-term conflicts of apparent intractability in which language, ethnicity and human rights play a part. In many ways, these two approaches represent not so much theory as such, but rather a disparate, at times quite speculative (albeit extremely popular and widely read), spectrum of opinion. The unifying, or at least common, features which these views share are, first, an assumption that violent conflict is an inevitable part of human interaction, second, that it can only be imperfectly prevented rather than avoided altogether and, third, that the root causes of conflictive behaviour are *in natus*, or present at birth, and are thus to be found in unchanging, or very slowly changing, features of human development or physiology. Conflict is, in other words, inherent; 'the potentiality for it always exists and actuality can only be obstructed' (Eckstein 1980: 139).

Socio-biology

The attribution of social ills to the fixed nature of humanity is far from new. Basing their work on the writing of Saint Augustine and others, Christian theologians have long promulgated the idea that humanity has inherited the original sins of Adam and Eve, the only two people born free of sin. People are thus not sinners because they sin, but rather people sin because they are sinners – or as John Calvin put it in the sixteenth century, humanity's 'whole nature is, as it were, a seed of sin' (1949: 8). In many ways, this view of human behaviour as immutably prone to, among other dysfunctions, violent conflict captures the essence of this chapter's topic. While the various ideas and approaches discussed below mostly have their origins in the less exegetic concerns of the nineteenth century, they share Christianity's tenet that, at their most fundamental, the causes of violence are to be found within human beings and not within the social dynamics of human interaction. Moreover, in policy terms, efforts to end the human propensity for violence are, for both old and new accounts, largely futile. So, although evolutionary change, ethological instincts, psychological drives and fixed socio-cultural imperatives have replaced divine ordinance and creationism as the primary determinants of individual action, the best that can be hoped for is that dysfunctionally conflictive behaviour may be temporarily arrested by ritual, cathartic release, religious or secular education, imminent or deferred punishment and therapeutic procedure.

A salient element of this literature is socio-biology, defined as 'the systematic study of the biological basis of all social behaviors' (Crawford 1987: 3), and its pioneer, Charles Darwin (1809–82). Its master-concept is the idea that organic adaptations, including patterns of behaviour, have their origins in an evolutionary course of change. This has two fundamental tenets: that variation exists at the outset of a process of achieving a better fit between organism and environment and that this character is transmitted between parent and offspring. As Patrick Bateson explains:

> The short-term steps in the process involve some individuals surviving or breeding more easily than others. If the ones that survive or breed more easily carry a particular version of the character, that version will be more strongly represented in the future generations. If the character enabled them to survive or breed more readily, then the long-term consequence is that the character will bear a close and seemingly well-designed relationship to the conditions in which it worked.
>
> (1989: 36)

Aggressive behaviour is one such character. In environments where the supply of food and mates is in short supply, aggressive animals are more likely to live longer and produce (and protect) greater numbers of offspring. As a result, aggression, along with other strategies such as cooperation, migration and so on, evolved in a process of natural selection as a means of pursuing these imperative goals. Although Darwin was careful not to include humanity explicitly within his *On the Origin of Species by Means of Natural Selection* (1859), the fact that, 'in the mid-nineteenth century, science, theology, philosophy, and social theory had not yet been severed from one another to form autonomous disciplines', meant that his biological theory quickly became 'a source of both scientific insight and scientized social philosophy' (Kaye 1997: 15–16). Indeed, in preparing *The Descent of Man and Selection in Relation to Sex* (1871), Darwin borrowed extensively from non-biological sources, including Thomas Malthus' *Essay on the Principle of Population* (1798) and William Paley's *Natural Theology* (1802) (Jones 1980). This cross-fertilisation of ideas persisted with writers such as Herbert Spencer (1820–1903) and William Graham Sumner (1840–1910) extending and popularising various, and often distorted, renditions of Darwin's postulates in Europe and the United States (Moore 1979). The result was, and remains, the belief that conflict and violence are fixed, rather than learned, patterns of behaviour caused by innate motor actions that can be controlled socially or pharmaceutically, but cannot be completely prevented other than by a change in the genetic process that created them.

An important concern of the period was thus to understand the social implications of evolution's genetic motor. In particular, it was hoped that society could be made less subject to violent conflict by controlling reproduction – manipulating natural selection to produce characteristics that, in Darwinian terms, better suit individuals to their social environment. In 1883, Darwin's cousin, Francis Galton, formulised this as eugenics which, in a speech to the Sociology Society at the University of London in 1904, he defined as 'the science which deals with all influences that improve the inborn qualities of a race'. While in Great Britain, eugenics organisations were primarily concerned with preventing the 'unfit' from having children by withdrawing welfare provisions (which were regarded as a distortion of natural selection principles), equivalents within the United States took up Galton's focus on ethnicity as a way of responding to domestic racial conflict. In 1906, for instance, the Committee on Eugenics was established with the expressed aim of stemming 'the tide of threatened racial degeneracy' and protecting America against 'indiscriminate immigration, criminal degenerates, and race suicide' (cited in Mehler 1978: 3). Supported by luminaries such as John Maynard Keynes and Julian Huxley (the first director of UNESCO), a large body of literature appeared tackling issues such as the distribution of intelligence within society (the infamous Bell Curve Theory), criminality and selective sterilisation programmes (imposed in 27 American states as well as Norway, Sweden, Denmark, Switzerland and Germany by 1935). By 1923, research had 'advanced' sufficiently for Fairfield Osborn (President of the American Museum of Natural History from 1908 to 1933) to claim that 'we have learned once and for all that the Negro is not like us' (quoted in Gould 1981: 231).

Widespread revulsion at the German use of such ideas following the Second World War did, however, acutely damage the reputation of eugenics in particular and socio-biology in general (Allen *et al*. 1976). The image of the dispassionate scientist was severely shaken – not least by the publication of an influential book establishing a clear correlation between the political preferences of the researcher and their stated position with regard to the nature–nurture debate (the left being more associated with the latter) (Pastore 1949). As Howard Kaye puts it, the dominant thinking of the day held that 'biological needs and processes paled into insignificance before human reason, inventiveness, and the pursuit of meaning as determinants of how we live' (1997: 1). Collective culture and international cooperation were, as a generalised vision of humanity, generally preferred to the selfish individualism implied by Darwinian theory. By the 1960s, however, the failure of social sciences' turn towards culture – evidenced in the abandonment of functionalist and modernisation theories – led to a renewed interest in socio-biology, now invigorated by the gradual elucidation of DNA as the psychochemical theory of heredity Darwin lacked (Fleming 1969). In many ways, the 1960s and 1970s were the heyday of socio-biology, to which current writing continues to owe much. By the 1980s, a concerted attack from social scientists had again caused it to retreat from much of its societal commentary (to be discussed in the next chapter). In 1997, for instance, Albert Somit and Steven Peterson felt compelled to entitle the first chapter of their book, *Darwinism, Dominance, and Democracy*, 'Prologue to a Predictably Unpopular Thesis'. In the mid-1960s, though, socio-biologists, while carefully distancing themselves from the overt racial overtones of the interwar period, were able to advocate large-scale social engineering programmes with an impunity not seen since the 1930s – Francis Crick, for instance, suggested reversible sterilisation and the licensing of 'people with the qualities we like' to bear children (quoted in Wolstenholme 1963: 295).

A potential quality to breed out of the citizenry at large was aggression. Studies by Guhl *et al*. (1960) and Scott and Fuller (1965) had shown that the aggressive behaviour, which, they argued, natural selection had endowed upon chickens and dogs, could be significantly diminished by interbreeding aggressive and more placid varieties together. To explain this, it has been proposed that 'all animals which show aggressive behaviour carry a number of genes which modify its level of expression [and it] . . . would be very surprising if human beings were different' (Manning 1989: 51). A genetic element that attracted particular attention was the Y chromosome. Carried only through paternal lines in mammals, its genetic patterning has been associated, in some studies, with differences in human behaviour (Maxson *et al*. 1979). In instances where males have received two Y chromosomes (XYY rather than the usual XY structure) – a condition affecting one in every 1,000 men – high levels of aggression have been observed. For instance, in a 1965 survey of 197 men detained for violent crime in a maximum security psychiatric unit, eight (30 times the background average) were found to possess two Y chromosomes – strongly suggesting that their propensity for aggression was genetically linked (Jacobs *et al.* 1965).

Vice versa, the study of behaviour has also been used to make assertions regarding the likely influence of genetic patterning on aggression and conflict. Ethology, defined by Barnett as the 'biology of behaviour' (cited in Nelson 1974: 292), emerged during the 1960s with an interest in 'the comparative study and analysis of instinctive or stereotyped movements of animals' (Thorpe 1974: 147). While, today, many ethologists adhere to the classic Darwinist position that, as animal evolution is independent, cross-species generalisation is impossible, others argue that the common ancestry of many species (such as the alleged connection between human beings and higher primates) and the commonality of behaviour patterns between unrelated forms suggest generically comparable selection pressures. Their overall aim is therefore to develop 'a scientifically defensible conception of man's nature' by looking at what they call 'fixed action patterns', which are 'largely unlearned and take place without demonstrable stimulation' (Willhoite 1971: 619; Berkowitz 1990: 25).

Numerous studies have helped to establish the importance of instinctive behaviour for lower order animals. Removing rhesus monkeys and weaverbirds from their parents at birth and rearing them in absolute isolation, for instance, proved that their demonstrable requirement for contact comfort and their ability to construct complex nests, respectively, must have been acquired innately (Harlow and Harlow 1986; Ferrell 1996: 39). The Nobel laureate, Konrad Lorenz, argues that human beings share comparably inherent proclivities. 'The instinct to aggress', he writes, 'is not a reactive one, but is a spontaneous activity within ourselves' (cited in Zillmann 1979: 47). In his book, *On Aggression*, he suggests that 'it is the spontaneity of the [aggressive] instinct which makes it so dangerous' and calls on society to provide ways in which this can be channelled away from violence (Lorenz 1966: 50). However, while humanity's primate ancestry continues to produce innately violent men, human society has, he proposes, lost the capacity to mitigate its consequences. Unlike other predators, we have neither the ritualised surrender nor the tournament-style organisation of the animal kingdom's intraspecific violence – no longer can we turn on our backs like dogs and expect mercy. Despite this, our highly evolved intelligence systems have given rise to complex weapons of mass lethality, thereby creating a fatal disjuncture between 'nature and efficacy [which] in a nuclear age are held to be potentially catastrophic' (Webb 1992: 70).

Beneath this veneer of precocity, however, Lorenz identifies an 'action-specific energy' originating in humanity's evolutionary hinterland. For some writers, such base instincts are to be found in the reptilian essence of the brain which, over millions of years, has been obscured by mammalian and human layers in a process 'somewhat like a house to which wings and superstructure are added' (MacLean 1967: 382). The spontaneity of human aggression and violence can thus be explained by the imperfectness of this evolutionary process. 'To the extent that primitive and limbic systems "dominate" overt behaviour, people may not be totally aware and in control of their reasons for behaving as they do, notably in times of stress that attend conflict' (Davies 1980: 33). Whether or not a violent response is discharged may be influenced by cultural and learned factors – to be discussed further below – which can constitute a 'specific inhibitory block' or, contrarily, a 're-leasing mechanism' (Brown 1965: 29; Eibl-Eibesfeldt and Wickler 1968).

Important here is the nature of the 'external releasers' or 'sign stimuli' within the environment (Nelson 1974: 293). Because behaving aggressively carries inherent risks, the aggressiveness of the response is likely to vary with the nature of the extraneous cue. For instance, while human beings may, in keeping with higher primates, engage in territorial behaviour (as a fixed action pattern) in response to a wide range of stimuli, greater aggressiveness is probable when there exists an acute threat to individual fitness – most obviously the maintenance of an adequate supply of material resources and potential mates. Studies of primate competition have, therefore, concluded that, as Freedman *et al.* point out, a 'high population density always leads to an increase in aggressiveness and that this also occurs in humans' (1972: 530). This tendency has frequently been found to be both more common and more intense among mammals that have already mated. Squirrels, for example, appear to be more likely to fight, rather than flee, when they have offspring and a nearby home (Barash 1980: 173). Such a tendency, dubbed 'the territorial imperative' by Robert Ardrey, is held to be a characteristic of human society (1966). David Barash, for instance, claims that it demon-strates that 'we fight most strongly for "what we believe in", and what we believe in is most likely to be closely related to our home and our family . . . [as a] reproductively relevant resource' (1980: 173–4).

Seeing the functionality of aggression in this way helps to resolve the longstanding problem of altruism for ethologists. As one of the pre-eminent socio-biologists of the twentieth century asks, 'how can altruism, which by definition reduces personal fitness, possibly evolve by natural selection' (Wilson 1975: 3)? Among insects such as ants and termites, Darwin noted the difficulty of explaining the behaviour of worker, neuter and soldier castes that seem to sacrifice their labour and lives in the service of the queen and the group as a whole. Acknowledging that such behaviour must have evolved through natural selection, he described the problem as 'a special difficulty, which at first appeared to me insuperable and actually fatal to the whole theory' (cited in Krebs 1987: 83). Subsequent studies have offered three types of potential answer. The first is that apparent acts of altruism might be aimed, in fact, at enhancing individual fitness. When faced with an imminent threat, many species of bird, for instance, will suspend their supposedly in-nate tendency to respond with either aggression or desertion and emit an alarm call that appears to warn others members of the flock at the expense of making the individual more conspicuous to the advancing danger. Studies by Hamilton (1964) and Charnov and Krebs (1974) have, however, claimed that the alarm call evolved in order to cause other members of the flock to take flight, thereby presenting a more difficult target to the threat and transferring attention away from the individual caller. More complex forms of 'reciprocal altruism' have also been noted among primates. As the development of social trust can promote individual fitness by storing goodwill and indebtedness within the group, baboon troops appear to have evolved sophisticated tit-for-tat arrangements that cohere the overall unit and discourage free-riding (Trivers 1971).

A second possible reason for the evolution of altruism is kin recognition. Animals may recognise their relatives through chemical phenotypes (believed to be important in ant colonies), associative imprinting (the recollection of littermates and so on), behavioural cues (such as greetings and ritual) and spatial awareness (associating progenies with nests and the like). Penguins, for instance, have been found to resist the tendency to respond more aggressively to territorial incursions near to their mate if members of their own kin group are involved. When relatedness is low within or between competing groups, then both conflicts and an overt lack of altruism are more apparent (Barash 1980: 174). Third, apparently altruistic behaviour may serve the evolutionary purposes of the group as a whole – the protection of which is vital for the selection of mates, the continuation of the gene pool and thus inclusive fitness maximisation. Wynne-Edwards noted in 1962 that many species reduce, or even abandon, reproduction when population densities begin to pressurise the availability of resources – a 'natural' adjustment related to Malthusian notions of 'balance'. However, in order to prevent a situation in which the altruistic simply die out, considerable cultural adaptation, or 'epigenesis', is required. This is defined by Albert Somit as 'a biologically transmitted tendency, evolved over the history of a species to learn, recognize, or behave in one fashion rather than another when faced with appropriate environmental stimuli' (1990: 562). It is particularly obvious in the human propensity for cooperation and reciprocity which, born of 'extreme selective pressures' upon our ancestors (for whom 'organized food gathering and hunts [we]re successful only if each member of the group knows his task and joins in with the activity of his fellows'), have 'become embedded to some degree in our genetic make-up' (Leaky and Lewin 1977: 125).

A fundamental epigenetic limitation upon human altruism is said to be familiarity (Ardrey 1970: 15). Necessary to underpin most social systems and likely to have originated in the small, extended family structures of ancestral humankind, it demarcates in-groups from out-groups. According to some, 'this xenophobic principle has been documented in virtually every group of animals displaying higher forms of social organization' (Wilson 1975: 249) and is thus likely to have a genetic basis which, as interaction becomes more heterogeneous, is being slowly eliminated (Rushton *et al.* 1985; Silverman 1987). Presently, familiarity outside kinship is thought to involve five 'recognition markers': physical appearance, descent, language, homeland and religion (Shaw and Wong 1989: 110). As these are held to act as inhibitors to aggression, it is predicted that diverse societies – particularly those in which overcrowding exacerbates territorialism – will be high on conflict and low on reciprocity. David Barash, for instance, proposes that 'a high immigration rate means, in general, a lower relatedness between individuals, which in turn means less altruism and more competitiveness' (1980: 174). Moreover, affiliation to in-groups can form a basis for tribal and national identities, providing considerable mobilising potential for inclusive fitness maximisation. This has important implications for both the ways in which social mobilisation occurs during conflicts (to be discussed further in Chapter 8) and the processes of 'otherisation' outlined in Chapter 4. It has also been used to explain the ethnic nature of politics in sub-Saharan Africa, the efficacy of organised religion and the urge for national self-determination.

To prevent such groupings from become cleavages upon which violent conflict may be grounded, Shaw and Wong conclude that cultural structures and 'incentives must be introduced to foster and protect inclusive fitness priorities' (1989: 110). Indeed, as David Barash notes, because human beings have a 'unique dichotomous nature as both biological and cultural creatures' (1977: 318), 'social evolution . . . [can] counter individual selfish tendencies which biological evolution has continued to select as a result of . . . genetic competition' (Campbell 1975: 1115). In most socio-biological accounts of human behaviour, however, this countering action takes many generations to take effect and, even then, there is, in Wilson's words, a limit 'beyond which biological evolution will begin to pull cultural evolution back to itself' (1978: 80). In 1981, in a book co-authored with Charles Lumsden, Wilson developed this notion of an intrinsic tension between biological and cultural processes into what has been termed 'the leash principle'. Here, the human 'dog' is restrained by the genetic 'master' through a cultural leash. The task for socio-biologists was now to determine the length of this leash – or the extent to which 'culturgens' can modify genetically predetermined behavioural tendencies. Such elasticity has allowed Wilson and others to respond to the severe criticisms that his and other socio-biological work began to attract during the 1980s and 1990s (looked at in Chapter 6) with less deterministic models of human behaviour (White 1999). In his more recent writing, for instance, Wilson claims that

culture is created by the communal mind, and each mind in turn is the product of the genetically structured human brain. Genes and culture are therefore inseverably [sic] linked . . . . The mind grows from birth to death by absorbing parts of the existing culture available to it, with selection guided through epigenetic rules inherited by the individual brain . . . . The quicker the pace of cultural evolution, the looser the connection between genes and culture, although the connection is never completely broken.

(1998: 127–8)

Culture, historiography and ancient hatreds

Socio-biology's turn towards culture is born, in part, of the perennial problem of variation. It has long been noted that conflict 'does not invariably or universally lead to the same behaviour' and that some societies display both higher frequencies and greater intensities of violence (Boring *et al.* 1939: 163). Indeed, as a subset of human action, conflict is relatively infrequent. While each of us may have disputes with other individuals quite regularly, aggressive behaviour is, for most people in most cultures, quite unusual and violence is rarer still. This is even true of the vast majority of XYY men (well over 90 per cent) who never acquire a conviction for violent crime and who respond well to interactive therapy (Manning 1989: 54–5). Indeed, as Keith Webb observes, modern people probably spend more time watching television than behaving aggressively, yet nobody is arguing that this is born of an innate propensity (1992). Moreover, at the state level, the majority of countries have experienced a declining rate of warfare over the last few centuries, despite considerable rises in human population (Levy and Morgan 1984). In fact, across the global system as a whole, the incidence of large-scale wars may be cyclical rather than deterministically constant – a proposition explored in Chapter 10 (Väyrynen 1987). In all, this suggests that 'whatever the bases of human aggression, it is within the capacity of humans to do away with it', or at least prevent its expression (Goldstein 1989: 15).

For psychologists and social scientists supportive of the innateness paradigm, the societal provision of individual cathartic releases may be one such way to prevent the expression of inner aggressive drivers. Here, psychoanalysis and the work of Sigmund Freud are important. He argued that individuals are born with an inherently self-destructive tendency, *Thanatos*, which works 'to reduce life to its primal state of inert matter' – the evolutionary origins of humanity, in other words (quoted in Strachey 1964: 75). Buried deep within the unconscious *id* (over which biological and cultural evolution has laid a thin veneer), the influence of *Thanatos* is, it is argued, reduced by displacing its destructive qualities on to other individuals, thereby causing conflict (Kull 1990). Society must, Freud argued, institutionalise cultural practices that can offer a functional outlet for pent-up emotion. This remains an important idea today and underpins much of the justification for competitive, including violent, sports as providers of a 'satisfactory outlet for the instinctive aggressive drive' (Menninger cited in Berkowitz 1990: 30).

Other writers argue that the cathartic control of inner aggression can be bolstered by developing complex social structures of dominance, defined as the 'probability that the dominant animal will have preferential access to some good to which both animals aspire' (Somit and Peterson 1997: 52). While also providing an enhanced means of reproductive success (for those who are on top), these structures serve 'to contain male aggressiveness and subordinate it to the needs of the group' (Corning 1971: 342). They do so by increasing the predictability of social relations and by obviating the need for continual disputes over resource access (Jolly 1985). As 'stark coercion, unsupported by other devices, is usually unsuccessful over time', it is concluded that dominance has evolved in order to ensure that male aggression is contained by norms of obedience and authority (Wilkinson 1969: 8). While modified by regime variation in a constant struggle between the strong and the weak, such an iron law of oligarchy is considered to be universal, ineluctable and, insofar as it ensures passivity, socially functional (Frank 1985).

The failure of some societies to institutionalise cultural patterns that control, or provide functional outlets for, male aggression is often seen as a fundamental explanation of substate level violence. Group formations are, for observers adopting this approach to conflict analysis, 'controlled primarily by the values, norms, or duties imposed by the sociocultural structure . . . distantly related to the basic propensities of individuals on which natural selection operated' (Hinde 1993: 49). As Umberto Melotti notes of the work of the evolutionary biologists, Richard Alexander and Gerald Borgia (1978),

> culture is the great unbalancer that reinforces human tendencies to live and compete in groups and to engage in an unusual (and unusually ferocious) group-against-group competition. Murder and war are likely to keep recurring only when their perpetrators are likely to gain, or at least believe that they will gain. Therefore, these phenomena are essentially human practices because culture alone leads frequently to imbalances that make such all-out aggression apparently profitable.
>
> (1987: 101–2)

So, as conflict causality is seen as innately embedded in the cultures of the protagonists, it is often treated in isolation from political or economic concerns (Harrison 2000: 296–9). The maxim that 'neither a democratic nor a capitalist economy is conceivable apart from certain cultural and moral habits' leads to the view that, in some 'cultures, people do not strive for progress or development' regardless of changes in their socio-economic position (Novak 2001: 169). The developing world is seen as especially guilty of not institutionalising functional systems of cathartic release and domination. Of the 29 countries identified by Albert Somit and Steven Peterson as having successfully channelled their citizenry's genetic propensity for conflict and violence into functional forms of dominance and catharsis (liberal democracies in other words), only four are from the South and just Botswana is from Africa (1997: 42). Faced with the 'powerful, immovable culture' upon which his continent's perpetual recidivism is said to be based, Daniel Etounga-Manguelle, a former World Bank adviser from Cameroon, asks 'what can we do to change Africa's destiny' (quoted in Huntington 1996: 75; see also Etounga-Manguelle 2000)?

An important representative of this view is the American travel writer turned social scientist, Robert Kaplan. His article entitled 'The Coming Anarchy' published in *Atlantic Monthly* in 1994 so impressed the White House that it was, according to Richard Holbrooke, faxed to every American embassy in the world (1999). In it, Kaplan claims that West Africa, defined in terms of 'disease, overpopulation, unprovoked crime, scarcity of resources, refugee migrations, the increasing erosion of nation-states and international borders, and the empowerment of private armies, security firms, and international drug cartels', represents a general vision of the future (1994: 46). Later, in a book extending this thesis, Kaplan explains how such a situation has come to pass: 'in places where the Western Enlightenment has not penetrated and where there has always been mass poverty, people find liberation in violence' (2000: 45). Such a pessimistic characterisation of non-Western culture, coupled with a reading of his earlier (and similarly deterministic) account of Balkan historiography, has proven especially influential in the analysis of civil wars (1993). It was, for example, seemingly instrumental in persuading the Clinton administration that the Yugoslav conflagration of the 1990s was an unavoidable consequence of 'ancient hatreds' and therefore best ignored (Tuastad 2003: 598).

Indeed, straddling Muslim, Slavic-Orthodox and Western civilisational fault lines, it was all but inevitable that a shift in geopolitical power of the scale of the Soviet Union's implosion would release, within the substate groups of the Balkans, 'a scramble for turf between . . . the inheritors of Rome, Byzantium and Islam' motivated by 'ancient political feuds as antagonistic and passionate as ever' (Gati 1992: 65; Ajami 1993: 7). Accordingly, these disputes were seen as a result not of contemporary political inculcation, but of the 'defrosting' of innate animosities which the Moscow-backed federation had 'officially suppressed but never fully extinguished' (Snow 1996: 38; Wimmer 2004: 3). Once awoken from this 'communist-inspired sleep', large-scale violence was 'inevitably resurgent given the almost genetic propensity to violence of the Balkan peoples' (Kaplan cited in Mueller 2000: 44; Finney 2002: 2). With such reasoning, it is only possible to conclude that 'the people of central and eastern Europe will go on living in countries . . . inspired by xenophobic nationalism and intolerance' (Hobsbawm 1997: 6).

At another level of analysis, the state, the influences of innate cultural features have interested analysts of geopolitics. The notion of a 'strategic culture', for instance, emerged during the 1970s as a challenge to realism's primary focus on international influences in the decision-making process of state elites – a topic considered at length in Chapter 9 (Rosen 1995: 8–14). Defined as 'a nation's traditions, values, attitudes, patterns of behaviour, habits, symbols, achievements and particular ways of adapting to the environment . . . with respect to the threat or use of force', it produces 'a historically imposed inertia on choice [which] makes strategy less responsive to specific contingencies' (Booth 1990: 121; Johnston 1995: 34). While the degree to which these features influence conflictive behaviour varies considerably from writer to writer, some have constructed highly deterministic accounts of state strategy in which rational reactivity and organisational mutability are severely limited by the innately acquired cultural baggage of political elites. Colin Gray, for instance, portrays a homogeneous American leadership for whom a deeply ingrained respect for humanity made a nuclear exchange during the Cold War unthinkable (1981). Comparable studies of Soviet strategy concluded that innate societal structures, ethnic characteristics, Bolshevism and historical experience produced an executive marked by an absence of restraint and a propensity for grand offensive strategies including a nuclear assault (Pipes 1977; Jones 1990). A fixed account of culture is, in both cases, seen as the most efficacious way 'to explain the persistence of distinctive approaches in the face of disconfirming evidence as well as distinctive patterns of learning that are coloured by pre-existing institutions and ideas' (Snyder 1990: 7).

Using such an approach can, it is claimed, cast light on very long-term intractable conflicts in which geopolitical power, language, civilisational history, religion, ethnicity, colonialism and minority rights play a part. These features have, as Table 5.1 illustrates, been identified as part of the dynamics of the Iran–Iraq rivalry, which escalated to war in the 1980s. These comparators, which can be compared with Table 2.3 in Chapter 2, reveal the enduring efficacy of ancient legacies. The antediluvian rivalry of two of the world's oldest Powers rests upon primordial enmities over historiography (the violence of the Shia schism, the Abbasid takeover of the Umayyad dynasty, the contest between the Safawid and Ottoman empires and differing

Table 5.1 The strategic culture of the Iran–Iraq war

Iran	Iraq
Persia long competed for influence in the Middle East	Babylonia long competed for influence in the Middle East
Farsi and its sister language, Urdu, were/are the languages of education in much of central Asia and the subcontinent	The Qur'an was revealed in Arabic, the language of Iraq, and to an Arab prophet. It is obligatory for Muslims to learn Arabic
Iran became one of the great Shia civilisations	Iraq became one of the great Sunni civilisations
Marked by resentment over the deaths of Imam Ali and Imam Hussein at the hands of Arabs in Iraq in the seventh century	Resentful over Shia attitudes to some early Muslim leaders such as Umar al-Khattab and Aisha as-Siddiqi
Disdainful of perceived Arab tendency towards excessive legalism in Islam	Disdainful of perceived Iranian tendency towards excessive mysticism in Islam
Competed with Ottoman control of Iraq for 400 years	Important part of Ottoman resistance to the Persian Empire
Proud of never having been colonised by the West	Suffered the humiliation of colonialism after the First World War
Unhappy about the treatment of Shias in Iraq for a long time	Unhappy about the treatment of Iranian Arabs for a long time

experiences of Western imperialism), culture (the different interpretations of Islamic exegeses), language (the Arab claim of linguistic and religious 'purity' versus the 'refinement' of urban Farsi), land (the administration of Iranian 'Arabistan' and Iraqi 'Khuzistan') and race (the Semites of Iraq opposed to the Indo-Europeans of Persia) (Grummon 1982; Ismael 1982; Ali 1984).

At the systemic level, the foremost account of the cultural innateness of such atavism is, perhaps, Samuel Huntington's 'clash of civilisations' thesis. First formulated in 1993, it argued that, in the new world order of the post-Cold War era,

> the great divisions among humankind and the dominating source of con-
> flict will be cultural. . . . [T]he principal conflicts of global politics will
> occur between nations and groups of different civilizations. . . . These
> include Western, Confucian, Japanese, Islamic, Hindu, Slavic-Orthodox,
> Latin American and possibly African civilizations.
>
> (Huntington 1993: 22, 25)

In a subsequent book of the same name, he defines culture both by 'common objective elements, such as language, history, religion, customs, institutions, and by the subjective self-identification of people', of which religion is the most important (1996: 43). Of these, David Welch presciently notes, 'Huntington dwelt at length on his (and, arguably, the American people's) favorite future foe: Islam' – a predisposition which has, unsurprisingly, enjoyed something of a revival since the attacks on the Pentagon and the World Trade Center in 2001 (1997: 198). In Ervand Abrahamian's words, 'the mainstream media in the USA automatically, implicitly and unanimously adopted Huntington's paradigm to explain September 11', thereby sending his book to the top of the bestseller list (Abrahamian 2005: 529). Even now, in 2007, it remains in *Amazon*'s top 4,000 (out of more than 2 million titles). The result has been a mainstreaming of previously more marginal discourses in which Muslim culture is seen as immutably incompatible with the West and innately prone to irrational outbursts of anger and envy (a proposition apparently confirmed by the suicidal nature of the 2001 mission). For instance, Osama bin Laden and Ayman al-Zawahiri are said to represent a 'nihilistic subculture' leading an 'assault on civilisation' with the ultimate aim of 'seek[ing] martyrdom' in a cathartic venting of 'Muslim rage', which the inherently repressive nature of their faith prevents them from expressing functionally (Kelly 2001: 2; *New York Review of Books* 17 January 2002). In this sense, 'the new barbarian threat, like that of old, grows out of civilisational backwardness', concludes Brink Lindsey from the Cato Institute (*National Review Online* 27 November 2002).

Is there any empirical support for such claims, though? Considerable amounts of evidence contradicting Huntington's assertion (citing Akbar (see 2002 for his thesis)) that, 'on both sides, the interaction between Islam and the West is seen as a clash of civilizations' (1993: 23) have been provided by Midlarsky (1998) and by Norris and Inglehart (2002). Although, in Midlarsky's study, a majority of adherents to Islam within the states he looks at is found to influence the type of incumbent regime, religious criteria are less significant than factors such as economic development. This leads him to conclude that 'there are certain compatibilities between democracy and Islam that deny the mutual exclusivity hypothesis' favoured by Huntington and others, thereby making civilisational conflict 'not likely in the foreseeable future' (Midlarsky 1998: 505). The latter study utilises the World Values Survey to compare the beliefs of individuals from 75 Muslim and non-Muslim countries. The result 'suggests striking similarities in the political values held in these societies', prompting the authors to 'urge strong caution in generalizing from the type of regime to the state of public opinion' (Norris and Inglehart 2002: 1, 16). Indeed, quantitative data suggest that the vast majority of large-scale wars have been fought over specific issues such as resources, boundaries, international law and so on, rather than supranational ideological concerns (Holsti 1991).

The Huntington thesis has thus been widely criticised for failing to explain why some states fight each other, but others do not. 'Civilisational clashes' have, for instance, been identified throughout history: between Assyria and Sumer, Rome and Persia, Spain and the Maghreb, the Ottoman and Habsburg Empires, and France and Germany. Yet, despite bloody pasts, these relationships currently suffer from relatively modest levels of conflict. Indeed, according to Melvin Small and J. David Singer, there were almost twice as many intracivilisational as intercivilisational wars (resulting in over three times the loss of life) between 1816 and 1980 (1982). This calls into question the very notion of homogeneous civilisational blocs. Here, Huntington's monolithic characterisation of Islam has been particularly pilloried – especially given the fact that he cited Saddam Hussein's invasion of Kuwait as an example of a cultural challenge to the West despite the Iraqi regime's overt secularism and the instrumental role Saudi Arabia (presumably a key element in Huntington's vision of the obscurant Muslim 'other') played in supporting the Western response. His assertions that Islam is uniquely belligerent and moving towards ever greater radicalism are also of doubtful validity. While evidence from India, the United States, Sri Lanka, Israel and Central America suggests that each of the world's religions is home to extremist groups, the overall picture is one of growing worldwide secularism (Mottahedeh 1995).

Indeed, it would appear that many of the features that Huntington ascribes to civilisational difference – communitarianism versus individualism, kinship status versus meritocracy, gender roles and so on – actually have more relevance to substate groups than to international relations. Even here, though, violence within groups is more common than violence between them – within families, within villages, within ethnic groups, within states and so on (Gurr 1994). In Bosnia, for instance, Cynthia Enloe has found that, in

1991, 34 per cent of all Sarajevo's marriages were multiethnic (2000: 142), while 85 per cent of Serbian reservists refused to be called up for military action (Denitch 1994: 63). Rather than an explosion of innately pent-up rage, then, it may be that Yugoslavia was 'deliberately and systemically killed off by men who had nothing to gain and everything to lose from a peaceful transition' following the fall of the Soviet regime (Silber and Little 1995: xxiii). Rudolf Rizman, for instance, argues that the collapse of communism's ideologically constructed and repressively maintained internal class enemy produced a political vacuum in which the radical right's search for moral safety filled the resultant 'psychological gap by introducing new lists of enemies toward whom the people should address their hatred' (1999: 149). Each of Yugoslavia's national communities was encouraged 'to imagine itself as an "endangered species" that urgently needed its own state in order to protect itself from other "species"' (Pesic 1996: 11; Judah 1997). This constructed and instrumental explanation of the Balkan conflagration is, for many, more convincing than Kaplan's deterministic account of 'a region of pure memory', in which it was 'only a matter of time' before grievances flared up (Kaplan 1991: 104; *New York Review of Books* 18 April 1993).

Indeed, this latter position, like its socio-biological cousin, tends to reinforce the idea of difference, leaving little room for progressive change and potentially promoting the forces of reaction. As Patrick Finney notes of eastern Europe, the 'tragic irony is that this representation of the causes of violence in the Balkans exactly reproduced the logic of the most extreme nationalist demagogues in the region who for their own purposes wished to declare ethnic co-existence an impossibility' (2002: 3). As such, it is, in the eyes of many, 'irresponsible and factually irrelevant to write off ethnic conflict as inevitable and unmanageable' (Ross 2000: 152). Moreover, in accepting that the search for successful multiethnic societies is futile, Kaplan's position also serves to legitimise inaction. After all, if conflicts 'are understood as no more than settled history or human nature rearing its ugly head, then there is nothing that can be done in the present to resolve the tension except repress or ignore such struggles' (Campbell 1998: 84). Indeed, if violence and conflict are eternal and immutable, the best that can be hoped for in policy terms is, like the greed thesis discussed in Chapter 8, a programme of defensive securitisation. It is unsurprising, then, that a perennial preoccupation of innate models of conflict is a call for an omnipotent leviathan to mitigate humanity's 'perpetual and restless desire for power' (Hobbes quoted in Hogenraad 2005: 151). This was, for instance, voiced in the seventeenth century and, during the 1990s, in the form of a call for Washington to impose 'a national policy of democratic indoctrination' aimed at alleviating a litany of American ills born of individuals' innate propensities (Somit and Peterson 1997: 111). Paul Shaw and Yuwa Wong reach the similar conclusion that, at the international level, a 'world government [or] some management force' imposed by 'a conquest state' will be necessary to save humanity from its innately self-destructive inclination and impose a 'truly monumental' re-education programme 'at least over the next few generations' (1989: 208–9).

This self-contradictory tendency of fundamentally static accounts of the human condition to include calls for extensive social change has become a way of offsetting their more deterministic features. Nature and nurture debates are thus held to be made commensurate by the inclusion of cultural adaptation (Lloyd and Feldman 2002). Variation in human behaviour in general, and violent conflict in particular, is therefore explicable by a complex interaction between the socially acquired and the natural – a position which has the happy corollary of absorbing all forms of social learning and thus resisting falsification (Miller 1986). As we shall see in the next chapter, however, this is not a coherent conflation of the two positions. That the social environment plays a part in determining human behaviour is undeniably obvious. The acknowledgement of this fact does not, therefore, move the writer on from the characterisation of violent conflict as an innate disposition. Simply accepting that internal processes are subject to extraneous modifications during expression cannot approach its *tabula rasa* antithesis – the idea that all human behaviour is socially acquired.

Consequently, the conflation of cultural adaptation and biological evolution has not succeeded in obviating the detractions of those who do not regard violent conflict to be a part of 'human nature'. For many writers, such a premise is based on a confused representation of our organic environment in which nature is associated with an incongruous blend of pristine simplicity and uniform regularity. In fact, Keith Webb suggests, the notion of 'the natural' is actually a normative supposition masquerading as, and obfuscated by, a discourse of empirics and 'hard' science (1992: 79–83). Are infectious diseases, insect plagues, droughts and violence to be regarded as natural, he enquires, while homosexuality, immunisation, peace, clothes, ungrateful children and selflessness are seen as (despite the frequency with which they are observed) unnatural? Choosing organisms from the natural world to study because they demonstrate some of the behaviour and functions of human life is, for Webb, no more likely to be illuminating than, in an analysis of transportation, to use a wheelbarrow to study an aeroplane. 'Hence', Webb concludes,

> it is an error to suggest that man is 'only' or 'merely' a more complex kind of animal, first, because there is a qualitative difference between the most advanced primates and man, and secondly, because in the specification of characteristics, those that are shared would not adequately characterise man. . . . [T]hose things that essentially characterize the human species – moral behaviour, inventiveness, symbolism etc. – are so far divorced from anything observed in the animal world that any such comparison is foolish.
>
> (1992: 81)

There is certainly a considerable amount of evidence to support such a conclusion. As long ago as the mid-1970s, many ethnographers and anthropologists were compiling extensive studies undermining many of ethology's and socio-biology's fundamental tenets (Peter and Petryszak 1980: 45–8). Marshall Sahlins, for instance, rejected Wilson's account of human kin selection based on biological fitness in favour of 'the entirely different calculus . . . [of] an egotistically conceived natural selection' (1977: 57). Similarly, the oft-reported tendency of animals (and therefore humans) to fight with greater intensity in proximity to their home territory has been brought into question by the work of Bruce Bueno de Mesquita, whose explanation rests on perhaps more plausible matters of logistics, the maintenance of technology, morale, national interests and the unfamiliarity of terrain (1981). Indeed, humans can, uniquely, overcome the fight-or-flight mechanism and, in conscientious objection for example, choose a pacific response that is neither surrender nor aggression. Similarly, evidence abounds that other apparently evolutionary imperatives can also be surmounted. Sustenance requirements can be modified by dieting, fasting or, in hunger striking, conquered altogether. Sexual behaviour has become detached from procreative functions and can also be reduced or eliminated through solitude or celibacy. In fact, all socio-biology can tell us with any certainty is that people are likely to eat and to copulate. This rather acute limitation has convinced many that, even if some social attributes are acquired through evolution, they are so heavily overlaid with culture as to be no longer genetically driven. Aggressive behaviour, violence and organised conflict may be, in other words, 'learned from others, primarily through socialization and enculturation, involving both teaching and learning by observation' – the underlying premise of the next chapter (Segall 1989: 173).

Conclusion

This chapter has considered the idea that conflict is *in natus*, or present at birth. A bedrock of the West's analysis of the 'ethnic' conflicts of the South and frequently implied in many other studies of contemporary conflict, this basic premise has its roots in Christian theology and the notion of transferable sin. Two bodies of work have been focused upon here. Although derived from a wide range of different disciplines and traditions, both draw on the acute impact that violent conflict has on the human psyche and the intense pessimism it can engender. Their basic postulate, that the innateness of the human propensity for conflict makes violence an inevitable aspect of social interaction, is sustained by socio-biology's scientific aura, which has remained an important part of the social sciences for much of the last 100 years. After all, refutation is, as Gerhard Lenski observes, difficult given the widely held belief that many social studies from outside the tradition of experimental science lack 'substantive conceptual links to established theories in other scientific disciplines [and are not] . . . falsifiable in the same unambiguous manner as theories in the natural sciences' (1988: 163).

The first section above looked at the biology of the human body, its evolutionary origins as well as its neurological, psychological and hormonal functions. The emergence of the discipline of socio-biology, as the inheritor of Christianity's understanding of the human tendency to violence, was traced alongside an account of its early and contemporary applications to the social sciences. Darwin's work, along with eugenics, genetics and ethology, was considered with a particular focus on the causes of conflict within human society. Especially important here are notions of dominance, altruism and kin recognition. These have been subject to concerted challenges seeking to rebut some of their more illiberal findings and to question the authority of natural scientists to carry social research, given the fact that they have spent several hundred years unsuccessfully endeavouring to elucidate the general laws they so frequently claim guide human society (Jacoby 2004a). Although frequently dismissed as an unscholarly attack orchestrated by 'the poets and artists among us', they have, nevertheless, obliged socio-biologists to incorporate more aspects of cultural adaptation (Blalock 1984: 25). Ideas such as the leash principle and the inclusive fitness of dominance and cathartic release have consequently been used to elaborate models of conflict and violence that emphasise adaptive influences.

The second body of work examined in this chapter relates to the way in which culture and historiography are understood as causes of violent conflict. Although this literature frequently owes its foundational assumptions to the 'hard' sciences of Darwin and his successors, it is, especially in its populist forms (from journalists and politicians), more commonly applied to the seemingly intractable dynamics of the 'new wars' introduced in Chapter 1. As the sustained popularity of Huntington's clash of civilisations thesis demonstrates (particularly since the attacks on Washington and New York of 2001), however, the idea of immutable cultural forces driving individuals to commit organised acts of violence does not only serve to explain substate conflicts. History also weighs heavily upon the level of the system which, in this characterisation, is marked by a millennial struggle between an inherently reasonable West and the immutable barbarism of the (frequently Muslim) 'other'. Here, the function of culture is quite different from the models looked at in the next chapter. Rather than formed by the settling of generations of broadly unchanging social practices, these regard culture as requiring constant substantiation and legitimisation in order to exert an influence on human behaviour. As individual action is not linked to hereditary endowments, conflict and violence are, as we shall see, regarded primarily as heuristic responses to contingent changes in the social environment.

6 Learnt

As we saw in the previous chapter, it has long been agreed that most forms of aggressive behaviour are influenced by learning. As early as the 1950s, the zoologist John Paul Scott was able to conclude that, among dogs, 'the motivation for fighting is strongly increased by its success, and that the longer success continues, the stronger the motivation' (1958: 194). Today,

> no one seems to deny that learning is critically involved in the acquisition and maintenance of hostile and aggressive modes of behavior. There is considerable disagreement and controversy, however, with regard to the adequacy of explanatory attempts that rest solely or primarily on the basic learning paradigms.
>
> (van der Dennen 2005: 1)

It is these latter attempts that will make up the focus of this chapter. In many ways, they are summed up in the Seville Statement on Violence of 1986. Signed by 20 scientists from 12 countries and from a wide range of disciplines, it put forward five basic postulates:

1 that we have not 'inherited a tendency to make war from our animal ancestors';
2 that 'war or any other violent behavior is not genetically programmed into our human nature';
3 that it is 'incorrect to say that in the course of human evolution there has been a selection for aggressive behavior more than for other kinds of behavior';
4 that it is 'incorrect to say that humans have a "violent brain"'; and
5 that war is not 'caused by "instinct" or any single motivation'.

(UNESCO 1986).

Although the Seville Statement offers an account of what the causes of violent conflict are not, it omits to include any alternative suggestions. This chapter seeks to redress this by looking at ways of viewing conflict causality that do not regard innate influences as of primary importance. Instead, environmental cues and stimuli are seen as the fundamental causal element in human behaviour generally and in violent conflict particularly. Although many socio-biologists and cultural determinists accept that learning from experience is crucial to a full understanding of social interaction, much of the work discussed below explicitly rejects an active role for intrinsic factors, leading to numerous important, and frequently tangential, points of departure between the two schools. This chapter explores, first, work derived from the behaviourist school of social psychology. In particular, it focuses on studies of peer pressure, authority and modelling as examples of the way in which the violent behaviour of individuals may be conditioned through reinforcement and deterrence. These studies have been especially important to constructivism, the focus of the second section. Here, the concern is to understand the ways in which conditioning occurs collectively – in other words, the means through which group identities are created, consolidated and used as a basis for violent conflict. These considerations have proved to be of particular interest to analysts of conflict and gender, the focus of the third section. Drawn from a wide range of disciplines, this writing emphasises both sexual differences and compatibilities in the study of violence at various levels of analysis. While these three broad areas of study represent a disparate and heterogeneous body of work, their common distinguishing thread is a focus on socially learnt or environmentally acquired behavioural factors.

Social learning

Theories of social learning generally work from the premise that behaviour in general and aggression in particular are acquired from the environment through conditioning rather than driven by innate features of human physiology or psychology. Such an idea is far from new. Edward Thorndike pre-empted the work of more famous behaviourists (such as Burrhus Skinner's analysis of external stimuli (1938)) with his studies of trial and error association published in 1898. According to this, and a growing body of more recent literature, behaviour can be conditioned in two ways. First, conditioning may occur *directly* through rewards and punishments experienced as part of an internalised process of heuristic experimentation. For instance, studies have found that children who respond aggressively to school bullying are more likely to increase their aggressiveness if they perceive the response to be successful – if, in other words, the bullying ceases (Fox and Boulton 2003). This may be taken as an indication of the reinforcing effects of either the reduction of annoyance or the attainment of a reward. Either way, aggression is reinforced not by satisfiers inherent to the aggressive act itself, but by its capacity to meet an individual's immediate needs which, in most cases, are not biologically essential (Tapper and Boulton 2005). As such, aggression is, according to many writers, deployed selectively in order to obtain a reward such as wealth, prestige or status, the value of which is, itself, reinforced by social learning mechanisms. This can be offset by negative punishment in the form of the withdrawal of a reinforcing influence or positive punishments such as the imposition of noxious sanctions. In Thorndike's early experiments, positive punishments were regarded as a symmetrical influence upon response – carrots persuade, sticks dissuade (1932). More recently, however, it has been widely accepted that the effectiveness of both forms of punishment depends largely on the identity of the punisher and on the punisher's assessment of desert. If the former lacks authority and legitimacy or the latter is found to be arbitrary and unwarranted, aggression is unlikely to be inhibited and may, in fact, be exacerbated or even instigated (Pisano and Taylor 1971).

The importance of legitimacy and authority in modifying behaviour has been famously demonstrated by the experiments of Solomon Asch and his student Stanley Milgram. The former presented a number of individuals (of whom all but one – the subject – had been prebriefed) with a flipchart upon which were drawn two lines of various lengths and two of identical lengths. He then asked each individual to tell the group which the identical lines were, leaving the uninformed subject until last. In keeping with Asch's earlier instructions, each individual initially identified the two identical lines correctly with the subject following suit. After some time, however, the group, again as instructed, all began to identify two obviously different-sized lines as identical, thereby pressuring the subject and causing them to doubt their own judgement. During 12 trials, 76 per cent of subjects went along with the groups' incorrect selections. When the experiment was repeated, first, using a secret ballot and, second, with another individual going against the group, the subject always identified the correct answer. Thus Asch concluded that individuals do not simply follow crowds blindly; rather, they assess the level of disapproval they are likely to face from challenging established, legitimate and authoritative norms (1951). If this can be mollified by political elites, then, as Chapter 4 revealed, the construction of internal foes and the pursuit of overseas distractions can be successfully deployed to buttress their leadership positions.

Stanley Milgram was interested in the extent to which this kind of social pressure could instigate violence (1963). He was inspired by the trial of Adolf Eichmann, who, having been responsible for the transportation and extermination of German Jews during much of the Second World War, had been captured by Israeli agents in Argentina in 1960 and returned to Jerusalem for prosecution. The world's media were in attendance and struggled to explain why he had done such terrible things: was he a deranged monster, as much of the press suggested, or, as Eichmann himself claimed, was he an ordinary person simply following orders for which he was not responsible (Wistrich 1997)? In order to examine the credibility of Eichmann's defence, Milgram placed a newspaper advertisement offering US$4.50 for one hour's participation in what was called a psychology experiment investigating memory and learning. Respondents (identified as 'S' in Figure 6.1) were introduced to a stern-looking experimenter in a white coat ('E') and a friendly co-subject ('A'), both of whom had been selected and briefed by Milgram. Fabricated lots were drawn to ensure that the subject 'S' took on the role of 'teacher' and the co-subject 'A' (who was taken to an adjoining room, strapped to a chair and attached to a fake electrode) was to be the 'learner'. The former was taken to a desk containing a generator, instructed to read a list of word pairs and then told to ask the 'learner' to read them back. If the 'learner' responded correctly, the 'teacher' should move on to the next word but, in the case of an incorrect response, the 'teacher' was directed to deliver an electric shock to the 'learner' using the equipment provided. This had 30 labelled switches in 15-volt increments up to 450 volts. Each switch also had a rating, ranging from 'slight shock' to 'danger: severe shock' (Blass 2004). The 'teacher' was told to increase the shock each time the 'learner' missed a word in the list (the equipment was, of course, harmless and the 'learner' was an actor feigning electrocution). Once the 'teacher' had been assured that the experimenter assumed full authority for the consequences of the experiment, 65 per cent delivered the maximum 450 volts, and none stopped before reaching 300 volts – demonstrating that, even in liberal democracies,

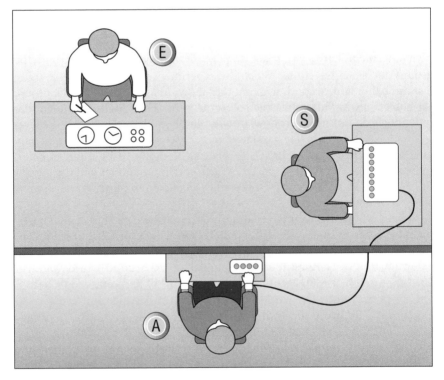

Figure 6.1 The set-up of Milgram's experiment on obedience and authority. Source: Redrawn from http://en.wikipedia.org/wiki/Milgram_experiment/.

people are willing to obey authority figures and commit acts of violence that they would normally find morally repugnant (Harrington 2004: 56; Post 2004).

A second type of conditioning may occur *vicariously* through the observation of models, which, if successful, have 'the effect of a positive reinforcement on the viewer' and, if unsuccessful, have a deterring outcome (Björkqvist 1997a: 32). Current writing in this area of social psychology owes much to the work of Albert Bandura. In his formulation, knowledge about the likely result of aggressive behaviour is acquired by witnessing its consequences upon others. This was demonstrated in a series of experiments using Bobo dolls (Bandura *et al.* 1961). These were large toys that were filmed being beaten and abused by adults. This was then shown to three groups of children accompanied by three different endings. The first film showed the adult being rewarded for his aggressive behaviour, the second showed the adult being punished and the third showed no consequences. The children who watched the video in which the person was rewarded for his actions were found to be more likely to duplicate the behaviour than those children who witnessed the adult either being punished or receiving neither punishment nor reward. From this, four conclusions were drawn regarding the power of such modelling: that it teaches new behaviour, that it influences the frequency of previously learned behaviour, that it may encourage previously forbidden behaviour and that it increases the frequency of similar behaviour (Bandura 1973).

Extrapolating these findings to the level of society, Bandura hypothesises that 'there are three major sources of aggressive behaviour [or models], which are drawn upon to varying degrees' (1976: 124). First, the correlation of anti-social behaviour in children with homes in which aggression, in words as well as deeds, is predominant suggests that familial influences are highly significant. Parents who attempt to influence their children using coercive methods are presenting a positively reinforcing model of aggression which conditions directly, if experienced by the child personally, or vicariously, if the child observes siblings adjusting their behaviour in response to parental aggression (McCord *et al.* 1959). Second, variations in the expression of aggression indicate that, where it is highly valued (often through competition, sport and historiography), violent subcultural influences may vicariously reinforce individual behaviour. Here, cultural features are not expressions of innate tendencies fixed by the weight of history, but influential only if perpetually reinforced by successful modelling (Wolfgang and Ferracuti 1967). Differences in violence levels between cultures are not then a consequence of the failure to institutionalise catharsis or dominance, but a result of continually constructed, socially contingent and constantly changing conditioning. A third factor, symbolic modelling, involves the legitimisation of aggression through the indirect example of leaders, celebrities, fictitious heroes/heroines, sports stars and so on – influences frequently intensified by favourable media portrayal. In this way, both children and adults have virtually limitless ways of receiving televisual and pictorial models of aggression, inputs that have been shown to have a demonstrable effect on both the quantity and the quality of interpersonal aggressiveness (Felson 1996).

Recent studies have extended Bandura's findings to establish more nuanced accounts of familial conflict. Kaj Björkqvist, for instance, finds that children are more influenced by their mothers' behaviour outside the home and their fathers' approach when they are angry at home. Moreover, while mothers generally exert greater reinforcing authority, sons tend to imitate the aggressive behaviour of their fathers more than daughters, who, outside the home at least, demonstrate a stronger maternal influence (1997b: 79–80). Analyses of a wide range of deviant behaviour, from terrorism to drug use, have also made use of Bandura's research (Ruby 2002; Lee *et al.* 2004). The criminologist Ronald Akers, for instance, finds that the 'probability that persons will engage in criminal and deviant behavior is increased and the probability of them conforming to the norm is decreased when they differentially associate with others who commit criminal behavior or espouse definitions favorable to it' (1998: 50). This may be the direct influence of rewards and sanctions or, as in the case of televisual portrayals of criminal aggression, desensitisation through vicarious observation (Eron *et al.* 1994). In direct contrast to the immutable characterisation of aggression of the last chapter, such an understanding of behaviour offers numerous methods of treatment (Cunningham *et al.* 1998). Rebecca Dobash and her team have, for instance, used social learning approaches to treat violent offenders by reinforcing alternative response models through education, self-assessment and peer pressure (1996).

These studies, along with those of Asch and Milgram, have also been of interest to military institutions. They, too, have sought to modify individuals' aggressive response through reinforcement and modelling. Rather than reducing aggression, though, they have used behaviourist experiments to overcome the perennial problem of non-firing. Of the 26,000 muskets collected from the field following the Battle of Gettysburg in 1863, for instance, over 24,000 were still loaded, 12,000 were loaded more than once and more than 6,000 were loaded between three and ten times (Lord 1976). This was particularly puzzling given the labour and time involved in preparing muzzle-loaded weapons for use. As Dave Grossman explains, 'the obvious conclusion is that most soldiers were *not* trying to kill the enemy. Most of them appear to have not even wanted to fire in the enemy's general direction' (1996: 22). A similar phenomenon was observed by Brigadier-General Marshall during the Second World War. He claimed that, of his study group of American combat soldiers, at least 75 per cent did not fire their weapons at all during battle (1947). It would appear that 'when soldiers discover their vulnerability then the fear of being killed, rather than killing, becomes the more oppressive problem' (Newsome 2003: 33).

Military institutions' response to this issue has been complex and varies considerably from country to country. Three general approaches can, however, be linked to theories of social learning. The first is group identity. As Asch demonstrated, individuals will conform to the views of a proximate group by assessing the level of disapproval they will incur by deviating. To increase such pressure and thus soldier participation on the battlefield, the United States army introduced small, cohesive fire-teams following the Second World War (George 1971: 297; Kennett 1997: 137). This could not, however, deal with the type of problem experienced at Gettysburg where the closeness of firing formations meant that 'if a man truly was not able or willing to fire, the only way he could disguise his lack of participation was to load his weapon . . . bring it to his shoulder, and then *not actually* fire' (Grossman 1996: 23). To tackle this problem, the United States army, in keeping with the findings of Milgram, adopted a second approach – the devolution of authority to these small companies of buddies. Non-commissioned officers, such as corporals, were trained to develop high levels of legitimacy with which to elicit commitment from their troops (Shalit 1988). Assuming the role of Milgram's 'experimenter', they both take responsibility for the actions of their soldiers and issue fire commands which, given their proximity and authority, are difficult to ignore – particularly given the extensive vicarious reinforcement of associating status with rank hierarchies. Both these factors – the intensification of group identity and the decentralisation of authority – have considerable implications for the mobilisation of social groups (looked at in Chapter 8) that are too large to be directly influenced by charismatic or zealous leaders.

Third, the conditioning of enlisted men before arrival at the combat arena has been revolutionised. The direct reinforcement of the need to engage the enemy on the battlefield has been stepped up through the increased use of medal citations (Kellett 1990: 220–1). Subcultural and symbolic modelling have also been developed in what Grossman calls the 'boot-camp deification of killing' (1996: 252). This has mixed the dehumanisation of the enemy through the constant use of derogatory language (thereby reinforcing a division between the collective self and the other) with highly repetitious and blood-thirsty chanting. Soldiers are thus 'being indoctrinated in the most explicit fashion (as previous generations were not) with the notion that their purpose is not just to be brave or fight well; it is to kill people' (Dyer 1985: 123). This type of conditioning has, in some cases (such as the preparation of Liberation Tigers of Tamil Eelam cadres in Sri Lanka), been accompanied by the use of televisual media through which highly graphic portrayals of battlefield violence are repeatedly shown to new or potential recruits with the joint intention of instilling feelings of anger and of desensitising.

Most armed forces have also replaced static target training with 'quick-shoot' ranges employing pop-up models of enemy soldiers. This has had two outcomes. First, it offers immediate gratification in that an accurate round produces an instant and very obvious indication of success (a reward positively reinforced by considerable regimental kudos and negatively reinforced by mild punishments). Second, 'in addition to traditional marksmanship, what is being taught in this environment is the ability to shoot reflexively and instantly. . . . The man shape popping up . . . [makes] the conditioned stimuli more realistic and the conditioned response more assured' (Grossman 1996: 254). The effect on the United States military was that, by Vietnam, firing rates had increased to between 90 and 95 per cent – thereby confirming Bandura's fundamental hypothesis that 'people are not born with preformed repertoires of aggressive behavior. They must learn them . . . either through observation of aggressive models or on the basis of direct experience' (Bandura 1976: 122; Holmes 1985).

Constructed identities

Such studies have had a profound effect on the way in which collective identity and its value in the eyes of political leaders are studied. Bandura's observation that societies which 'provide extensive training in aggression and make it an index of manliness or personal worth' spend more 'time threatening, fighting, maiming and killing each other' than 'cultures where interpersonal aggression is discouraged and devalued' underpins the idea that the efficaciousness of violence is constructed (or learnt) rather than innate (1976: 128). Constructivism, as an approach to the analysis of collective identity (national, religious, ethnic, gender and so on), therefore rests on the assumption that both the categorisation of, and the boundaries between, social groups are fluid and subject to constant manipulation. As Jennifer Sterling-Folker notes, 'this means that there is no "middle ground" between the biological and the social in most constructivist narratives. Human interaction is instead treated as if it springs forth from some unknown source that has no implications for species-wide behaviour' (2002: 92). So, rather than offering a static account of fixed antagonisms, constructivism seeks to explicate 'a *specific process* by which identities are produced and reproduced in action and speech' (Fearon and Laitin 2000: 850). In keeping with their behaviourist roots, collective identities are therefore expected to be stronger 'the greater the tangible rewards, perceived tangible rewards or expected tangible rewards associated with the ingroup and the loyalty to it' (Rosenblatt 1964: 132). 'Rather than reflecting deep, historic passion and hatreds', civil wars between self-identified groups are, accordingly, more usefully considered to be a 'result of a situation in which common, opportunistic, sadistic, and often distinctly nonideological [sic] marauders [a]re recruited and permitted free reign by political authorities' (Mueller 2000: 43).

Such leaders might 'construct' and demarcate a collective identity for a wide range of strategic reasons, some of which (including diversionary motives) have been discussed in Chapter 4. The concern for constructivists, however, is more 'how' this is achieved than 'why'. The latter is mostly assumed to follow the basic tenets of rationality – self-preservation, material profit, status acquisition and so on (Tambiah 1996). Assuming that rigorously exclusionary collective identities do not serve popular interests, the challenge is, therefore, to understand the ways in which leaders convince people of abstractions such as nationalism, racial purity, gender roles and such like and then persuade them to act upon these beliefs. One of the simpler ways in which elites might achieve this is, as Milgram demonstrated, to create a sense of moral resignation by using their authority over their immediate followers to provoke cycles of violent action and reaction (Kalyvas 1999). In cases in which their constituents stand to prosper from a collapse in civil order or from a redistribution of wealth, such a tactic can reduce internal dissent within, and external pressure upon, the in-group by appearing to consolidate the idea that support for the existing leadership structure is the only viable way to preserve its collective identity (Kapferer 1988: 102).

In Rwanda, for instance, Gérard Prunier argues that Hutu extremism was based, in part at least, on the need to demonstrate both to the peasantry and to international donors that their policies (and not those of moderate Hutus who had negotiated a ceasefire with the Tutsi-influenced Rwandan Patriotic Front two years earlier) were the only feasible means to protect the majority of Rwandans (approximately 80 per cent of whom were Hutu) and thus to bring stability to the country as a whole (1995: 141–3). To reinforce this idea, the President's wife, Agathe Habyarimana, and her three brothers established small death-squads which, by selectively killing Tutsis, succeeded in ending the ceasefire, fomenting an environment of acute fear and gathering support for the Hutu *Interahamwe* militia (Gourevitch 1998). The resultant sense of collective peril among Hutus reduced perceptions of individual responsibility for the escalating violence and enhanced the authority of the extremists (despite the fact that over 90 per cent of Hutu men did not actively take part in the genocide) (Des Forges 1999).

It has frequently been observed that a key element in the construction of such conflictive social identities in general, and in Rwanda in particular, is the control of the mass media (Hobsbawm 1990: 141–2). Although graphic televisual portrayals of violence have long been shown to be among the most powerful vehicles for vicarious behavioural reinforcement, literary and verbal communication of violently exclusionary ideas, commended by decentralised, non-state authorities, can also exert a subcultural and symbolic modelling effect on opinion and thus potentially on behaviour (Lagerspetz 1989; Brass 1997). Studies of the United States, for instance, have, as per Milgram, shown that the public is swayed most powerfully by the testimony of authoritative and legitimate experts (Page and Shapiro 1992: 339–54). This can both negatively reinforce out-groups (thereby demobilising opposition to the elite's version of reality) and positively reinforce the character and boundaries of in-group self-perception. Such a process may occur either as part of a restrictive environment in which 'official control of information makes public opinion highly manipulable' or 'during incipient democratization, when . . . the state and other elites are forced to engage in public debate in order to compete for mass allies in the struggle for power' (van Evera 1994: 26–33; Gagnon 1995; Human Rights Watch 1995: xiv; Snyder and Ballentine 1996: 6).

In Rwanda, both scenarios were apparent during the build-up to the genocide. The abandonment of the state's media monopoly in 1990 had produced 'an explosion in the number of newspapers and journals' which, in presenting polarised interpretations of the unfolding conflict, radicalised and pressurised the incumbent government and helped to manipulate public opinion (Africa Rights 1994: 150). The extremist Hutu journal *Kangura*, for example, 'warned Habyarimana not to flinch from the destruction of the Tutsi' (Snyder and Ballentine 1996: 33). With only around 60 per cent literacy, though, a more important vehicle of persuasion was the radio, over which Hutu extremists obtained a virtual monopoly. For example, the *Radio-Télévision Libre des Mille Collines*, established by Agathe Habyarimana, became an instructive voice of elite Hutu radicals through which the boundaries between Rwanda's ethnic groups were redrawn. From Kigali and then from within the French army-controlled zone, it helped to mobilise the genocide through a combination of authority, threatened punishments and promised rewards – leading Holly Burkhalter, the director of Human Rights Watch in Washington, DC, to conclude that 'the one action that, in retrospect, might have done the most to save Rwandan lives' would have been the censure of its broadcasts (1995: 53).

At a more diffuse and general level, access to mass media outlets can also help to establish what James Fearon and David Laitin call 'social construction by discourse'. This, they continue, relies on 'symbolic or cultural systems that have their own logic or agency . . . . [I]ndividuals are pawns or products of discourses that exist independently of the actions of any particular individual' (2000: 851). These ideological frameworks provide meaning to actions and can thus assist in explaining how individuals come to imagine themselves to be part of an exclusive collective group – or, put another way, how 'the multiple identities of individuals come to be expressed in terms of one dominant identity' (Jabri 1996: 120). Here, models of social learning blend with accounts of globalisation and post-modernity to produce analyses of conflict less based on truth, or causality, and more concerned with the rise of fragmented supra- and substate identities and the content of the competing narratives that they develop (Bilig 1995: 131). These, it is suggested, tend to be ignored by commentators whose focus on 'modern' conflict attributes – professional military structures, scientific strategy, field tactics, technology and clear war aims – causes them to overlook the post-modern character of contemporary warfare (its diverse armed groups, ethnicised politics, ritualised violence and transnationality) and to regard it as an abnormality or social pathology evident simply in manifest adversity (Duffield 1998a; Kaldor 1999).

In reality, many argue, today's conflicts are a direct result of the routine actions, cultural references and linguistic content of all collective identity (Giddens 1984: 60). Often banal, subliminal and self-affirming, these combine to construct what Vivienne Jabri calls discourses of 'exclusion' and 'origins' (1996: 128–41). The former relates to the dichotomous representation of out-groups, and the latter refers to the homogenised traditions of forebears. Each is held to be imaginary (and thus impervious to rational analysis) and both are thought of as constituent parts in the legitimisation of conflictive relations. In attitudinal terms, the conflict engendered by these is therefore what Mitchell (considered in Chapter 2) might describe as 'unrealistic' as, like the cathartic release of inner aggression, it is not caused by the demonstrable pursuit of incompatible goals. Rather, the dynamics of the conflictive discourse are represented in symbols, ritual, art, emblems, remembrance and sovereignty as well as notions of societal interest and social difference (Onuf 1989). These are then disseminated by 'the casting of thought in language [which] makes the private and the individual public and collective by accommodating individual experience and subjectivity' (Norton 1988: 46).

Gender

The gendered nature of this language has proved of particular interest to feminist writers on violence and conflict. As Table 6.1 illustrates, commentators from what Ted Hopf calls a 'critical constructivist' background have identified binary gender oppositions within theories of conflict themselves (1998: 181–6). These, it is argued, undermine the claim to truth inherent in more positivist studies of conflict and identity and provide a challenge to the implied gender essentialism of socio-biological research examined in the previous chapter – both of which may be said to disguise their masculinised character behind an afflatus of normality and 'scientific' authority (Peterson and Runyan 1993: 22–5; Jacoby 2004b). In emphasising the intersubjectivity of meaning, the reflexivity of the self and the concealment of patriarchal discourses, 'feminism and constructivism [thus] share an ontology of becoming' that resists the 'natural' in favour of the socially acquired (Hoffman 1987; Locher and Prügl 2001a: 111). In this sense, constructivism's account of social identity has helped to establish mechanisms of individual agency within a 'naturalised' social structure, while feminism has informed analyses of the construction process by more fully incorporating gendered forms of

Table 6.1 Gender binaries in the language of social enquiry

Masculine/subject	*Feminine/object*
Knower/self/autonomy/agency	Known/other/dependence/passivity
Objective/rational/fact/logical/hard	Subjective/emotional/value/illogical/soft
Order/certainty/predictability	Anarchy/uncertainty/unpredictability
Mind/abstract	Body/concrete
Culture/civilised/production/public	Nature/primitive/reproduction/private

Source: Adapted from Goldstein (2001: 49).

social power (Locher and Prügl 2001b). In practical terms, both are generally concerned with the social structures that ensure that women do two-thirds of the world's labour (mostly in the home) for around one-tenth of the world's wages and one-hundredth of the world's property (Tickner 1992: 75; Ehrenreich 1997: 125).

Some feminists argue that the reasons for such acute inequality and the apparently more aggressive character of male identity can be found in gendered patterns of childhood conditioning. Across a wide range of cultures, parents give girls baby dolls and boys toy weapons to use as the basis for their play and, therefore, their formative learning. It is argued that the kind of behaviour that this encourages tends to divide children according to their genders with boys constructing social relationships around autonomous individuals interacting according to agreed rules and group responsibilities. Maccoby suggests that the types of material (guns, swords, monsters, dinosaurs and so on) and themes (peril, struggle, assertion and the like) that emerge from boys' play prefigure the male proclivity for war (1998: 167). It is suggested that, in some cultures, prowess in these areas, established through competition followed by status or ridicule, reinforces and stabilises dominance and submission structures within groups of boys. In contrast, dominance hierarchies in groups of girls have been found to be less pronounced, not so grounded upon success in competitive fields and subject to daily fluctuation (Hartup 1983). Girls, it is said, tend to use play in order to establish more stable friendships based around issues of connection, individual rights and caring (Gilligan 1993). In adulthood, then, women are more likely to be apprehensive about competitive threats to their web of empathetic social interactions, whereas men may be more prone to fearing a loss of autonomy within an imagined hierarchical order (Tannen 1990: 24–5).

The disconnected, and therefore violence-prone, character of male identity is, for some feminists, a consequence of men's lack of engagement in child-rearing, which might be considered to be the embodiment of the peaceful resolution of incompatible goals (Ruddick 1989). Women's primary role in giving life to very young infants is, the argument goes, so profound as to make violence almost inconceivable; whereas men's realisation of their biological marginality gives them a sense of purposelessness, low self-esteem and a craving for authority that is expressed through violence and an insistence upon female obedience (Runyan 1994: 201; Byrne 1996: 33). After all, as Mussolini explained, 'war is for men what maternity is for women' (quoted in Schoenewolf 1989: 86). Resultant forms of hierarchical organisation may therefore 'be more uniquely male than female' and may serve to naturalise the gendered nature of violent conflict (Abernethy 1978: 7; van Creveld 2000a: 844). They might also be regarded as an important means of incorporating women, as producers of 'new lives for the nation to replace its lost members', into national efforts in times of war (Peterson and Runyan 1993: 82).

To resist this, feminists argue that, while it may be axiomatic that 'men are distinguished from women by their commitment to do violence rather than to be victimised by it', there is no inevitability to male domination (Dworkin 1981: 51). Peace is possible but, for many writers, it must (as the work of Galtung discussed in Chapter 3 holds) remove or transform the structurally violent relations of female subordination – particularly the male project of fighting wars in defence of the patriarchy and its foremost organisational form, the nation-state (Carroll and Welling-Hall 1993: 16). Constructing the idea of the nation that must be defended is, it is argued, a device designed to perpetuate male supremacy by moving women's identity away from the world's primary cleavage – gender – and towards a socialised male fear of the dominance of another nation. By disproportionately emphasising the views of those women who do support war and by portraying male identity in terms of the protection of women, political elites can motivate men towards the war effort (Lake and Damousi 1995). This pressure may, in ways related to the manipulation of public opinion highlighted in Chapter 4, take the form of depicting a unified home front by 'otherising' women who do not comply with their roles as mothers and sweethearts. It may also misrepresent the masculine nature of the war itself by dispatching female impresarios and nurses to the field and then disproportionately focusing upon their involvement (Leonard 1994). For feminists, such cynical obfuscation has long been resisted. As Virginia Woolf puts it,

> obviously there is for you some glory, some necessity, some satisfaction in fighting which we have never felt or enjoyed . . . As a woman I have no country. As a woman I want no country. As a woman my country is the whole world.
>
> (1938: 9, 166)

There is evidence to support the idea that women are socialised towards greater passivity then men. For instance, although local variations are considerable, only around 3 per cent of the 23 million or so uniformed soldiers worldwide are women – of these, combat troops are 99.9 per cent male. In a large scale study of values and policy preferences, Benjamin Page and Robert Shapiro were able to conclude that in 'practically all realms of foreign and domestic policy, women are less belligerent than men' (1992: 295). Indeed, a survey of 285 American polls showed a regular male preference for a 'more violent or forceful option' (Smith 1984: 384–95). As Table 6.2 illustrates, this has been, in many cases, at a surprisingly consistent level, suggesting that states in which the participation of women is high are less likely to take part in wars than those where women are less prominent. Having reviewed over 2,000 military incidents between 1960 and 1992, Mary Caprioli supports such a view. She concludes that 'higher levels of gender equality correlate with lower levels of military action to settle international disputes' (2000: 65).

Indeed, the prominent role that women's organisations have played in peace and civil rights movements and anti-nuclear campaigns, along with eco-feminism's attempts to institutionalise less structurally violent ways of

Table 6.2 Gendered survey support for American policy

Year	Issue	Percentage in agreement	
		Men	*Women*
1939	Take strong measures against Japan	56	42
1960	Adopt a tougher policy towards the Soviet Union	60	46
1968	Step up effort in Vietnam	50	32
1975	Wars are necessary to settle differences between countries	55	38
1991	Use force to remove Iraqi troops from Kuwait	63	41

Source: Adapted from Goldstein (2001: 49); Nincic and Nincic (2002: 559).

transforming and utilising nature, would seem to substantiate the idea that 'in most societies boys are encouraged more than girls to behave aggressively' (Segall 1989: 179). The apparent ubiquity of such gender differences has led some to conclude that, once social development has 'modernised' gender relations, a more pacific, and consequently less resilient, environment will emerge (Fukuyama 1998: 27, 36). As Martin van Creveld puts it, 'if only because research shows that going into combat is the last thing that military women want [one study found that 52 per cent of female soldiers would probably or definitely leave the service if forced into combat positions (O'Beirne 1998)], the more of them there are around the less capable those military are of acting as effective combat units' (2000b: 442).

For many feminists, however, seeing the socialisation of women in pacific terms unwarrantably universalises the experience of the Western middle classes and serves to essentialise gender roles in ways similar to the biological determinism of innate theorists. They point to research demonstrating that a significant proportion of domestic violence is initiated by women against men, against their own children or, in the case of same-sex relationships, against other women (James 1996). In J. Ann Tickner's view, then, 'the association of women with peace renders both women and peace as idealistic, utopian, and unrealistic: it is profoundly disempowering for both' (2002: 338). So, rather than seeking to reinforce male–female dualisms which, they suggest, replicate the rigid and restrictive nature of the patriarchy, many feminists see individual rights, freedom of choice and institutional access as key to the advancement of women's status. Their exclusion from warfare is thus emblematic of a broader tendency to discount both the potential and the actual contribution of women – a feature (of developed and developing polities) more likely to provoke cynicism and withdrawal than peace activism (Tobias 1990: 181–2).

Where women have been permitted to participate in violent conflict, their performance has been, it is argued, limited primarily by the discriminatory and inhibiting effects of masculine identity. This was demonstrated on the

home front during the World Wars when women in the United States contributed actively to military production despite being restricted to a 'menial
type of corps of low-grade personnel' (Treadwell 1954: 12). In combat units,
it has often been argued that women perform better in guerrilla armies,
where a comparatively decentralised format and an ostensive commitment
to 'fundamental alterations in the socio-political order' produce a working
environment less conditioned by male identity than states' imperative 'of op-
timising military effectiveness' (Enloe 1988: 161, 164). Although their duties
have often replicated the divisions of domestic labour, some revolutionary
movements have also made extensive use of female troops on the front line
(O'Gorman 1999: 92–6). The armed wing of the Nicaraguan Sandinistas,
for instance, was made up of 30 per cent women (Jones 1997: 103).

Women also demonstrate considerable support for wars in which their
participation is limited. Survey data on the Arab–Israeli conflict, illustrated
in Table 6.3, shows, for instance, no significant gender differences across the
Middle East. In the United States, too, differences in support for the hypo-
thetical use of force have been found to be slight. They are, Pamela Johnston Conover and Virginia Shapiro conclude, 'certainly not large enough to
warrant making the kinds of sweeping statements differentiating men and
women that have long been part of stereotype' (1993: 1095). Indeed, this is
indicated by the vociferous campaigns that women have led to gain access
to the armed forces. In a challenge to the constitutional legality of all-male
military registration, the American National Organization of Women, for
example, argued that 'the military is so central to the entire social order that
it is only when women gain access to its core that they can hope to fulfil their
hopes and aspirations' (cited in Elshtain 1985: 43; see also Elshtain 2000:
445).

The grounds for resisting such access primarily rest on the biological
theses put forward in the previous chapter. It is claimed that the innately
'superior ability of men to add muscle to their bodies' makes them better
soldiers regardless of the social conditioning an individual has received

Table 6.3 The relationship between gender and attitudes towards the Arab–Israeli
conflict (all figures in percentages; date of survey in parenthesis*)

State	Palestine (1996)		Kuwait (1988)		Jordan (1994)		Lebanon (1994)		Israel (1991)	
Attitude	F	M	F	M	F	M	F	M	F	M
Highly supportive	35	34	24	25	33	34	36	36	35	32
Somewhat supportive	36	37	33	29	15	26	19	28	37	35
Not supportive	29	29	43	46	52	40	45	36	28	33

Source: Tessler *et al.* (1999: 527).

(Zorpette 1999: 48). Various surveys have, for example, shown that, when compared with men, women are, on average, 12 centimetres shorter and 14.3 kilograms lighter, as well as possessing 28 per cent less aerobic capacity and a morphology less adapted to violence (Morris 1977: 239–40; Mitchell 1998: 141–2). While some feminists accept this as evidence of the innate social and moral superiority of women (a few have even suggested that the men should therefore be treated surgically or pharmaceutically to reduce their inherently violent capabilities), others have pointed to the influence of social learning both on the way women eat and exercise and on how strength is measured (Okin 1990). It is suggested that the dichotomised imposition of body shape norms upon both sexes in most cultures, combined with the gendered access to nutrition in many poor societies, produces small women and large men (Floud *et al.* 1990: 226). This can, however, be overcome through the ascription of societal value (rural African women appear to have a much greater capacity for manual work than Western urban men) and the utilisation of women's generally higher levels of fat reserves which, as Joshua Goldstein notes of the 1997 New York marathon, means that 'the great majority of men finish well behind the fastest women, and the great majority of women finish well ahead of the slowest men' (2001: 163).

However, apart from specific tasks where lighter body weight, smaller frame and technological aptitude rather than force is at a premium (such as tolerance of the cramped cockpits and gravitational pressures of fighter aircraft), the great majority of violent tasks are carried out by men (Richman-Loo and Weber 1996: 151). To explain this purely in terms of socially acquired inputs is, even for many constructivists, perverse and unnecessarily pedantic. For some, demonstrating the important influence of modelling and reinforcement on the formation of individual and collective identity reaffirms the basic truth that social acts and human behaviour 'occur at the nexus of biology, psychology, and sociology' (Ferguson and Mansbach 1996: 35). Constructivists such as Alexander Wendt and Rodney Hall, for instance, talk (respectively) about 'intrinsic, self-organising qualities' such as the 'fundamental, even primordial, motive (or "interest") of self-preservation' (Wendt 1994: 385; Hall 1999: 38). At the international level of analysis, this echo of the leash principle discussed in the previous chapter is, in many ways, a concession to the enduring salience of realism and its emphasis on the perennial character of group competition and the inevitability of collective conflict (Bloom 1990: 29–39). As such, actors are seen as driven by a mutual fearfulness and a belief that a state's position in the geopolitical order is determined by a universal and fixed blend of zero-sum competition over diminishing resources and individual fitness (in the form of weaponry, security, economic strength and so on) (Thayer 2000).

At the substate analytical level, too, innate theorists remain unconvinced by the idea that behaviour based on social identity is purely learnt. Reversing a criticism also levelled at socio-biology, they argue that such ideas tend to imply some sort of idyllic 'natural' state of being for humanity which, even in less complex acephalous societies, is obviated by subliminal structures of domination and submission. The fact, they suggest, that attempts to remove violent conflict from our environment through social means since the time of Plato have culminated in a century of unparalleled bloodiness tells us that the liberal optimism of the social learning school is misplaced and even dangerous. Moreover, as the emergence of hierarchies and dominance appears to occur in very young children (before the socialisation process could have had a chance to work), it is argued that, contrary to Milgram's premise that people only have the 'potential for obedience' (1974: 125), people are born with 'a readiness to comply with a submissive role', which is then influenced, and not determined, by environmental conditioning (van der Molen 1990: 63). It is concluded, therefore, that the ease with which humans can be indoctrinated is better explained by selection pressures than the false dichotomy of juxtaposing nature and nurture. Such compliance does, after all, allow individuals 'to enjoy the benefits of [group] membership with a minimum of energy expenditure and risk' (Wilson 1978: 187). Indeed, this innate suggestibility explains, for Somit and Peterson, the cross-cultural nature of 'sanctioned massacres' in Vietnam, Poland, Armenia, Rwanda and elsewhere (1997: 69–70). It also recasts military training as more effectively centred upon directing intrinsic combat motivations (such as the proclivity to obey) than attempting to produce conditioned responses based on reward, sanction and peer pressure (Newsome 2003: 38–41).

Conclusion

This chapter has reviewed a number of ways of approaching the causes of conflict and violence from the perspective of human learning. Although none is, in any sense, uniform and, together, they are far from representing a coherent position, all share an appreciation of conflict causality as fundamentally derived from the social environment. The tendency to behave aggressively is acquired from individuals' socialisation experience and deployed selectively as part of a range of possible responses to given stimuli. Early expressions of this basic premise can be found in the work of behaviourists such as Thorndike, Skinner and Asch, whose conclusions regarding the functions of rewards and punishments – both material and non-material – paved the way for later experiments aimed at understanding the role of groups, obedience and authority figures. These established that behaviour could be significantly affected by both direct and observational influences. So, given the demonstrably compliant character of social interaction, such a combination of experiential and vicarious pressures and inducements can be seen as the primary or sole determinants of a considerable proportion of interpersonal violence. Conflict may thus result directly from authority and instruction as part of a direct relationship, as famously demonstrated by Stanley Milgram, or vicariously from the symbolic and subliminal power of society and culture.

At the level of the individual, this helps to extend and elaborate Mitchell's conflict triangular introduced in Chapter 2. The common patterns of expectation, emotional orientation and perception that, he argues, accompany involvement in a conflict situation can, perhaps, be more clearly understood as not simply subjectively experienced states of mind, but collectively developed imprints of the broader social environment that surrounds conflictive situations. In this sense, conflictive attitudes such as anger, resentment and suspicion are not simply associated with other cognitive processes such as stereotyping and selective approaches to new information, but products of the formation of social constructs, which is, itself, guided by the expediencies of the conflict dynamics. So Mitchell's observation that the development of conflictive attitudes frequently proceeds in a self-perpetuating and exclusionary manner may be true but, without an account of *how* previous experiences are used to reinforce or exaggerate individual outlooks, his model lacks explanatory power – a criticism also pertinent to the apparently cohering and distracting properties of conflictive situations presented in Chapter 4.

At the collective level, similar forces may shape the construction, content and delimitations of identity groups. Unlike innate models, these require perpetual reinforcement to remain influential and are thus liable to change markedly and rapidly. Such ideas have had a major influence on the way in which soldiers are recruited and trained – both in a formal sense and in the mobilisation of combat irregulars during the build-up to civil wars. Indeed, the notion that the roles and identities that underpin wars are constructed and ascribed rather than inflexible and fixed has been used to argue that the patriarchal structures that underpin women's vision of, and participation in, conflicts are not biologically based, but grounded upon the differing socialisation experiences of boys and girls. This can, when either polarised by elite manipulation or organised by seemingly benign social institutions, result in both behavioural and structural violence. As such, the way in which we learn to accept conflict and violence is difficult to separate from a general acceptance of inequality and injustice. Clearly, the process of redrawing the boundaries between ethnic groups in Rwanda, for example, cannot be fully distinguished from the rise of Hutu political and socio-economic power. The fact that such ascendancy relied, in Galtung's terms, upon Western penetration, segmentation, marginalisation and fragmentation necessitated an accompanying ideological effort to ensure that the powerless remain partially informed, passive and disunited (1990: 294). The learning methods that underpin the formation of identity are therefore closely connected to the notion of structural violence as a facilitative element in behavioural violence. Their capacity to create an atmosphere of ordinariness can lower social barriers to individual acts of violence (as Grossman points out), to collective tyranny on a grand scale or, in keeping with Leo Strauss' account of liberalism's mass malleability, a strata of political elites devoid of value–fact distinctions.

7   Grievance

In the previous chapter, various ways in which political elites organise conflict and violence were considered. In Chapter 4, some of the reasons why leaders might wish to do this were discussed, along with a range of benefits that might accrue from such endeavours. As these mostly emerge once the decision to become involved has been made, more analysis is needed to understand what motivates participants in the first place. Here, research goes back many years. Writing over 2,000 years ago, Aristotle, for instance, noted that much social conflict was a result of grievances caused by the combined effects of the fundamentally unequal nature of Athenian society and of the perceived weakness and incompetence of the city's leaders in responding to this inequality. Comprehending the impact of grievances on human behaviour in general, and on the causes of conflict in particular, has made up a key element of the social sciences ever since. This chapter looks initially at the range of work, mostly emerging after the Second World War, which focuses both on understanding the ways in which grievances are formed and on the analysis of causal linkages between grievance formation and conflictive behaviour. Of key significance here is the notion of relative deprivation and its proposed relationship with frustration, action and rebellion – at the level of both the individual and the group. The way in which these factors change over time is also a fundamental concern. As the second section highlights, it has often been noted that societies going through processes of 'modernisation' or 'development' may be subject to greater disparities between the satisfaction of human needs and the general desire of the citizenry to acquire the perceived benefits of modernity. This can be seen as an important cause of grievance formation, collective frustration and conflict.

Relative deprivation and revolution

For many writers, the development of relative deprivation as a research programme represents one of 'the most important advances of social science theory during the twentieth century' (Tyler and Lind 2002: 44). Despite being 'extensively used in social psychology, sociology, and other social sciences for more than half a century', it remains 'a hot topic of research, being used primarily to understand the processes of social identity and the responses to disadvantage by both disadvantaged minorities and privileged minorities' (Walker and Smith 2002a: 1; 2002b: i). It was first put forward by Samuel Stouffer and his team in an investigation of differential pay and conditions in the American armed forces (1949). This, and a subsequent study by Robert Merton and Alice Kitt (1950), concluded that the perceived denial of wants, expectations and rights is likely to lead to a sense of deprivation, disappointment and injustice respectively. As Robin Williams notes, the basic postulate of these studies (which remains broadly intact today) was 'deceptively simple: persons may feel that they are deprived of some desired state or thing, in comparison with some standard, or with the real or imagined condition of other people' (1975: 355). In this sense, the ideas that underpin relative deprivation theory, as deployed to explain various forms and structures of social conflict, are very old – being both fundamental to Marx's notion of immiseration as the motor of collective action and central to de Tocqueville's account of rising expectations as an important factor in the causes of the French Revolution (Gurney and Tierney 1982: 33). In other words, individuals' lack of personal fulfilment, both material and non-material, and the growing realisation of others' wants, as perceived within their reference group (or a combination of the two), can be a motivational factor in various forms of conflictive behaviour.

A commonly cited means through which the formation of grievances is translated into individual and collective action is the frustration–aggression mechanism. The most important formulation of this relationship was published in 1939 by John Dollard and colleagues from the Institute of Human Relations at Yale University. They suggested that, when goal-directed behaviour is obstructed, frustration results. In their work, this always leads to aggression, although its expression may be modified by heuristic learning, transference, social institutions and catharsis (Miller *et al.* 1941). Much also depends on '(1) the strength of instigation to the frustrated response, (2) the degree of interference with the frustrated response, and (3) the number of frustrated response-sequences' (Dollard *et al.* 1939: 28). The result may therefore be fixation, regression and resignation, as well as aggression (Maier 1949). In instances where observable aggression does result, however, it is regarded as having been promoted by an external cue, stimulus or instigator, which then replaces the original goal-directed drive and becomes an end in itself (Maier 1942: 587). Aggression directed at the perceived cause of this cue is therefore a way of reducing frustration, which, if successful, reinforces the tendency to use aggression in the future (as part of a process of direct modelling) (Feshbach 1964). A similar sequence may occur in response to a perceived threat. This can act as an anticipated frustration if the hazard cannot be easily avoided or if it impinges upon the attempted attainment of particularly valuable goals (Berkowitz 1962: 45). If, in other words, the threat imminently imperils a basic human need.

Identifying these needs has produced, over the years, a wide array of characterisations and taxonomies. Abraham Maslow, for instance, ordered human needs into a four-point hierarchy in which lower-order needs will not emerge until those of a more fundamental nature are met (1943). At the top – and therefore most likely to provoke the most acute motivational responses – are the physical imperatives of sustenance, shelter, procreation and bodily comfort. Secondarily, yet still predicted to exert a very significant influence over individual and group behaviour, are needs of safety and order. Once these are met, a third category of needs can emerge – those of love and belonging – followed by a fourth layer involving needs of self-actualisation driven by the inherent satisfaction that people derive from using their minds and their labour. No stratum within Maslow's hierarchy is, of course, fully discrete, and none can be completely distinguished from one another. The lower-order needs of self-actualisation, for instance, are said to be vital to the realisation of higher order needs such as physical sustenance and human security.

Survey data, however, commonly confirm the hierarchical ordering of peoples' needs, suggesting a varied relationship with frustration intensities and, by extension, aggressive or conflictive behaviour. Hadley Cantril's rank ordering of respondents' concerns from 12 countries surveyed between 1957 and 1963, for example, finds that material stability, house ownership and health were the most commonly reported personal needs, followed by fears of war and disorder and then, subsequently, desires to see more representative and just government as well as aspirations of greater communality, interpersonal reciprocity and the fuller pursuit of personal interests (1965). Indeed, since Maslow's initial formulation, theories of human needs have appeared in a great number of guises, each with its own schematic structure and each with a different implied or explicit relationship with human behaviour. Some writers, particularly those from a Marxist tradition, have suggested that economic needs, once frustrated, are the most important element in understanding conflict and violence (Ridker 1962). Others, such as Hannah Arendt, have suggested that the frustration of political needs (participation, self-determination, freedom of expression and so on) is the primary cause of collective conflict (1963).

Multicausal models that incorporate both these traditions are, however, more common. Ted Gurr, for instance, drew heavily on various human needs theories to develop the founding proposition of his highly influential research in the late 1960s: that relative deprivation 'with reference to any class of commonly held welfare, power, or interpersonal value can lead to collective violence' (1974: 68–9). For Gurr, these values, which are broadly synonymous with Maslow's needs, may represent a measure of capability – in terms of what people 'have actually been able to attain or have been provided by their environment' (their value position in other words) – or an assessment of potential: what people 'believe their skills, their fellows, and their rulers will, in the course of time, permit them to keep or attain' (1974:

27). Put another way, an awareness of deprivation may be derived from an externalised view of what one thinks one ought to have relative to what one feels others, within a referential framework, have/are getting. Alternatively, a sense of deprivation may arise from an internalised comparison of one's promise relative to one's own apparent capabilities. This is an important distinction for, as Robin Williams writes,

> a primary response to a gap between personal aspiration and attainment is 'frustration' or 'disappointment', whereas the response to a gap between what one receives and what is received by reference individuals or groups is more likely to involve envy, resentment, and a sense of being unjustly treated.
>
> (1975: 357)

As David Aberle points out, these perceptions may be experienced personally without reference to collective groupings or by individuals who identify themselves, and their sense of deprivation, with a broader sense of identity (1962: 210). This is important in terms of both the research questions that are asked and the behavioural outcome that may result. Gary Runciman highlighted such a distinction by questioning respondents on how well they believed they were doing, first, in relation to family members and peers and, second, in relation to groups of which they did not perceive themselves to be a part. His objective was to establish whether the subject felt 'dissatisfied with his position as a member of what he saw as his group . . . [or felt] dissatisfied with what he saw as his group relative to other groups in the larger system' (1966: 31). The first he called egoistic deprivation. Findings here have suggested that, if deprivation is experienced at an individual level, then people tend to react in individualistic ways. This may lead to a reinvigorated pursuit of personal goals, but the fact that the cognitive condition that grievances induce 'is a psychologically upsetting state that generates attempts to reduce the dissonance' may mean that individuals, devoid of a clear and viable means of value attainment, are more likely to lower their expectations and manifest withdrawal and apathy (Morrison 1971: 682).

It is, for example, the view of many writers that the isolation, humiliation and under-representation of (as well as active discrimination against) Arab Israelis through Tel Aviv's inequitable residential, infrastructural, land use and employment practices have led to an acute sense of individual relative deprivation (Bernstein 1984; Rouhana 1997). In the absence of viable alternative strategies of resistance, though, the egoistic deprivation experienced by Arab Israelis 'strengthens their sense of helplessness (or fatalism) . . . reduces their ability to influence their life course or the social context that defines their options . . . [and] decrease[s] the[ir] instrumental sense of control' (Moore and Aweiss 2003: 194).

Alternatively, 'a collective consciousness may develop among individuals who share the same resentment (e.g. a group of economically deprived individuals), or it may develop among people with different resentments if they define themselves as having the same oppressor' (Sayles 1984: 452). This is 'fraternal deprivation' (the second of Runciman's models), which, many suggest, 'uniquely generates agitation for or against structural change' (Dion 1986; Taylor 2002: 15). In a study of American political opinion, for example, Reeve Vanneman and Thomas Pettigrew found lower levels of support for non-white mayoral candidates from white people who believed that African American groups were prospering to the detriment of white Americans than from those who saw their socio-economic situation as related to the position of other white people (1972).

Indeed, the formation of this type of collective or participatory response may be especially likely if group leaders are able to issue effective pleas for action. As Will Moore and Keith Jaggers note, appeals can instigate a

> process by which an individual develops a fraternal identification . . . with a larger group via their category. [In this way,] . . . the core group is able to construct a psychological bond among individual potential group members, and a bond between them and the group itself.
>
> (1990: 23)

Such appeals may, they continue (building on Gurr 1974: 229–31), take five forms: (1) the establishment of a categorical identity, (2) the mustering of an individual's sense of relative deprivation, (3) the association of the existing order with the source of discontent, (4) the normative defence of collective action and (5) the utility of collective action. Although, in many cases, these may be conceptually detached from the grievance–motive–action sequence that underpins the approaches discussed here (and will therefore be returned to in the next chapter), they remain an important element in understanding how social movements maintain 'an ongoing sense of legitimacy and efficacy among movement cadres and members' (McAdam *et al.* 1988: 722). This is necessary not only to pursue group objectives (or values), but also to ensure that deprivation continues to be associated with the level of the group and not at the more dissonant level of the individual, which, as we have seen, tends to provoke feelings of futility and self-doubt, leading to the perception that a grievance may be a result of unrealistic expectations, personal shortcomings or the failure of the group to achieve a change in circumstance (Turner 1969).

Much, of course, depends on the dynamic circumstances in which grievances are formed. As we saw in Chapter 2, conflictive situations may change rapidly. This is true not only of actual conditions, but also of individuals and groups whose expectations can also grow sharply, thereby intensifying perceptions of both egoistic and fraternal deprivation. After all, 'the more intensely people are motivated toward a goal, or committed to an attained level of values, the more sharply is interference resented and the greater is the consequent instigation to aggression' (Gurr 1968: 257–8). Assuming that there is a notional equilibrium point at which a society is able to meet its needs and therefore conflate, or at least narrow, any discrepancy between its citizenry's expectations and its capabilities (or vice versa), it is possible to imagine a norm from which various scenarios of change – or growing disequilibrium – can be distinguished. Gurr, after the work of Morrison and Steeves (1967), points to three (1974: 46–58). The first, 'decremental' deprivation, is illustrated in Figure 7.1. Here, expectations have not significantly changed during a period in which people perceive themselves to be decreasingly able to meet their needs. Such a sense of declining capabilities might be caused by sudden shocks such as an economic recession, a collapse in civil order, a natural disaster or a foreign invasion. It might also be the result of incremental changes in the norms or beliefs of society leading to a lessening of reciprocity and social capital or a gradual erosion of civil liberties by a political elite. In either instance, people subject to decremental deprivation develop grievances and become frustrated (and therefore prone to conflictive behaviour) by the loss of what they once had.

John Booth's study of Central America offers a comprehensive account of decremental deprivation during the 1970s and early 1980s (1991). As Table 7.1 illustrates, the entire region (except for Costa Rica) suffered both a significant decline in real wages and a marked increase in unemployment levels. In many areas, the concentration of land ownership intensified as high cotton prices and an enlargement of beef production forced small-scale farmers off their land and into saturated urban labour markets (Brockett 1988: 72–4). In Guatemala, for instance, the availability of arable land fell from 1.7 to 0.8 hectares per capita between 1950 and 1980 (Hough *et al.* 1982). Costa Rica, in contrast, developed a comparatively successful land reform programme and, like Honduras, maintained higher welfare and lower military expenditure levels than its neighbours. These factors combined to reduce the impact of the 1970s energy crisis and to lessen rural labour volatility. The result was that, in Nicaragua, El Salvador and Guatemala, vibrant

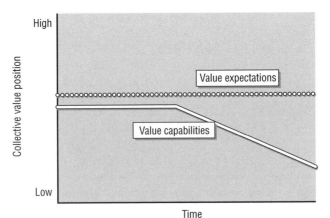

Figure 7.1 Decremental deprivation. Source: Redrawn from Gurr (1974: 47).

Table 7.1 Unemployment levels (percentages) and real working class wage indices in Central America 1970–84 (1972 = 100)

Year	Costa Rica		El Salvador		Guatemala		Honduras		Nicaragua	
	Unemp.	Wages	Unemp.	Wages	Unemp.	Wages	Unemp.	Wages	Unemp.	Wages
1970	3.5	93	16.0	98	4.8	102	8.8	–	3.7	106
1980	5.9	125	24.0	87	5.5	79	8.8	101	17.8	56
1984	6.6	107	30.0	61	9.1	79	10.7	93	16.3	40

Source: Booth (1991: 42–3).

and eclectic protest movements emerged from social groups most affected by the economic downturn. White-collar workers, proletarianised by a sharp drop in living standards, appeared alongside peasant groups and Church-led organisations already opposing incumbent regimes and their cabal of clients. While an increase in social activism was also noted in Costa Rica and Honduras during this period, political fragmentation was mostly avoided and instances of irredentist violence and state brutality remained significantly fewer than in the rest of region. Booth concludes thus:

> The evidence strongly suggests that Central America's rapid growth of export agriculture after 1950 and industrialization after 1960 markedly reduced the relative and absolute living standards of many members of the working class, who then mobilized to demand redress of their grievances. Where the state responded accommodatingly and with limited repression (in Costa Rica and Honduras), opposition mobilization stagnated or subsided. Where the state did not ameliorate growing inequality and employed heavy repression (in Nicaragua, El Salvador, and Guatemala), opposition mobilization and unity increased and led to a broad, rebellious challenge to regime sovereignty.
>
> (1991: 60)

Absent from Booth's analysis, however, is an account of the impact of Central American impoverishment and resistance on collective expectation levels. As we have already seen in Figure 7.1, Gurr's model of decremental deprivation rests on the assumption that value expectations remain broadly stable. Yet, it may be possible that expectations deteriorate in parallel with capabilities, thus rendering the 'want-gap' constant and making rebellion unlikely. Although this possibility may legitimately be excluded from an account of grievance-led action on the grounds that there is no conflictive phenomenon to explain, it is important to acknowledge that, theoretically at least, it is feasible to envisage a situation in which increases in value expectations (through the expansion of higher education opportunities or apprenticeship schemes for instance) coincide with a period of capability decline resulting from an economic recession or some other imminent event. Such a possibility is dealt with by another of Gurr's grievance models – 'progressive' deprivation.

This is adapted from James Chowning Davies' J-curve (depicted in Figure 7.2), which predicts that revolutions, or large-scale collective violence, 'are most likely to occur when a prolonged period of objective economic and social development is followed by a short period of sharp reversal' (Davies 1962: 6). In many ways, this is a combination of the classic positions of Marx (who saw revolution as the result of the growing exploitation and desperation of the workers) and de Tocqueville, who concluded that 'the regime which is destroyed by a revolution is almost always an improvement on its immediate predecessor. . . . Evils which are patiently endured when

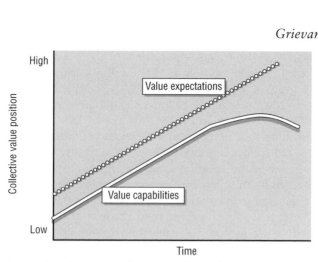

Figure 7.2 Progressive deprivation. Source: Redrawn from Gurr (1974: 53).

they seem inevitable become intolerable when once the idea of escape from them is suggested' (1856: 214). Davies suggests that, during times of perceptible improvement, expectations increase alongside capabilities, thereby maintaining a tolerable gap between individuals' wants and their ability to achieve satisfaction. When an acute downturn occurs, however, there is, he continues, an inevitable lag between material change and the collective readjustment of expectation, producing a widening, and therefore increasingly intolerable, gap between wants and satisfaction. Indeed, conflict participation, for Davies, 'requires the continued, even habitual but dynamic expectation of greater opportunity to satisfy basic needs perpetuation' (1962: 8). The continued growth of expectation through the period of decline is, in other words, necessary for frustration and a fraternal sense of deprivation to occur.

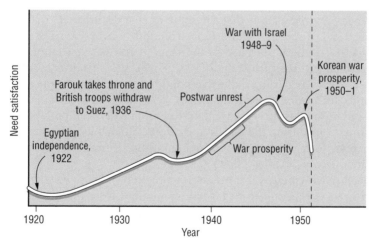

Figure 7.3 The Egyptian revolution of 1952. Source: Redrawn from Davies (1962: 13).

There have been numerous applications of the J-curve. Davies himself points to the Egyptian revolution of 1952 as illustrative of the motivational effects of progressive deprivation (his model is presented in Figure 7.3). He argues that a growing sense of collective expectation began in Egypt following the British decision to confer a degree of independence on Cairo in 1922. This fillip to local political aspirations coincided with a period of urbanisation and industrialisation which, he suggests, led to a comparative improvement in the material standing of many peasant migrants and to the emergence of an urban entrepreneurial class. Downturns during the 1930s were damaging, but they were, he continues, largely blamed upon the British, who maintained a substantial garrison of troops and considerable administrative influence. A sizeable influx of foreign soldiers during the Second World War, coupled with a worldwide increase in agricultural prices, maintained this relative growth in collective capability and expectation. The end of the war, however, saw a sharp downturn in the economy, leading rapidly to mass redundancies, a series of industrial disputes and a rise in political radicalism. Defeat in the 1948 war with Israel directed disquiet at King Farouk himself, which, Davies contends, became irresistible following a collapse in cotton prices (previously buoyed by the Korean War) in March 1952, prompting a coup 4 months later. In other words, it was, Davies concludes, the combination of nearly 25 years of steady improvement followed by 7 years of decline that led to the Egyptian revolution and the sweeping away of Farouk's regime.

Davies has also sought to apply his model to the race riots that affected a number of American cities during the 1960s. Using aggregate data on family income and education (as respective proxies for capability and expectation), he shows that the difference between Afro-American want–get gap levels and that of the population as a whole remained broadly stable amid an overall improving trend during the 1940s, before growing sharply in the 1950s. This leads him to conclude that the spate of civil disturbances that affected cites such as Los Angeles, Newark, Detroit and elsewhere during the 1960s 'appears to have been preceded by the same J-curve of expectations that are first gratified and then frustrated' (1970: 717). It is, however, problematic to use evidence regarding collective conditions to comment on individual grievance, frustration levels and motives. When individual data, drawn from heads-of-households surveys, are used to evaluate deprivation levels among Afro-Americans during the 1950s and 1960s, a much less coherent picture is apparent. Instead of a J-curve configuration, 'frustration varies without consistent pattern' (Miller *et al.* 1977: 968).

Indeed, what emerges is a long-term situation of acute instability in expected need satisfaction, with black communities from the northern states of America suffering the greatest fluctuations. Such uncertainty may become an important source of frustration in itself. A society 'in a state of social disarray, where things appear in flux, changing rapidly in all directions at the same time, where the past performance of the social system appears quite inconsistent, where social policies of many sorts seems haphazard', is, according to Ivo Feierabend and colleagues, 'a very explosive state of social affairs' (1973: 407–8). In political terms, for instance, they find that oscillations in regime coerciveness, as measured by the number of policy reversals per year, are positively correlated with guerrilla activity, revolts, large-scale arrests, riots and assassinations. Of the 20 most fluctuating countries between 1945 and 1966, 13, they conclude, were rated in the top two most unstable categories and none appeared in the top two most stable categories (Feierabend *et al.* 1970).

Development and inequality

Anther pattern of grievance formation, which may have a demonstrable effect on political stability, arises when improvements in expectation levels are not matched by comparable changes in capability levels. This can be modelled in two ways. The first, illustrated in Figure 7.4, occurs when a social stratum suffers a low standard of living for a long period of time – concurrently demonstrating a low level of expectations – and then experiences a rapid improvement in conditions leading to a great increase in expectations. These almost inevitably prove to be unrealistic and quickly give way to disappointment, grievance and frustration. Ivo Feierabend and colleagues illustrate such a state of affairs with the example of the Hungarian revolution of 1956, which, being preceded by an extensive 'thawing of totalitarianism', 'exaggerated hopes' to the extent that 'what seemed like spectacular change to the observer was too little and too late to meet the expectations of the insurrectionists' (1973: 407).

A similar scenario is outlined by Gurr in the third of his models of deprivation. As Figure 7.5 shows, 'aspirational' deprivation describes a broadly

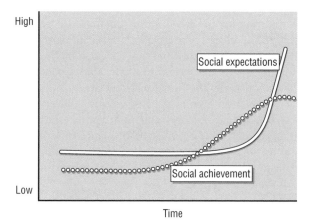

Figure 7.4 An improving J-curve. Source: Adapted from Feierabend *et al.* (1973: 407).

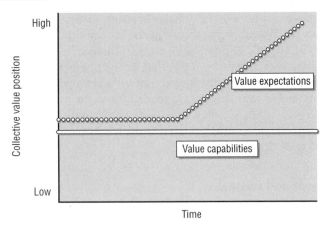

Figure 7.5 Aspirational deprivation. Source: Redrawn from Gurr (1974: 51).

analogous situation in which individuals or groups, while not anticipating or experiencing a significant loss of what they have, 'are angered because they feel they have no means for attaining new or intensified expectations' (Gurr 1974: 50). The result, as before, is an intolerable gap between expectations and capabilities. Commonly, such a process is associated with the impact of modernisation and its capacity either to introduce or to emphasise new ideas and material resources to people previously accustomed to different (and often less desirable) conditions. This can be an important motivator of collective action. As Norman Cohn notes of the consequences of industriali-sation in medieval Europe: when 'social and economic horizons expanded, hardship and poverty and dependence ceased to appear the ineluctable fate of common folk' (1961: 27–8). Similarly, it is clear from Stephen Kent's study of the English Civil War that many parliamentary soldiers believed that they were fighting for the freedom of religious conscience and the vol-untary support of the clergy. Cromwell's announcement that compulsory tithes would be abolished if victory were secured at the Battle of Dunbar in 1650 led to a marked rise in expectations. The subsequent failure of parlia-ment to end tithes following the Royalist defeat produced an extensive sense of aspirational deprivation among the Roundhead soldiery, a section of the political elite, Cromwellian farmers and radical protestant clergy. Further-more, as Kent concludes, 'this deprivation only intensified hostility between the predominantly rural tithe-payers and sympathetic sectarians on the one side and ecclesiastical and civil authorities, impropriators and other wealthy land-owners on the other' (1982: 532).

Such patterns have considerable relevance today. Developing countries experiencing rapid change and the passing of traditional society often under-go what David Learner called a revolution of rising expectation (1958). As the Feierabends put it, the arousal of an under-developed society to awareness of complex modern patterns of behavior and organization brings with it a desire to emulate and achieve the same high level of satisfaction. But there is an inevitable lag between aspiration and achievement which varies in length with the specific condition of the country.

(1966: 257)

This may happen in a number of overlapping ways. First, it is often the case that such a change is prompted by the demonstration effect of modernisation processes' differentiated influence. Some groups, in other words, benefit disproportionately from change, leading to increases in inequality, envy and resentment, grievances and on to conflict and violence (Nafziger and Auvinen 2002: 156). Second, developmental processes inevitably involve greater media linkages between the North and South and within developing countries themselves. This makes previously unconnected people aware of each other's lives – particularly the apparently inspirational lifestyles of local and Western elites.

Third, population increases and land shortages, which frequently result from the modernisation of the agrarian sector, expose rural migrants arriving in cities within developing countries to the Western lifestyles of the urban wealthy and the expatriate community (Gurr 1973: 366). Fourth, political leaders may blame foreign powers and comprador classes (such as the Gujarati community in Uganda during the 1970s) for domestic problems, thereby highlighting differences in standards of living previously unnoticed or disregarded. Fifth, the low administrative, economic and social capacities of many developing countries may prevent the state from responding to development-led changes, with the consequence that capabilities fall behind expectations (Holsti 2000). Finally, leaders may utilise the benefits of development to increase their own prosperity or the material position of their clients. This, in turn, can give rise to a social stratum of inordinate wealth which then becomes a source of grievance and unmatched expectations (Keen 2000a: 292–4). As these changes are likely to occur in societies undergoing rapid social change, frustrations may have a curvilinear relationship with development. Countries at either end of the supposed tradition-to-modernity continuum are, in other words, likely to be more stable than those in transition. As the Feierabends explain,

it is at this middle stage that awareness of modernity and exposure to modern patterns should be complete, that is, at a theoretical ceiling, whereas achievement levels would still be lagging far behind. Prior to this theoretical middle stage, exposure and achievement would both be lower. After the middle stage, exposure can no longer increase, since it already amounts to complete awareness, but achievement will continue to progress, thus carrying the nation eventually into the stage of modernity.

(1972: 144)

To test this proposition cross-nationally, the Feierabends measured gross national product (GNP) and calorific intake per capita and the number of doctors, telephones, newspapers and radios per 1,000 people as indicators of satisfaction. This was then divided by each country's coded urbanisation and literacy scores (as indicators of a society's exposure to modernity and thus level of want formation) to give an enumerated estimate of a country's want–get gap for the years 1948–55. Assuming that there would be a lag between the emergence of grievances and calculable frustration, the Feierabends then collected data on political stability levels for the years 1955–61 – measured by quantifying violence levels, regime support and changes of office. As Table 7.2 demonstrates, the results do not show support for a curvilinear relationship between development and instability. Low literacy and urbanisation rates (as the basis of a traditional society) are, in other words, not associated with stability, leading to the Feierabends' hypothesis that the entire 84-state sample may have already been exposed to modernity in other ways. What is certain, they continue, is that, once a country meets an eight-point criterion ((1) 90 per cent literacy, (2) 65 radios per 1,000 people, (3) a newspaper readership of 120 per 1,000 people, (4) telephone ownership of 2 per cent of the population, (5) a calorific intake of 2,525 per person per day, (6) 1,900 people per doctor, (7) a per capita GNP of $300 and (8) 45 per cent of the population living in urban centres), 'there is an extremely high probability that the country will achieve relative political stability' (Feierabend and Feierabend 1972: 145–6).

In countries exposed to modernity, yet still mainly agrarian, the failure to redistribute land is frequently seen as a key cause of political instability. This tends to reinforce post-colonial polities in which wealth is concentrated within the hands of small, urban elites whose access to political authority makes entrance to the public sector the only viable source of individual material and status advancement. In particular, the resilience of highly unequal patterns of rural property ownership throughout the period of decolonisation is regarded as an important source of civil unrest in Latin America (Kling 1956). Figure 7.6, which Bruce Russett constructs by ranking each farm according to its size and then plotting the percentage of Austrian and Bolivian land that each decile of farmers actually owns, certainly suggests that the concentration of land in the region may be far from equitable. The top 10 per cent of farmers in Austria own 65 per cent of the land, whereas in Bolivia the top 10 per cent own nearly 95 per cent of the land. Indeed, once a Gini index is calculated by measuring the area between a country's curve and the line of equality (which represents a situation in which each decile of farmers owns an equal share of the land), a picture of acute inequality is apparent across Latin America. As Table 7.3 illustrates, this would appear to correlate quite closely with political instability – measured by the number of people, per million, killed by civil violence between 1955 and 1962 (Russett 1964).

Getting beyond a correlative relationship towards a specification of the

Table 7.2 Political stability/instability and indicators of satisfaction

	Literacy (%)		Radios (per 1,000)		Newspapers (per 1,000)		Telephones (%)		Calories (per capita per day)		Doctors (people per)		GNP ($ per capita)		Urbanisation (%)	
	< 90	> 90	< 65	> 65	< 120	> 120	< 2	> 2	< 2,525	> 2,525	< 1,900	> 1,900	< 300	> 300	< 45	> 45
Unstable	48	5	45	6	48	5	35	6	39	10	40	13	36	8	38	6
Stable	10	19	9	20	6	10	7	18	8	20	6	19	9	18	11	15

Source: Adapted from Feierabend and Feierabend (1972: 147).

Table 7.3 Political instability and Gini indices of land distribution in seven Latin American countries

Country	Cuba	Bolivia	Colombia	Argentina	Venezuela	Honduras	Guatemala
Gini index	79.2	93.6	84.9	86.3	90.9	75.7	86.0
Political instability	2,900	663	316	217	111	111	57

Source: Adapted from Russett (1964: 451).

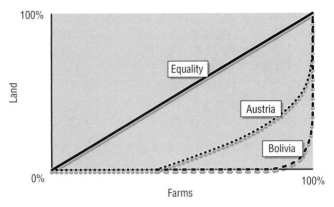

Figure 7.6 Land distribution in Austria and Bolivia. Source: Adapted from Russett (1964: 446).

precise link between inequality and conflict is, however, very problematic. As Jonathan Goodhand has recently noted, 'while there is some agreement in the literature that conflict causes poverty . . . the argument that there is a causal relationship in the reverse direction is more contentious' (2003: 633–5). Findings generally disagree with one another, and single studies frequently produce contradictory results. Ranveig Gissinger and Nils Petter Gleditsch, for instance, begin their study of the relationship between globalisation and conflict with the comment that 'a high level of trade does generate more domestic peace; at the same time, direct foreign investment also creates conditions conducive to political instability' (1999: 327). Much may depend on the nature of the material basis for such change and the kind of inequality that is produced. The extraction and transformation of natural resource endowments, an important concern of the next chapter, may, for instance, lead to new grievances over issues of wealth distribution or, as in the case of Angola, to an intensification of long-held political grievances (Cramer 2003: 406). In such circumstances, heavily skewed patterns of land ownership may, in situations where 'the peasant lives in poverty and suffering', make conflict 'likely, if not inevitable' (Huntington 1968: 375). This, like ethnic or other communal linkages, may be considered a horizontal inequality, while disparities of income (also found to be an important causal element in conflictive behaviour (Alesina and Perotti 1996)) can be regarded as a vertical index of inequality (Murshed and Gates 2003).

In contrast, some writers have suggested that acute inequality does not lead to conflict at all. Indeed, Paul Collier and Anke Hoeffler, pointing to a statistically significant inverse relationship between the two variables, argue that 'greater inequality significantly reduces the risk and duration of war' (quoted in Cramer 2003: 399). This, they explain, is because acute inequality implies the existence of a politically entrenched elite that is likely to back, both materially and ideologically, the repression of any challenge to the status quo – from which the elite continues to prosper. Moreover, in keeping with the premises of what Mark Irving Lichbach calls 'the rational actor scientific research program' (also discussed in more detail in the next chapter), potential protagonists are dissuaded from initiating conflicts aimed at redistribution by observable increases in governmental/elite strength born of inequality (1989: 459). As Collier concludes, 'conflict is not caused by divisions, rather it actually needs to create them' (2000a: 13). These, as Alejandro Portes notes of Santiago de Chile, may result from 'the *post-factum* self-legitimation of successful revolutionary movements' (1971: 26). Consequently, claims regarding preparticipatory grievances cannot be taken as evidence of individuals' actual motivations. This tends to undermine the idea (central to the relative deprivation model generally and studies by Maro Ellina and Will Moore (1990) and Douglas Hibbs (1973) in particular) that political repression, as a grievance-inducing input, should be positively correlated with conflictive behaviour.

The result is, in many cases, an arbitrary tendency to classify people as deprived and to see a wide range of post-frustration responses as aggressive. In other words, comparatively affluent researchers may make social judgements based on their own feelings of affinity and sympathy when recording the sentiments and observing the behaviour of the poor (Bandura and Walters 1963). Indeed, Richard Walters and Murray Brown (1963) found that observers could be trained to adjust their evaluations of post-frustration responses and that many used different criteria, based on past experiences, to judge what amounted to 'aggression'. Such objectivism can, as we saw in defining conflictive situations and in the measurement of structural violence (looked at in Chapters 2 and 3 respectively), become based upon overly broad social judgements. These may then be deployed to label any individual or group that, perhaps deliberately and contentedly, does not possess 'sufficient' material goods as inclined to behave aggressively and therefore a potential threat to the established order. As Leonard Berkowitz puts it, 'people have learned to categorise an individual's rigorous behaviors . . . as aggressive even when the frustrated person does not intend to commit injury' (1965: 306).

In fact, it would seem that, in empirical terms, the 'vast majority of the disadvantaged do not engage in disruptive public protest' (Bandura 1973: 169). Throughout the urban upheavals in the United States during the 1960s, for instance, it is estimated that only 15–20 per cent of residents from socially deprived areas actively participated in the disturbances (Bowen *et al.* 1968). The possible reasons why the poor (and, therefore, presumably aggrieved) do not engage in conflictive behaviour are, however, largely ignored. As Rod Aya notes of the work of the Feierabends, relative deprivation theorists generally do not 'specify the conditions under which expectations may be frustrated *without* producing rebellion. [Instead] . . . they simply presume a direct connection between frustration and revolt, and thus beg the question they profess to have answered' (1979: 57). Given that a number of studies have indicated that passivity is highest among the most deprived, this criticism is particularly damaging. Edward Mitchell's study of South Vietnam, for instance, found that governmental control was highest (and the recruitment powers of the Viet Cong were weakest) not in areas of comparative prosperity, but in provinces where 'few peasants farm their own land, the distribution of landholdings is unequal, no land redistribution has taken place, large French landholdings existed in the past, population density is high, and the terrain is such that accessibility is poor' (1968: 438).

Another key problem in associating frustration with conflict is the great difficulty in measuring an individual's (let alone a group's) needs. How can an accurate study of the social requirements for love and respect be adequately operationalised? Even physiological needs are difficult to ascertain, and there is little consensus among theorists on the comparative standards used to analyse dissatisfaction. The notion of a need hierarchy of sustenance, sexual gratification, self-actualisation and so on (which is fundamental to many relative deprivation theorists) is especially problematic. As Peter Lupsha points out, such an ordering is likely to be 'subject to change without notice as one's needs are satiated and others rise to the fore', thereby making longitudinal studies difficult to assess, compare and corroborate accurately (1971: 93). Measuring and relating satisfaction levels are similarly challenging. What one subject might find highly satisfactory, another might consider intensely frustrating. Yet writers such as Davies illustrate expected need satisfaction as a straight-line function into which various revolutions are made to fit. To do this, he and others are obliged to work backwards from the event using post hoc and inferential methods, thereby undermining the prognostic potential of their models.

An example of this kind of problem is the failure of the Feierabends' basic assertion – that 'once traditional societies are exposed to the modern way of life, without exception, they desire benefits associated with modernity' (1972: 144) – to predict instability levels in the South. It is generally acknowledged, for instance, that the last 30 years have seen a significant increase in both adult literacy rates and the combined primary and secondary school enrolment ratio across much of the developing world. This, according to the Feierabends' reasoning, has enlarged the numbers of people in contact with non-traditional concepts, thereby exacerbating a 'process during which former patterns of behaviour, outdated technologies, established roles, status and norms must all give way to new, unfamiliar patterns' and widening 'the inevitable lag between aspiration and achievement' (Feierabend and Feierabend 1972: 144). The expected rise in 'disruption, chaos and personal discontent', however, does not seem to have materialised (Feierabend and Feierabend 1972: 149). Transitional countries are not, despite the apocalyptic visions of Robert Kaplan and others discussed in Chapter 5, now demonstrably more unstable than they were in 1970. Although there has been an increase in civilian casualties that has disproportionately affected the developing world, this is not a result of recent trends, but because poor and transitional countries have been home to the bulk of civil wars for most of the post-Second World War era. Indeed, rather than a function of modernisation or development, these conflicts may be mainly a consequence of Great Power policy, the spread of small arms, the enduring despotism of tiny privileged elites often based on traditional societal structures or, as Stathis Kalyvas contends, microfoundational logic (2006).

At the heart of this problem is, for critics of the relative deprivation research programme, a basic confusion between a society's tendency to develop along modern lines and individuals' concerns about their own life that 'often occur within a still viable traditional context in which provision of a minimum of economic, social and psychological security dampens whatever frustrations unfulfilled demands generate' (Oberschall 1969: 9). Indeed, in Nigeria and Uganda, it was found that a high degree of exposure to urban life and the media, which supposedly 'prepare men's minds for new desires more rapidly than those new desires be satisfied' (de Sola Pool 1966: 106), made 'no marked difference in satisfaction level' (Oberschall 1969: 12). Previous positive correlations between these two variables tended to overlook a basic difference between desires (such as owning a tractor) that are not seen as likely to materialise and expectations (such as earning enough to feed one's family) which can be regarded as an imperative right. As Table 7.4 illustrates, more subjects did not want, for instance, a car or truck than wanted one and expected to get one. Consequently, Anthony Oberschall concludes that the lack of ownership of a car or truck could not be regarded as an example of relative deprivation. This, he explains, is because people living in developing or transitional countries are unlikely to orientate their expectations towards members of a comprador or overseas elite with whom they have little or no social interaction. Instead, it is more likely that the assets of their own immediate contacts will make up the primary reference against which their own position is judged (1969).

Indeed, Derek Birrell reached a similar conclusion in his study of deprivation levels in Northern Ireland (1972). Despite long being the poorest

Table 7.4 Material possessions, desires and expectations in Uganda (percentages)

Item	Owners	Does not own it, wants it and expects to get it	Does not own it, wants it and does not expect to get it	Does not own it and does not want it
Blankets	92	3	3	1
Land	85	3	8	1
Bicycle	63	10	16	4
Tin roof	52	16	26	3
Radio	46	18	28	15
Electricity	5	13	50	28
Car/truck	4	9	58	24

Source: Adapted from Oberschall (1969: 15).

region in the UK – a fact extensively disseminated by political leaders – there was, he suggested, little evidence that deprived groups compared their situation with people on the mainland. Nor, he continued, did they relate themselves to people in the Republic of Ireland; only 13 per cent of Catholics (the province's most deprived group) expected their position to improve through a united Ireland. Instead, he argued that people were more likely to assess their own positions in relation to their neighbours, and it is this that focused attention on the wealth disparities, differential levels of political representation and divergent traditions and symbols of the Catholic and Protestant communities, thereby intensifying the dynamics of the Northern Irish conflict.

Conclusion

This chapter has looked at some of the key debates regarding the formation and marshalling of grievances as a causal element in individual and collective conflict. First, it considered the notion of relative deprivation as a development of human needs theory and the frustration–aggression mechanism to which it owes much of its conceptual heritage. At its simplest, this is the idea that people participate in conflicts because they are unable to satisfy needs such as sustenance, security, affection and self-actualisation. There is, in other words, a direct connection – initially conceived of in terms of frustration always leading to aggression – between the inequitable distribution of resources (both material and non-material) and the causes of conflict and violence. Although this chapter has attempted to retain some of this explicability within a particularly abstruse and fragmentary section of the literature, it is important to note that the proposed relationship between perceived needs, a frustrating instigator, a sense of grievance and conflictive behaviour is, in fact, very complex.

There is, for instance, little agreement on whether or not perceived grievances are derived from frustrated needs that are innate or socially acquired, universal or culturally specific, rigid or fluid. Nonetheless, most writers are agreed that those whose needs are not met may develop grievances in two ways. The first – egoistic deprivation – is internally experienced and thus tends to lead to individual responses such as a lowering of expectation, withdrawal or, conversely, a reinvigorated pursuit of personal goals. The second – fraternal deprivation – is experienced collectively and is therefore likely to produce participatory responses including social movements, political parties, trade unions and the like. In a sociological process related to the integrative effects of conflict participation looked at in Chapter 4, much depends on how deprivation is experienced and the web of group affiliations with which an individual identifies.

Also relevant are the ways in which need satisfaction and individual or collective expectations are changing over time – the primary concern of this chapter's second section. The ability of people to meet their needs may decline in relation to static expectations amid economic recessions. Equally, people's expectations may grow in a way that outstrips need satisfaction during times of growth. The latter pattern is particularly relevant to periods of political liberalisation, economic modernisation and social development, all of which can increase expectations while also creating or exacerbating collective differences – and therefore fraternal deprivation – within societies. As we saw in the case of Rwanda (discussed in Chapters 3 and 6), such changes may lead to 'transition' periods in which inequality levels, collective frustration, structural violence and the redrawing of social divides all intensify, leading to a rise in instability, conflict and violence.

Specifying the causal dynamics of such relationships is, however, extremely difficult. As most countries might be said to be amid a period of modernisation or development, instances of social instability do not reveal any particular determinative influence. Indeed, problems in measuring human needs, deprivation and frustration (at the level of the individual, the group and the state), coupled with the more fundamental problems of objectivism, have produced a contradictory body of inconclusive findings that are difficult to link together longitudinally. Such problems have led some analysts to question the value of basing analyses of conflict and violence on the premises of need and frustration at all. Walter Korpi, for instance, states that an overemphasis on grievance as a motivational cause of conflict and violence 'overlooks the actual possibilities for achieving the desired change' and ignores the fact that achieving such an objective is 'determined primarily by the difference in power resources between the parties concerned' (1974: 1569). This focus on the dynamics of collective mobilisation, along with an associated emphasis on the expected utility of conflict participation, represents something of an elemental challenge to grievance-based approaches and is thus the topic of the next chapter.

8 Mobilisation

Our starting point in the previous chapter was Aristotle's assessment of the causes of Athenian conflict and violence. For Aristotle, these were not, however, simply the result of the unequal nature of Athenian society and frustration at the municipal administration's weakness and incompetence. They were also driven by the desire for the wealth and privilege that holding political office entails. This chapter looks at the influence that this desire has on the individual and the ways in which it is organised collectively. The first section considers the initial challenge to the grievance paradigm that first emerged during the 1960s. This emphasises the importance of rational calculations of likely success, the opportunities for mobilisation and the resources at the disposal of group participants. A particular focus here is the difficulty of overcoming the problem of free-riding, or the assurance that individuals will receive collective benefits whether or not they become involved in organised conflict. The second section looks at one of the key ways in which this is surmounted – by the control and distribution of selective benefits to group members. This suggests that individuals will take part in collective conflict in order to receive these rewards rather than to achieve social and political objectives (the premise of the previous chapter). Here, the presence of lootable natural resources within states unable to manage their extraction and distribution effectively is seen as an important incentive for conflict participation.

Individuals, groups and rationality

During the 1960s and the heyday of grievance-based explanations of conflict and violence, writers began offering dissenting theses challenging what they perceived to be the dominant precepts of the day: 'that movement participation was relatively rare, discontents were transitory, movement and institutionalized actions were sharply distinct, and movement actors were arational if not outright irrational' (Jenkins 1983: 528). More plausible, it is suggested, is the view that the decision to participate in social movements, protest groups and rebellions is 'not as a consequence of predisposing psychological traits or states, but as the result of rational decision processes whereby people weigh the costs and benefits of participation' (Klandermans 1984: 583). By the early 1970s, this concern had produced a heterogeneous body of work known as resource mobilisation theory (Etzioni 1968; Leites and Wolf 1970; Wilson 1973; McCarthy and Zald 1973).

According to David Snyder, this had five basic premises, which, as Table 8.1 illustrates, have given rise to approaches to conflict analysis quite different from the work of grievance theorists looked at in the previous chapter (1978: 504–6). First, variations in grievance are either unrelated (Jenkins and Perrow 1977), or only very weakly related (McCarthy and Zald 1977: 1214–15), to collective political action in general and violent conflict in particular. Second, the organisation of conflict is of utmost importance in explaining how people come to participate in collective action. This is also a feature of other approaches, but, for writers such as Snyder and Tilly (1972), the key element is the manipulation of participants by elites and not merely the command of discontent. Third, group membership levels, along with 'tangible' resources (weapons, money, communication links and so on), act as constraints upon, or facilitators of, conflictive behaviour (Gamson 1975; Freeman 1979: 172–5).

Table 8.1 A comparison of relative deprivation and resource mobilisation theory

Relative deprivation theory	Resource mobilisation theory
The fundamental disposition of individuals (or groups) is towards the avoidance of violent conflict	The fundamental disposition of individuals (or groups) is to maximise power and resources
Inclinations towards pacific politics may be blocked by aberrant events/conditions	Pursuing this objective may involve the use of violence
Primary problem is to explain why collective violence occurs as often as it does	Primary problem is to explain why collective violence does not occur more often
Assessment of environment is other-regarding in terms of both motivation and expectation	Assessment of environment is self-regarding in terms of both motivation and expectation
Engagement in collective violence is likely to be affective rather than coolly calculated	Engagement in collective violence is likely to be a result of rational, tactical considerations
Factors such as power balances and available resources are therefore expected to play a minimal role	Factors such as power balances and available resources are therefore expected to play a major role
Conflict may be heavily influenced by culture and learning as these fundamentally affect the way grievances are perceived and communicated	Cultural factors are not significant, but learning may play a role in influencing cost–benefit calculations

Source: Adapted from Eckstein (1980: 142–3).

Fourth, individuals and groups attempt to bring these resources to bear in order to achieve their objectives in a rational manner. The basic postulate here is that violent conflict

> is a purposeful form of contention for political power and, therefore, no matter how frustrated people are by conditions of relative deprivation, they will not contend collectively for political power unless the likelihood of success of rebellion is high and the expected benefits of rebellion exceed the expected costs.
>
> (Muller and Weede 1994: 41)

The individual is thus treated as a unitary actor proceeding on a single set of assumptions and preferences (grounded upon the ability to rank potential outcomes with a scale of value) in pursuit of well-defined goals. It is assumed that behaviour is based on the self-interested pursuit of clearly identifiable aims and that individuals have the time, rational capacity and emotional detachment to choose the best course of action, no matter how complex the choice (Finkel *et al.* 1989). Course *a* is preferred to *b* (and to *c*, if *b* is preferred to *c* as well) if it can be observed to have been chosen; no other mental processes are considered. People thus seek to pursue their own interests through a calculated assessment of the costs and benefits of any given course of action. Revolutions are supported because people expect the results to include a material improvement for themselves (not for the good of the collective) and that these will outweigh any expected costs. 'Participants will', in other words, 'spend an extra unit of their time on dissident activities only if the private reward from dissident activities is greater than the private reward from [other] economic activities' (Lichbach 1989: 460). Fifth, conflicts emerge because collective violence is an effective way to compete for scarce resources with other groups (including the state). Obtaining, or opponents losing, control over these resources is, it is suggested, therefore important as both a motive and an object of conflictive behaviour (Tilly 1975a).

In this sense, then, 'mobilization refers to the process through which individual group members' resources are surrendered, assembled, and committed for obtaining common goals', for defending group interests and for challenging existing structures of domination (Oberschall 1978: 306; 1973). Here, contenders are, as Charles Tilly notes, of two kinds (1978). Some are located within the polity and therefore enjoy routine, low-cost admission to the levers of power, whereas others are involved in attempting to gain access to the political centre and a share of its resources. Supported by, or consisting of, existing elites, the former group of contenders endeavours to exclude challengers and to maintain its preferential position. For a challenge to overcome these entrenched interests and succeed, there must be support for contenders' claims from within a significant section of the polity's population and there must be an inability or unwillingness to suppress both the challenger and any generalised support for its claims – a factor particularly important if 'coalitions between members of the polity and the contenders making the alternative claims' have emerged (1973: 441). When a challenge is successful, the newly inducted group adapts the system to recognise its position and to lower the costs of access for its constituency. The civil rights movement in the United States, for instance, was able, once it had secured a place within the polity, to wind down its direct action programme and transfer the costs of desegregating the public sphere to the Justice Department and other public sector organisations.

In this sense, then, varying levels of deprivation are not seen as an important element in the organisation and success of collective conflict. For instance, in their study of Europe during the nineteenth and early twentieth century, the Tillys find no positive association between rises in misery and poverty – frequently observed during periods of rapid urbanisation – and collective violence. They conclude that, while industrialisation and government centralisation certainly provoked conflicts (some of which were quite extensive), this was because the state was making claims upon resources that were previously the reserve of groups with sufficient internal solidarity to mobilise resistance. Price rises, conscription and tax increases all produced conflicts, but these occupied the most organised and purposeful and not the most deprived and dispossessed (Tilly *et al.* 1975). As a whole, though, modernisation, contrary to the work of the Feierabends and others discussed in the previous chapter, is said to depress 'the level of social conflict, because it weakens many groups' means of mobilization for collective action faster than it creates other groups with a high mobilizing capacity' (Oberschall 1978: 302).

Of crucial importance in the prevalence of collective conflict, then, is the nature of the polity in which it occurs. This is, as Edward Muller and Erich Weede note, because regime structures provide 'a set of constraints and opportunities that influence the benefits, costs, and likelihood of success of all kinds of collective political action' (1994: 43). Such an influence can work in three ways. First, as 'mobilization depends upon the coercive, normative, remunerative and informational resources that an incipient movement can extract from its setting and can employ in its protest', variables such as the availability of data, the accessibility of media outlets and the efficiency and extent of communication infrastructures can all have an important impact on collective conflict (Kitschelt 1986: 61). Second, the institutional relationship between civil groups and political elites may, through the formulation and implementation of rules and conventions, shape collective demands. As agents of social control are rendered, according to rational choice assumptions, as 'an exogenous variable captured by the cost function', mobilisation is likely to be encouraged by conciliatory responses and impeded by reactions that are more forceful (Oberschall 1994: 97). Third, mobilisation may be affected by the presence or absence of other mobilising groups. The perceived success of one group may exert a demonstrable influence over others, while the concurrent appearance of many such groups can help to determine the type of response preferred by the polity (Tarrow 1998).

Variations in such political opportunity structures give rise to open or closed polities (Eisinger 1973). In his study of anti-nuclear protest movements in Europe and the United States, Herbert Kitschelt concludes that liberal democracies with very open polities and effective administrations are more likely to contain non-violent and innovative forms of social mobilisation, whereas less assimilatory types of social mobilisation are probable in closed and ineffective systems (1986: 63–4). When extrapolated to non-democratic polities, this finding is broadly in keeping with the hypothesis that 'the incidence of collective violence should be relatively high under conditions of intermediate regime repressiveness and relatively low when the regime is either very repressive or very open' (Muller 1985: 48). Rational actors should prefer non-violent participation in open polities because it is less costly, easy to organise, more predictable and likely to lead to benefits.

Equally, in highly repressive systems, rational actors should abstain from political engagement as, although the potential benefits may be great, the expected costs are extremely high, the likelihood of success is very low and the difficulties of mobilisation are acute. However, in polities where prevailing political opportunities either permit some groups to mobilise or tolerate a low level of general mobilisation (but then prevent these from effecting changes), rational actors may be likely to adjudge the benefits of violent rebellion as outweighing the benefits of non-violent participation. They may also decide that the costs of rebellion are not inordinately high and that there is sufficient social space and available resources to mobilise a successful collective challenge (Muller and Weede 1990). This inverted 'U', or curvilinear, relationship between regime repressiveness/polity openness and levels of collective violence contrasts with the positive linearity of many grievance theories (for instance, Hibbs' premise that a lack of political participation acts as a frustrating instigator (1973)) and the negative linearity of work based only on the deterrent value of repression (Coleman 1990: Ch. 18).

For many writers, however, such a characterisation of participative, rational and measured collective responses to changing political environments does not fit with the way in which individuals actually make decisions – not least, because only around one in five rebellions has been successful (Gurr and Goldstone 1991). Part of the problem at the level of the individual (we shall look at the difficulties of reaching collective decisions in Chapter 9) is the issue of free-riding. Why should a rational individual join any collective action when most conflicts are fought over public goods (such as greater political representation, lower taxes and so on) that everyone will enjoy? Furthermore, it is extremely unlikely that any one person's decision to join a rebellion will have any effect on the outcome. As Mark Lichbach puts it, 'on the cost side (1) rebels face many social causes with which to become involved; (2) rebels have many personal demands on their time that have priority . . . [and] (3) participation is often quite costly and dangerous' (1994a: 386–7). In all, the 'rebel's dilemma' presents prospective dissidents, like all group members, with strong incentives to free-ride even though they, like their peers, stand to benefit from the outcome of mobilisation (Tullock 1971).

As such incentives can be obstructed or promoted by structures internal to the group itself, regardless of its position relative to the power structures of the existing polity, the nature of the relationship between individuals and collectives is important – particularly the benefits that the former cannot obtain for themselves and that may accrue from participating in the latter. Jack Goldstone summarises these thus:

> the unattached individual making choices in the free marketplace is un-likely to obtain much more than his or her preferred balance between consumer durables and disposables . . . . For locating and obtaining an enormous variety of crucial economic and affective goods and services – information, support for collective causes, status and career opportuni-ties – individuals depend on their involvement with identifiable groups.
>
> (1994: 144)

In return for these benefits, individuals therefore come to value the preser-vation of their group. They may overlook the opportunity to free-ride and, for reasons of time, money and the need to pressure others to conform, they may decide to commit their resources to the interests and objectives of the group (Hechter 1987).

For Lichbach, this can happen in four, overlapping ways (1994b: 11–19). The first he calls 'uncoordinated market exchange relations'. These may act to increase the benefits accruing to individual participation. If, for instance, a group contains a high proportion of zealots (individuals for whom the benefits of their contributions exceed the costs), then it is likely to mobilise more easily – particularly if the object of mobilisation is made more valuable through scarcity or policy (Olson 1971: 49). Similarly, a group's capacity to reduce or repay an individual's participatory costs, such as start-up expenses or forgone income (to be discussed in greater detail in the next section), may permit it to mobilise with less difficulty (Rogowski 1985). Obviously, this will be more likely to occur if the group can increase its resources, suggesting that mobilisation becomes more probable when organised by prosperous sections of society or when supported by larger concerns such as national organisations, wealthy diasporas, sympathetic patrons or overseas states (Azam 2001).

Additionally, an individual's decision to participate may be influenced by the perceived efficiency of the group's manifesto, resources or plans; if, in other words, more benefits can be obtained for a fixed cost (in terms of time, money and so on) through advances in technology and refinements in tactics (Muller and Opp 1986). These factors relate closely to the tendency, examined in Chapter 4, of conflict to exert a cohering effect upon members of participant groups. The use of incomplete or deliberately manipulated information, for instance, can be crucial in portraying groups' objectives favourably and improving their perceived likelihood of success, thereby solidifying internal support and bolstering external recruitment. Misapprehensions regarding the potential costs of becoming involved might inspire zealotry and increase risk-taking, while a misleading impression of the group's internal structure can convince individuals that their participation could make a material difference to the outcome of mobilisation (Moe 1980). Restricting information or other material resources can also prevent individuals from selecting alternative options and increase general perceptions of competition and polarisation (Gates 2002).

A second, inter-related solution to the free-riding dilemma is to be found in groups that enjoy high levels of solidarity, strong institutions and a widespread sense of common purpose (Taylor 1988). Here, the dissemination of knowledge is important in the construction of a collective ideology, which can promote conformity and the experience of self-actualisation, enhance an individual's capacity to endure hardship and add ethical dimensions to the goals of mobilisation (Defronzo 1991: 314). Indeed, groups that contain shared expectations based upon qualitatively similar ideas tend to make comparable assessments of utility, especially if their members are subject to appeals and pleas for action of the type discussed in Chapter 7. Additionally, a broadening awareness of this mutuality through the evident engagement of others can produce sequential forms of mobilisation known as bandwagon, threshold or critical-mass examples (Oberschall 1979). Third, free-riding may be overcome through the establishment of authoritative rules within the mobilising group. These are, as Chapter 5 highlighted, particularly important if groups are drawn from overcrowded and socially diverse environments where personal autonomy is expected to be high and reciprocity low. At a political level, such an oversight can help to ensure the contingent cooperation of individuals who fear that their involvement will not be matched by others, while, at an economic level, the enforcement of exchange conventions can assist in solidifying a group's resource base and further consolidate mobilisation (Ostrom 1990).

Fourth, 'a little power, authority, and, yes, dictatorship, can go a long way toward solving the Rebel's Dilemma' (Lichbach 1994b: 17). In addition to the institutionalisation of doctrinaire regulations, personality cults around charismatic and authoritarian leaders can facilitate mobilisation by consolidating interpersonal bonds of expected reciprocity and thus helping to alter an individual's assessment of the potential costs of trusting others (Hardin 1995). This may be strengthened by making the group more exclusive through the formation of a centralised, compact revolutionary bureau, the greater involvement of zealots or the establishment of a decentralised network of small, highly coherent cells (Weede and Muller 1998: 45–9). Top-down coercion, in the form of punishing desertion and sloth and enforcing stringent barriers between the group and the broader context in which it operates, can, along with the types of direct and vicarious conditioning considered in Chapter 6, increase individuals' sense of identity and lead them to believe that successful mobilisation is dependent on their participation (Moore 1995: 440–2). In Mozambique, for instance, young men recruited to the *Resistência Nacional Moçambicana* (the Mozambican National Resistance – RENAMO) were reported to have been forced to attack their home village, thereby permanently severing their societal links and rendering them more reliant on the group (Cohn and Goodwin-Gill 1994: 23).

Although these four sets of measures may be successful in offsetting the effects of free-riding, they do not fully overcome a fundamental difference in preference between the mobilising elite and the mobilised masses. As Patrick Regan and Daniel Norton observe, 'leaders seek authority and control . . . they view success in terms of a new distribution of political power, whether that is through a power-sharing arrangement or outright and total control over the bureaucracy'. Those enlisted, they continue, 'are motivated by personal gains in the form of a minimally accepted improvement in their personal standard of living', suggesting that the distribution of 'protection and resources in the provision of selective benefits' is extremely important for sustained mobilisation to occur (2005: 323). This is very significant because, as we shall see in the next section, 'an observable increase in the *self-financing* nature of combatant activities' since the end of the Cold War has led to further inroads in the predominantly grievance-based idea that warfare represents a frustrating breakdown in the supply of economic or political public goods and is thus an instigator of restorative action (Ballentine and Sherman 2003: 1). Rather, the imperative of ensuring an unbroken supply of remuneration is seen as the primary means of ensuring group integration, thereby transforming a war-affected economy into 'an alternate system of profit, power and protection' (Berdal and Keen 1997: 797). As Michael Pugh and colleagues conclude, 'the conditions of war present new commercial opportunities for the exploitation of assets, investment, services, marketing, and welfare. Indeed, . . . armed factions are remarkably adept at economic diversification and at seeking optimum gains in the changing contexts of their struggle' (2004: 19).

Greed and natural resources

Three factors are said to promote the emergence of war economies. The first is the gradual reduction in Great Power competition within the developing world since the 1980s. As we saw in Chapter 5's account of 'the new barbarism', it has often been noted that a decline in Superpower patronage led to a reduction in the expected costs of challenging previously supported regimes, lifting 'the lid on long-standing tribal, ethnic, and national rivalries' (Keen 2000b: 20–1). Hitherto, the 'confrontation between the two systems' had allowed developing countries 'to play one side off against the other to obtain aid', leading to favourable lending terms and limited conditionality (Singh 2002: 298). The West's geopolitical imperative of excluding Sino-Soviet influence, for instance, ensured that both the International Monetary Fund's Articles of Agreement and the General Agreement on Tariffs and Trade permitted developing economies to erect barriers to capital movement, to adjust importation tariffs, to control their balance of payments and to establish a degree of policy autonomy. This, for many economists, helps to explain why average annual growth within developing countries rose from 0.5 per cent for the period 1900–50 to 5.5 per cent from 1950 to 1980 (Patel 1992). These greater resources were then available to be used to repress or incorporate domestic dissent, thereby strengthening the state, increasing the costs of challenging the status quo and reducing the benefits of confrontational mobilisation.

As patronage declined, Southern regimes also became more susceptible to Western capital penetration. The imposition of extensive conditionalities on development assistance led to severe cuts in public expenditure, while private financial flows to the South grew from US$36 billion in 1988 to US$251.1 billion in 1997 (Thérien and Lloyd 2000: 27). Consequently, domestic elites turned to foreign firms and commercial lenders for support. As internal dissent grew, they also tended to institute polices aimed at debilitating potential challengers. As William Reno observes, 'removing public goods, like security or economic security, that are otherwise enjoyed by all, irrespective of their political or economic situation, is done to encourage the individual to seek the ruler's personal favor' and to offset the appeal of 'strongmen who have appropriated prerogatives of official office for their own benefit' (2000a: 47; 2000b: 439). As Table 8.2 shows, this has led to an acute weakening of the public sector. Such a decline in state capacity has, as Chapter 1 highlighted, been compounded by a proliferation of weapons made abundant and affordable by now cash-strapped former patrons seeking to reduce the running costs of their own domestic arsenals (Gamba and Cornwell 2000: 163–4).

Indeed, the availability of such resources has been greatly enhanced by a second change in the geopolitical context, globalisation. This has diminished the regulatory mandate of the state by increasing the power of supranational multilateral financial institutions and substate civil society organisations, both of which, in many cases, now have the authority to override national economic planning (Held *et al.* 1997). The result, Mark Duffield suggests, is a power vacuum in which 'political actors have been able to control local economies and realize their worth through the ability to forge new and flexible relations with liberalized global markets' (2000: 72). When this coincides with a proliferation of inexpensive weaponry, the potential costs of collective violence decrease, its benefits increase and the likelihood of elites securing political and further economic objectives grows. Mobilisation may thus take the form of internationalised criminal networks, supported as much for their ability to provide a pacific trading and social environment as

Table 8.2 Annual government spending on education and health in various African countries (US$ per capita/percentage of GDP)

	1980	1987	1994
Cameroon			
Education	32.3/12.4	34.3/12.0	21.5/9.1
Health	17.8/6.8	14.2/5.0	8.1/3.4
Kenya			
Education	18.4/19.6	22.2/19.8	18.0/13.8
Health	12.2/13.0	10.3/9.2	9.8/7.5
Zambia			
Education	15.8/10.2	8.6/5.8	5.5/4.0
Health	7.2/4.6	4.3/2.9	1.2/0.9
DR Congo			
Education	5.6/2.9	1.1/2.0	0.0/0.0
Health	3.9/1.8	0.7/1.2	0.0/0.0
Congo			
Education	56.5/18.7	39.5/9.8	19.2/4.9
Health	21.2/7.0	14.2/3.5	12.0/3.1

Source: Reno (2000b: 441).

for the selective benefits that they bestow. It may also result from collective attempts to control the supply of commodities across borders and frequently on to Western markets (Cater 2003: 32–3). In each case, the dynamics of mobilisation are 'deeply interconnected with both regulated and unregulated global trade and financial flows' (Pugh *et al.* 2004: 19).

Here, the presence of natural resources – a third factor in the emergence of war-affected economies – is held to increase the destructiveness of conflicts once they have begun (de Soysa 2000). The availability of primary commodities may, it is suggested, 'encourage [the] raiding of civilians to meet the needs of the fighters', giving rise to 'competition and conflict over access to and distribution of the economic proceeds of resource exploitation' (Keen 1997: 72; Sherman 2003: 225). As Table 8.3 illustrates, these commonly include oil, natural gas, timber, gemstones, narcotics and timber. For instance, the *União Nacional para a Independência Total de Angola* (The National Union for the Total Independence of Angola – UNITA) has controlled over 70 per cent of the country's diamond exports during much of the country's civil war (Berdal and Malone 2000: 5). Similarly, the National Patriotic Front leader, Charles Taylor, is said to have made hundreds of millions of dollars a year (between 1992 and 1996) from his organisation's administration of

Table 8.3 Civil conflicts linked to resource wealth, 1994–2001

	Duration	Resources
Afghanistan	1978–2001	Gems, opium
Angola	1975–	Oil, diamonds
Burma	1949–	Timber, gems, opium
Cambodia	1978–97	Timber, gems
Colombia	1984–	Oil, opium, coca
Congo	1997–	Oil
DR Congo	1996–	Copper, cobalt, diamonds, gold, coltan, coffee
Aceh	1975–	Natural gas
West Papua	1969–	Copper, gold
Liberia	1989–96	Iron, diamonds, gold, timber, coffee, palm oil, cocoa, rubber, marijuana
Papua New Guinea	1988–	Copper, gold
Peru	1980–95	Coca
Sierra Leone	1991–2000	Diamonds
Sudan	1983–	Oil

Source: Ross (2003: 49).

rubber, gold and timber extraction in 'Taylorland' – a territory (carved out of Liberia and eastern Sierra Leone) replete with its own currency, telecommunications network, airfield, port and banking system (Reno 2000c).

The availability of these resources has important implications for the manner in which conflicts are undertaken. While the presence of lootable resources (such as alluvial diamonds, timber, agricultural products and so on) can lessen free-riding by making mobilisation privately profitable, it may additionally obstruct the ultimate achievement of political objectives by turning local commanders into autonomous despots unmindful of the broader aims of the group (Herbst 2000a: 276–81). Such a constraint on the elite's chain of command also makes mobilisation difficult to bring to an end. As David Keen notes, 'winning may not be desirable: the point of war may be precisely the legitimacy it confers on actions that in peacetime would be punishable as crimes' (1998: 20). From an elite's point of view, this is efficacious as long as its objectives are limited to material acquisition and not political hegemony. However, if the natural resource is difficult to loot (such as oil, deep-mined gemstones and minerals) or if transportation links are easy to obstruct, then merely seeking to control and redistribute the wealth of one part of a country is not sufficient to ensure group loyalty. In such cases (of which Angola, Aceh, West Papua, Papua New Guinea and Sudan are cited as examples), wider political ambitions (separatism, ethno-nationalism and so on) may be more common (Ross 2004).

Much depends on the propinquity of the resources in question. As Peter

Le Billon notes, if the resource is near to the government's seat of power ('proximate' – as in the case of Angola's oil deposits, which are predominantly offshore and thus acquirable only through the deployment of naval power) and concentrated in one area ('point' resources), then, as Table 8.4 illustrates, it is likely to be necessary for a mobilising group to initiate wideranging political ambitions, such as the organisation of a coup d'état or other forms of enforced state control. In contrast, if the resource is 'diffused' and 'distant' from governmental power, its market value is comparatively easy to realise, producing a plethora of competing mobilised groups. This often diminishes if widely dispersed resources are nearer to urban centres, leading to lower intensity forms of irredentism (such as rioting and localised rebellions). If, however, distant resources are concentrated in one region, the result may be a more coherent and politicised form of mobilisation pursuing separatist or secessionist objectives (2001: 569–75).

This is especially likely if the region in question does not receive what it perceives to be an equitable share of resource revenues or, conversely, if it allocates disproportionate levels of public investment. Both scenarios can intensify competition for extraction rights and contracts between local elites, leading to the emergence of provincial 'mini-states' seeking to expand in to weaker regions (Smith 2004). These may be acutely divisive if supported by external Powers – particularly richer countries pursuing globally important resource endowments (as Winston Churchill observed, 'God put the West's oil under Middle Eastern feet'). The mobilisation of separatist sentiment in the Democratic Republic of the Congo, for instance, was partly a result of

Table 8.4 Resource geography and conflict type

	Point	Diffuse
Proximate	State control/coup d'état Algeria (gas) Angola (oil) Chad (oil) Liberia (iron, rubber) Nicaragua (coffee) Rwanda (coffee) Sierra Leone (rutile)	Rebellion/rioting El Salvador (coffee) Guatemala (cropland) Palestine (water) Mexico (cropland)
Distant	Succession Caucasus (oil) DR Congo (copper, cobalt, gold) Indonesia (oil, copper, gold) Biafra (oil) Papua New Guinea (copper) Sudan (oil)	Warlordism Afghanistan (opium) Angola (diamonds) Burma (opium, timber) Cambodia (gems, timber) DR Congo (diamonds, gold) Liberia (timber, diamonds) Peru (coca) Philippines (marijuana, timber) Sierra Leone (diamonds)

Source: Adapted from Le Billon (2001: 573).

neighbouring states seeking raw materials and involved the tacit support, if not active involvement, of French and Belgian corporate capital (Strizek 2004).

Such predation is said to be particularly hard to resist if internal trade networks have been diminished or weakened by the effects of an economy based on natural resource rents. Increases in currency values driven by resource booms tend to make exports less competitive, thereby depressing manufacturing sectors and constricting domestic commerce (a phenomenon known as Dutch disease after the adverse impact of natural gas income on the Netherlands' economy in the 1960s) (Lam and Wantchekon 2004). On the longheld liberal assumption that trade establishes reciprocal relationships that are mutually advantageous and, as Chapter 1 highlighted, intrinsically 'peaceful', it is possible that states benefiting from one another's exports are less likely to go to war than those without extensive commercial links (Russett 2002). It may also be true that a collapse in internal trade born of adverse exchange rates can also make civil conflict more likely by diminishing the income that individuals would forgo in order to join a mobilising group and by lowering reciprocal links with other proximate groups.

Moreover, as the income derived from rents originates exogenously and therefore does not require the support of a productive class, the limited number of individuals involved in the allocation of revenue tends, it is suggested, to give rise to oligarchic administrations with few incentives to seek civil support beyond those necessary to nourish patronage networks and offset domestic political pressures (Moore 2004). As taxation is comparatively inconsequential within *rentier* economies, there are few instruments to restrain the autonomy of the state and little incentive to monitor public sector decision-making (Fearon and Laitin 2003). Moreover, because replacing such a small elite is comparatively straightforward (as well as highly lucrative), resource-reliant regimes are held to be frequently volatile and insecure and thus inclined to rely on repression and surveillance, typically funded through the rents themselves (Mahdavy 1970). As such, the presence of natural resources may be a 'permissive' cause of conflict made possible by acquisition, but driven by other goals. Alternatively, if the conflict is inspired simply by the prospect of acquiring a selective benefit, the resource in question may constitute a 'root' cause (Humphreys 2005: 512).

For a number of economists, however, such a distinction is largely irrelevant. They argue that, because human goals are infinite, their relationship with the finite resources available to fulfil these goals is likely to be more or less constant in all societies. As the way that this is perceived is unobservable, expected utility and not motive must be used to explain conflict and violence. Insofar as individual self-interest can be evaluated, selective benefits can be assumed to be the underlying purpose of conflictive behaviour. These, it is suggested, will be expressed only in the form of group mobilisation if conditions are perceived to be conducive – as assessed by rational cost–benefit analyses (Grossman 1991). Variables such as natural resource endowments and regime type are therefore simply seen as facilitators or inhibitors of individual and collective avarice, which groups attempt to conceal behind loud, yet spurious, orations on injustice, inequality and a range of other grievances. As Paul Collier, the former director of the World Bank's Development Research Group and foremost proponent of this 'greed' thesis, puts it, 'rebellion is large-scale predation of productive economic activities' accompanied by a wide variety of obfuscatory discourses that provide 'no informational content to the researcher as to the true motivation for rebellion' (2000a: 3; 2000b: 92; 2001a: 146). According to some, then, the presence of grievance discourses may be positively correlated with conflict, but they cannot be used as an explanatory variable. In fact, income inequality and land distribution are, it is claimed, five times less likely to cause conflicts than 'greed' proxies such as the availability of lootable primary commodities (Collier and Hoeffler 1998).

To demonstrate this, Collier and Anke Hoeffler used an updated version of J. David Singer and Melvin Small's dataset (1994) covering 161 countries and 78 civil wars. To quantify opportunity, they developed seven indicators measured at 5-year intervals to establish 'episodes' which can then be categorised as 'conflict' or 'conflict-free' (Collier and Hoeffler 2001). The first was the ratio of primary commodity exports to a country's overall gross domestic product (GDP). Reiterating the earlier findings of Muller and Weede (1990), they predicted that this would be an inverted 'U' relationship, as low levels of resource availability would offer little expected utility, and governments controlling very high levels of resource abundance (such as the Kingdom of Saudi Arabia) may be so well financed as to make rebellion too costly to be feasible. The second indicator was the presence of transferable diasporic resources, measured as the proportion of a country's population living in the United States. Remittances from these expatriate groups have long been noted as an important element in a variety of civil conflicts – particularly the Liberation Tigers of Tamil Eelam in Sri Lanka (Venugopal 2003).

A third predictor of enhanced opportunity structures was the availability of finances from foreign governments. This may be regional states seeking to destabilise potential challengers (as in the Great Lakes region of Central Africa) or global Powers supporting ideological allies (the involvement of the United States in the Middle East and Central America for instance). Fourth, opportunities for mobilisation were found to increase considerably when the income individuals must forgo in order to participate is atypically low – of which periods of economic recessions or lulls in agricultural production are examples. To measure this, Collier and Hoeffler augmented rudimentary income per capita data with male secondary school enrolment and the growth rate of the previous 5 years in order to calculate prospective income opportunities.

A fifth indicator was the presence of unusually cheap, conflict-specific inputs such as the availability of weapons, military communication equipment, personnel, skills, armoured vehicles and so on. If the timespan since the last conflict was great, Collier and Hoeffler proposed that these would have become scarcer and thus more expensive to acquire. Sixth, an obstructive topography (mountains, large areas of dense flora, wetlands, desert and the like), as well as a widely dispersed pattern of population settlement, may impede policing, increase local autonomy, diminish the state's capacity to govern and therefore improve the opportunities to rebel (Herbst 2000b). Finally, Collier and Hoeffler pointed to social cohesion within mobilising groups as a key opportunity booster. Here, there was some evidence to suggest that an ethnically or religiously diverse recruitment base may create problems for elites attempting to impose a coherent chain of command (Collier 2001b). To calculate the possible impact of this, fractionalisation indices were used to determine the probability that two individuals selected at random from any given location would share the same religious and ethnic background.

In order to evaluate the predictive quality of these seven criteria, Collier and Hoeffler compared them with four factors indicative of what they called 'objective grievances' (those that can be quantified independently of an individual's subjective experience). The first was social polarisation – the idea, drawn from the socio-biological premises of Chapter 5, that ethnically diverse societies that become divided along political grounds are more prone to the expression of grievances (Bardhan 1997: 1390–2). This was measured by combining the fractionalisation indices used above with calculations of income to develop a scalar assessment of intragroup homogeneity, intergroup heterogeneity and the distribution of significantly sized groups within a given state (Esteban and Ray 1994). Second, Collier and Hoeffler used a ten-point scale of political rights (drawn from the work of Jaggers and Gurr 1995) to measure repression as a grievance-inducing pressure and, after the findings of Håvard Hegre *et al.* (2001), predicted a curvilinear relationship with the occurrence of conflict. Their third measure of objective grievance was 'ethnic dominance'. Here, conflicts are predicted to be more common when one ethnic group has a narrow numerical advantage over other groups, which it uses to govern the political sphere. Fourth, using the data of Klaus Deininger and Lyn Squire (1998), Collier and Hoeffler recorded the Gini coefficients of income quintiles and land ownership to examine the possibility that the 'poor may rebel to induce redistribution, and rich regions may mount secessionist rebellions to preempt redistribution' – a notion connected, at the state or systemic levels of analysis, to the 'preventative' wars considered in Chapter 10 (2001: 7).

Having applied these factors to data on civil wars from 1960 to 1999, they conclude that the availability of finance, especially that drawn from natural resources, is particularly likely to be correlated with the outbreak of civil war within any given 5-year period. In fact, they calculate that, for countries in which 32 per cent of GDP is obtained from natural resource-derived exportation, the risk of civil war is about 22 per cent, while for a country with 0 per cent of such exports it is 1 per cent. Overseas remittances, low male secondary school enrolment and stagnant growth rates – leading to low forgone income – are also found to be statistically associated with the onset of rebellious mobilisation. Dispersed settlement patterns also appear to contribute to the likelihood of civil war – a factor long associated with the conflict in the Democratic Republic of the Congo, where much of the population lives near the border – while mountainous terrain was a more weakly associated variable (Herbst 2000b). Of the deprivation variables, only ethnic dominance was found to be significant and this was offset by the placatory effects of social fractionalisation. Consequently, Collier and Hoeffler are led to comment that 'a model that focuses on opportunities for rebellion performs well, whereas objective indicators of grievance add little explanatory power' (2001: 16).

Collier's core conclusion, that rebellion is 'a quasi-criminal activity . . . in which the rebel objective is to loot natural resource rents on a continuing basis' (2000c: 839–41), has, however, been widely challenged by those concerned at what is perceived to be an expansion in the domain of classical liberal economics since the end of the Cold War (Fine 2001). It has been claimed that such studies tend to produce 'probabilistic statements of conflict risk rather than factual descriptions of actual conflict dynamics' (Ballentine and Sherman 2003: 5). Aggregated economic data may be able to 'indicate whether mobilisation levels tend to increase in prosperous times, but *not* whether that occurs because individual members *of those groups* have more resources upon which collective claims can be made' (Snyder 1978: 516–21). Analysts are thus unable to specify precisely under what conditions rebellious groups may form, so 'inevitably end up presenting a static, culturally blind and profoundly ahistorical picture of civil wars' (Berdal 2005: 690).

To overcome such constraints, it is, for many writers, necessary to give an account of 'the relations of force rather than just choices of violence' – where, in other words, 'the "players" come from, other than as the product of relevant economistic calculations' (Cramer 2002: 1858, 1847). It is, for instance, vital to disaggregate the parties to a conflict in order to understand both the political context in which they operate and the sociological conditions of collective action. In particular, it is important to acknowledge that only a proportion of civil violence results from insurgency and much is a consequence of the policies and actions of the governing administration. As Kalevi Holsti points out, these elites may, like insurgents, also 'use their positions and access to resources to plunder the national economy through graft, corruption and extortion' (2000: 251). States, for instance, might utilise resource rents to finance repression, thereby weakening rebel resolve – yet, contrary to the greed model, increasing the ratio of primary commodities to overall GDP (de Soysa 2002: 398–9).

Indeed, it is surely too simplistic to regard mineral extraction as intrinsically damaging to an economy. Australian development was, for instance, heavily reliant on zinc and lead exports and its mines were, in 1913, producing 22 per cent of the world's share of both. The United States' economy was also dependent on its natural resource endowment during its most productive period. Between 1890 and 1914, for instance, it became the largest mineral economy in the world. By 1913, it was producing 56 per cent of the world's copper, 43 per cent of the world's phosphate and 39 per cent of the world's coal (David and Wright 1997). Moreover, if natural resources are considered in terms of per capita value (rather than simply in terms of export reliance), mineral-rich countries are not among the least developed or most undemocratic. Of the top 12, eight are listed as 'free' by *Freedom House* and only Papua New Guinea and Jamaica are outside the top 60 on the UNDP's 2003 Human Development Index. Indeed, number one on this index was Norway, the world's second largest per capita exporter of oil after the Kingdom of Saudi Arabia (Wright and Czelusta 2004).

Decentralised non-belligerent groups may also use the proceeds of natural, as well as diasporic, resources to increase the income that individuals would have to forgo in order to mobilise (Menkhaus 2004). The tendency of remittance receipts and timber sales to 'aid rather than hinder conflict reduction' in Burma has, for instance, been well documented (Sherman 2003: 225). Indeed, for many apparently resource-based conflicts, it would appear that the avaricious motives of political elites have been overstated. Leaders do not generally withdraw from the extraordinarily dangerous business of insurrection once a personal fortune is garnered, but continue to pursue ostensibly political objectives. In fact, many of the better known and ultimately successful rebel mobilisations (such as the Mau-Mau uprising in Kenya, the struggle for Zimbabwean independence, Algerian resistance to French colonialism and Namibian opposition to the Republic of South Africa) have occurred despite the prospect of confronting overwhelmingly more powerful opponents (Herbst 2000a: 276–7). To downplay the ideological and political components here may not only lead to impoverished explanatory and analytical frameworks, but also contains the danger of arbitrarily dismissing the possibility of legitimate protest and resistance, thereby ultimately propounding a conservative endorsement of existent power relations. As Jeffrey Herbst enquires, is it really plausible that Nelson Mandela spent nearly three decades in prison just 'to steal from the gold and diamond mines, and that his criticisms of apartheid were not related to his own personal and political struggle' (2000a: 282)?

In overlooking the actual complexity of conflict causality and perpetuation in the developing world, the international order can, it is claimed, justify simplistic interventions that do not engage with the more abstruse difficulties of ethnicity, the role of Western consumers in determining productive relationships, political ideologies, coercion (as a constraint on individuals' choice between action and withdrawal) and colonial legacies (Guáqueta 2003). Peace, in other words, is, as we discussed in Chapter 1, believed to be achievable 'through technical measures that in the short- to medium-term will reduce both the accessibility and profitability of lucrative economic resources to combat groups' (Ballentine and Nitzschke 2003: 14).

The potential hazards of such a view were summarised in a speech given by Ibrahim Kamara, the Sierra Leonean ambassador to the United Nations:

> We have always maintained that the conflict in Sierra Leone is not about ideology, tribal or regional differences. It has nothing to do with the so-called problem of marginalized youths or, as some political commentators have characterized it, an uprising by rural poor against the urban elite. The root cause of the conflict is diamonds, diamonds and diamonds.
>
> (*New York Times* 6 July 2000)

It may be that such distinctions between greed and grievance, as well as those concerning theories of resource mobilisation and relative deprivation, have been exaggerated. There is, for instance, a clear conceptual connection between expected utility and the ways in which existing power relations are perceived. In other words, it is rational for actors who believe themselves to be relatively deprived to consider their own societal position when calculating the potential costs and benefits of joining social groups and participating in insurgent mobilisation (Korpi 1974: 1572–4). Conflict entrepreneurs can therefore be regarded as those best able to balance these considerations, as part of what psychologists call value–expectancy theory (Jackson and Johnson 1974; Atkinson 1982). Here, 'behaviour is a function of the strength of one's intentions and the possibility of carrying out those intentions, while intentions are a function of the attraction of the perceived consequences of the behaviour in question' (Klandermans 1989: 119). This has been described by Maurice Pinard and Richard Hamilton as internal motive (push factors such as aspirations, deprivation and so on) and external motive (pull factors such as expected utility, selective benefits and so on) which, when combined, are associated with collective participation rates of 92 per cent (1986). The presence of natural resources and low forgone income may therefore be as likely to engender grievances as greed.

Conclusion

This chapter has traced the emergence of a fundamental challenge to the grievance model of explaining the causes of conflict. Rather than viewing collective violence and social movements as emotional, cathartic and affective, they are seen as rational, considered and self-regarding. Proceeding from a Hobbesian premise of the avaricious nature of humankind, conflicts may be seen as loosely organised predation with the availability of lootable resources a key consideration in individuals' cost–benefit analysis of the prospects of participation. Owing much to visions of human behaviour drawn from the study of economics, these accounts stress the importance of resources – both as a requisite element in the instigation, and as an objective, of mobilisation. The key determining factor in the causes of conflict behaviour, then, is not the provision of public goods, the meeting of human needs or the management of expectation, but the quality of the regime in which mobilisation occurs. A highly repressive political system will, it is thought, act as a deterrent by imposing high costs upon, and offering little likelihood of success to, prospective protagonists. Similarly, a very open polity may offer dissenters alternative and lower risk/cost strategies through which to pursue change. It is, therefore, regimes that are sufficiently exclusionary to provoke reaction, yet insufficiently oppressive to deter action, that are predicted to suffer the highest levels of irredentism.

Much, of course, also depends on the way in which mobilising groups are internally organised. Elites may seek political objectives and positions of power, whereas foot soldiers are seen as more likely to be concerned with short-term material gain and remuneration. Here, then, greed and grievance may not be fully separable. As we saw in Chapter 7, the capacity of leaders to establish a categorical identity and to associate the existing order with discontent as a normative defence of collective action might be as much a means of mustering an individual's sense of relative deprivation as persuading her or him of the utility of collective action. It could be, then, more prudent to follow Jonathan Goodhand's advice to 'account for greed, but don't ignore grievance' and thereby to adopt a more nuanced account of the causes of conflict and violence (2001: 39). As Will Moore and Keith Jaggers conclude,

> before participation in armed rebellion is a viable alternative for a given individual, he or she must (1) have some grievance he or she wishes to rectify, (2) feel a sense of corporate identity with other members of a rebel group, (3) identify and hold the state responsible for rectifying his or her grievances, (4) believe that taking up arms is both an acceptable and effective method for addressing those grievances, and (5) join with others in a group which is able to channel collective resources into an armed revolutionary movement.
>
> (1990: 27–8)

It is not, however, simply the apparently arbitrary distinction between greed and grievance that has attracted criticism. The general characterisation of social mobilisation as fundamentally grounded upon materialism, avarice and pragmatism has also been extensively challenged. It would seem, for instance, that many of the ways in which individuals are encouraged to overlook the obvious advantages of non-participation (beyond a simple, and often not very credible, promise of financial remuneration) impinge directly on the rational calculations that the model frequently assumes. The presence of zealots manipulating information and coercing group members may be a plausible way to reduce free-riding and a commonplace feature of irredentist movements and other social collectivities, but their origins, ideas and influence are not easy to explain through the narrow parameters of instrumental rationality and economic gain. Consequently, a number of writers have argued that, in order to understand the way in which decisions are reached (especially during periods of comparative duress), a more sophisticated account of expected utility and collective pressure is needed. This will make a key component of the following chapter.

9 Crises

In the previous two chapters, we have looked at the somewhat oppositional, although perhaps not entirely incommensurate, debate between analyses of collective action which, on the one hand, tend to emphasise affectivity, motive, grievances and the desire for peace and those that stress rationality, power, issues of collective mobilisation and acquisitiveness on the other. In many ways, a similar debate is apparent at the level of the state. As Chapter 1 put forward, a divide exists between liberal and realist understandings of the international arena – particularly in the areas of security and decision-making (the two main topics of this chapter). In terms of conflict and violence, this debate is arguably most significant when considering the ways in which states respond to a crisis, defined as a 'change in type and/or an increase in intensity of . . . hostile verbal or physical interactions between two or more states, with a heightened probability of military hostilities' (Brecher *et al.* 2000: 39, emphases removed from original). The elements that make up these disruptive interactions are complex, varied and much debated. Little consensus exists over precisely what causes crises to escalate into war. Nonetheless, it is clear that two topics have received the greatest attention over the modern era of international studies: the acquisition of armaments and the signing of alliances. As such, these will make up the focus of the first section of this chapter. In order to discover how this 'funnel of causation' actually moves from negative reciprocity to outright warfare (Wayman 2000: 225), however, it is necessary to understand processes of individual agency and collective decision-making processes – the focus of the second section of this chapter.

Arms, alliances and escalation

Crises are normally triggered by a combination of four forms of interaction experienced by the actors themselves or their allies: verbal acts (threats, accusations, demands and so on), economic sanctions (the withholding of trade or aid), political measures (such as the covert support of sedition) and military coercion (border clashes, training manoeuvres, assassination and the like). The capacity of these to threaten basic values, to impose severe time constraints and to portend the imminent use of (further) force means that the responses of state leaders are difficult to predict with any degree of certainty (Snyder and Diesing 1977). While it is clear that such a complex environment is subject to a wide range of features, six inter-related considerations appear to influence whether or not a crisis escalates into a war.

The first is the capability of the actors involved – a feature not simply reducible to military prowess. Political elites from countries with highly productive economies, large currency reserves, balance of payments surpluses and the like may (especially if supported by allies and endowed with internal stability, low food prices and a broad revenue base) be more inclined to react robustly to perceived threats than those in weaker states (Rummel 1968). Leaders of large states may also believe themselves to have well-developed capacities to deal with crises, yet find themselves involved in more disputes than their counterparts in smaller states. This may be because of a state's relative imperviousness to successful land invasion (such as Russia and China), combined with the high numbers of borders that it shares with other states (East 1973). Indeed, numerous studies have suggested that proximity may enlarge threat perceptions (Starr and Most 1978: 444), reduce the costs and increase the probability of success of warfare (Boulding 1962). Of around 2,000 interstate disputes between 1816 and 1992, for example, more than half were between adversaries with contiguous borders and, of 79 wars over the same period, 53 occurred between states that share at least one boundary (Hensel 2000: 64), indicating 'a significant and strong relationship between the presence of a territorial dispute between states and the likelihood of militarized conflict and war' (Huth 2000: 85).

A second pertinent factor in crisis escalation is the age of the state or states in question. Recently decolonised countries such as Namibia and Guinea-Bissau may respond differently from those decolonised in the first (Palestine, Iraq, India) and second (most of Africa) waves of imperial withdrawal and these might behave in ways unlike states that gained their independence and joined the international order earlier (East and Herman 1974). Also important here is the duration of the regime within which the decision-maker operates. Recent constitutional changes, coups, popular revolutions and territorial secessions may all, in materially altering both the stability and the character of the administration, have an impact on a political elite's response to a crisis. A competitively elected government in a long-established liberal democracy, for instance, reaches collective choices in very different ways from autocracies that have recently assumed power (Levy 1988).

Third, much depends on the type of threat posed. The construal that an actor is facing high levels of damage or even complete destruction over a wide range of interests (political, military, cultural and economic) is likely to produce decisional outcomes dissimilar to those based on less severe threat perceptions (Sample 2000: 179–81). In assessing these, states are, like the individuals considered in the previous chapter, bounded by environmental 'characteristics which provide a context as well as a set of opportunities and constraints' (Brecher and Wilkenfeld 1982: 410). Most obviously, the distribution of power within the international system will have a major bearing on the way in which response strategies are developed. The Cold War, for instance, was marked by a stable concentration of force in two countries, which were, along with a small number of other major Powers, able to veto a great variety of decisions made by nearly all lesser states (Baldwin 1979).

Fourth, the severity, duration and outcome of previous disputes all constitute significant elements in leaders' assessment of their operating environment and play an important part in the dynamics of future interactions (Geller 2000). An actor's prior defeats, victories, compromises and stalemates, or those experienced by allies, are an especially significant influence on decision-making processes during crises. These and resultant agreements (tacit or formal, official or covert, imposed or consensual) can have a marked effect on tension levels and expected outcomes. Actors may, for instance, demonstrate greatly different levels of satisfaction with the new order (as in the case of the United Kingdom and Egypt following the 1951 Suez settlement) or, conversely, they be mutually pleased with post-crisis revisions (such as Italy and Yugoslavia after the 1953 Trieste dispute) (Vasquez 1993: 283). Decisive here is the manner in which actors behaved during the preceding crisis. This may range from the early and extensive use of violence to immediate compliance or submission to arbitration.

Indeed, the intervention of a third party is a fifth important consideration. Those seeking to defuse a crisis may engage in preventative diplomacy (political activity aimed at reducing the likelihood of escalation), peace-making (political, diplomatic and sometimes military interventions directed at bringing parties to agreement), peace-keeping (the provision of intercessional military forces to monitor compliance with agreements and foster mutual confidence) or peace-building (the promotion of institutional and socio-economic measures to address the underlying causes of the crisis) (Sanderson 2002). Of course, other states or multilateral organisations may intervene in support of one or more of the protagonists, leading decision-makers to expect a swifter abatement of tensions or a more protracted dispute, depending on the perceived balance of forces and the envisaged nature of the intervention.

Sixth, the configuration of the international power hierarchy (in terms of alliance structure, relative power, membership and stability – or what Zeev Maoz calls 'the focal state's politically relevant international environment' (2000: 114)) appears to be a particularly important consideration in leaders' thinking during crises. This is because, when changes in the international system 'are perceived as posing a long-term threat', decision-makers commonly respond 'by attempting to increase their military power through alliances and/or a military build-up' (Vasquez 1987a: 117). The former, defined as 'a formal agreement between or among states stipulating a manner of consultation or joint action in a number of prespecified contingencies', may take a wide variety of forms (Maoz 1990: 193). Defence pacts consist of documents or arrangements that oblige states to intercede on behalf of an ally attacked by another party. Non-aggression treaties are mutual commitments intended to prevent allies from attacking one another, while ententes and friendship agreements promote reciprocity, cooperation and consultation (Walt 1987). As such understandings inevitably involve a loss of autonomy, there is a trade-off between states' capacity to take decisions independently and their ability to respond effectively to perceived threats.

This tension can be analysed at three levels. First, studies of state behaviour show that, just as individuals are said to make calculations of expected utility before participating in social groups, countries that perceive themselves to possess a comparative military advantage are predicted to feel less insecure and therefore to seek fewer alliances. Similarly, if potential signatories are few and already aligned or if the overall milieu is conflictive and thus a treacherous setting in which to give assurances, leaders may also decide not to pursue overseas agreements. However, when viewed from a second level of analysis, the dyad (or 'relational factors for pairs of states that engage in conflict'), these features can make the formation of alliances more probable (Geller and Singer 1998: 22). An unaligned state with strong military capabilities within a volatile and mostly already allied international system may be regarded as a particularly good prospective candidate for an affiliation. Third, if international interaction is considered from the systemic level, then the pursuit of alliances can be construed as an attempt to establish a balance of power (such as Cold War bipolarity) or a multilateral normative regime (such as the United Nations). Both these structures can, in preventing predation upon potentially allied minor states and ensuring the perpetuation of major Powers' dominant positions, dissuade those with perceptible military advantages from initiating potentially costly and destabilising conflicts (Kegley 1991).

Military build-ups can also be analysed at each of these levels. The purchasing of arms, for instance, can occur unilaterally. States may embark on extensive armament programmes without having been stimulated by an identifiable external hazard. Most commonly here, political elites perceive themselves to be at risk from internal dissent (Altfeld 1983). In seeking to intensify levels of domestic repression, however, states may alter the international balance of power, thereby prompting others to arm themselves. Typically, this leads to dyadic military build-ups in which hostility and fear – frequently exaggerated by leaders in order to legitimise inward expropriation – are the main drivers of state behaviour (Singer 1958). At the level of the international system, existent alliance configurations and the distribution of capabilities may be structured so as to encourage states to initiate arms purchasing programmes or, conversely, to desist from engaging in military competition (Waltz 1967). While the struggle of multilateralism to mitigate the geopolitical arena's intrinsic anarchism, the varying intensity of Cold War polarity and the transfer of weapons of mass destruction between allies may have been among the postwar era's most salient factors, their influence was taken as both a reason for disengagement and an incentive to escalate tension. In the case of the latter, for instance, it is not clear whether 'the advent of nuclear weapons fundamentally alter[ed] the nature of interstate relations, as some argue, making war between major states rationally incredible' (Sample 2000: 166) or the mutual desire to avoid nuclear war led 'each side to perceive the other as having a greater tolerance for bullying' and brinkmanship (Leng 2000: 238).

At the heart of this question is the notion of deterrence; in other words, the idea that states respond to crises by building their military capabilities and signing alliances in order to prevent 'other nations from using military force by making it too risky for them to do so' (Morgenthau 1960: 30). Assuming that opponents will not pursue their objectives if the expected costs of achieving these are calculated to outweigh the expected benefits, such measures are, in the absence of a legitimate international arbitrator, seen as the only rational way to protect one's interests. Moreover, acquiring weapons and aligning oneself with powerful friends also has the added benefit of being already prepared for war if the opponent turns out to be irrational, misinformed or stronger than one's own assessment (Jervis 1978). Alliances, for instance, can reduce uncertainty by clarifying the position of previously unaligned states. In aggregating capabilities, they can prevent or restrain unilateral actions by powerful states and obstruct destabilising shifts in power, such as the collapse of previously influential states. Similarly, advanced and extensive arsenals may prevent opponents from obtaining strategic objectives and portend heavy punishments for those who challenge the existing order (Snyder 1961). Crises are therefore thought to be unlikely to escalate into wars so long as the combined force of allies favouring the status quo outweighs that of the revisionist state or states (Wallace 1982: 39–40). Such a preponderance of strength ensures, as Table 9.1 illustrates, that the great majority of disputes are resolved 'far short of war or the threat of war' (Huth and Russett 1988: 29). As the ancient aphorism goes, if you want peace, then prepare for war.

However, it may be that, through this reasoning, 'states are driven to acquire more and more power in order to escape the impact of the power of others. This, in turn, renders the others more insecure and compels them to prepare for the worst' (John Herz cited in Skillen 1982: 86). In a spiral

Table 9.1 The frequency of violence in international crises, 1918–94

No violence	105	25%
Minor clashes	114	28%
Serious clashes	102	25%
Full-scale war	91	22%
Total	412	100%

Source: Wilkenfeld and Brecher (2000: 283).

of negative reciprocity, a dilemma emerges in which the rational pursuit of security leads to an irrational outcome – greater insecurity, both perceived and real. This could be simply a consequence of growing international tension, or it may result from the emergence of hard-line leaders prospering from the new, militarised environment. Such an atmosphere often leads to collective paranoia and the view that warfare is an inevitable result of existing crisis dynamics. 'States that prepare for war' are, in other words, likely to get not peace, but 'exactly that for which they prepare' (Bremer 1992: 318). Rather than deterring aggression, alliances may, for instance, 'destabilize international peace because they increase the level of international confrontation, spread hostility, and reinforce systemic polarization' (Attinà 2004: 3). Similarly, during periods of military build-up, a growing sense of general concern can prompt minor disputes to intensify rapidly. The risk of this happening as a result of misperception, inadequate and inaccurate information or ideological proclivity is said to be particularly high. The aggressive acquisition of armaments thus makes it more likely that, during a dispute, at least one party will not assess another party's comparative resolve and military capability correctly and that the boundary between coercive bargaining and mobilisation will become blurred, making escalation into war more likely (Blainey 1973: 122).

This may occur 'vertically' in terms of the rate, magnitude and intensity of the escalation process. Rate refers to 'the rapidity with which coercive behavior increases over the course of the crisis . . . [and] provides the best predictor of events running out of control' (Leng 2000: 240). Magnitude offers a way of assessing how close hostility levels are to outright war, while intensity represents the magnitude of a crisis over time. Escalation may also occur 'horizontally' in the sense that it increases the scope for others to participate in a dispute, thereby expanding its geographical and social sphere (Schelling 1960: 5). Both forms of escalation, which may be compared with Mitchell's methods of adding dynamic elements to his triangular model of behaviour, attitude and situation examined in Chapter 2, are thought to occur under at least four conditions (Vasquez 2000b: 378). First, the intensification of a crisis becomes more probable if vital issues are threatened, particularly 'if a group is reduced to a point where it starts to fear for its future existence' (Gochman and Leng 1983; Kriesberg 1998: 159).

A second factor is a history of previous crises between the protagonists – especially if the leadership remains unchanged (Leng 1983). As Willem Jaspers observes, 'new (less motivated) actors might be inclined to respond to positive or negative inducements aimed at de-escalation because their attitudes are not yet hardened by the conflict' (2005: 21). Third, and related to this, is the presence of inflexible and hard-line elites within the leadership of at least one side (Vasquez 1987b). Fourth, escalation becomes much more likely if a hostile spiral of negative reciprocity occurs – a feature of various levels of analysis, as Table 2.2 illustrates. Such conflictive processes can move from mutual name-calling, to diplomatic withdrawal, to embassy closures, to economic sanctions, to military mobilisation and so on and, although violence is not an inevitable conclusion, it is commonly suggested that, once under way, 'the process of escalation requires more effort to be stopped or reversed, than it does to be started' (Holsti *et al.* 1968; Smoke 1977: 19).

The relationship between escalated crises (in the form of alliance polarisation and arms races) and warfare is subject to great controversy. Empirical evidence is, at best, inconclusive. As Randolph Siverson and Paul Diehl remark of military build-ups, 'if there is any consensus among arms race studies, it is that some arms races lead to war and some do not' (1989: 214). Similarly, 'while previous studies share the theme that there is a relationship between alliances and wars, these same studies reveal little agreement over the form of the relationship' (Ostrom and Hoole 1978: 215). Consequently, 'no clear support has emerged for the argument that alliances improve the prospects for peace through effective deterrence nor that they kindle the flames of war' (Leeds 2003: 427). On the one hand, Jack Levy has found that 81 per cent of alliances during the twentieth century were followed by war involving at least one of the signatories within 5 years (1981: 597–8). Similarly, Randolph Siverson and Joel King have demonstrated that, of 188 participants in wars between 1815 and 1965, 112 (of which 76 had signed prewar commitments) fought as part of a coalition and only 76 (of which 52 had no prewar alliances) did not, suggesting that crisis escalation will tend to be horizontally less extensive in systems with fewer alliances (1979: 45). On the other hand, using data similar to those employed by Siverson and King, Michael Wallace finds that a curvilinear relationship exists between the severity of polarisation and nation-months of war. He concludes that bipolar systems and systems with no alliance blocs are most prone to high-magnitude wars, with moderately polarised systems enjoying the lowest incidence of severe war (1973).

Bruce Bueno de Mesquita takes a rather different line by arguing that it is changes in the 'tightness', or internal coherence, of existing alliance blocs that are the most significant indicator of war proneness. Building on the reasoning of Morton Kaplan (1957), he tests the proposition that

> when all the members of a bloc are substantially committed to each other, it is difficult for any one member to venture on an independent foreign policy course that involves commitments to nations outside the bloc. . . . Hence, the more tightknit the system's blocs are, the less likely that hostile sentiments between blocs will be mitigated by friendly interaction between individual members of different blocs. Consequently, . . . the higher the probability of war.
>
> (1978: 248)

Rejecting the countervailing hypothesis that such tightness may decrease systemic uncertainty and therefore make it less likely that war can emerge from crisis escalation, Bueno de Mesquita concludes that 84 per cent of wars in the twentieth century began following periods of rising intrabloc coherence. In direct contradiction of such findings, however, are studies that emphasise the very low reliability rates of alliances (Sabrosky 1980). In fact, the incidence of honouring state commitments during times of war may be as low as 25 per cent (Leeds *et al.* 2000: 686). Whatever the truth, the relationships that these present are, of course, correlative rather than causal and so other factors cannot be excluded as possible determinative influences. It may be, then, that, as other accounts have proposed, 'alliances neither limit nor expand conflicts any more than prevent them' (Liska 1962: 138).

Similar problems afflict the study of warfare's relationship with arms races. Michael Wallace finds that, of 28 crises involving arms races between 1816 and 1965, 23 escalated to war, whereas, of the 71 crises that occurred unaccompanied by arms races over the same period, only three resulted in war (1979). He goes on to argue that arms races are significant predictors of wars regardless of which of the parties acquires the greater or more effective weapons (whether or not, in other words, a major Power or revisionist states emerge as superiorly equipped), thereby rejecting the peace-through-strength maxim of deterrence theory (1982). Almost immediately, however, these figures were challenged. Paul Diehl, one of the researchers who compiled the dataset that Wallace used, 'discovered that only one-fourth of the disputes preceded by military build-ups resulted in war, while ten of the thirteen wars [under analysis] occurred in the absence of joint arms increases by the dispute participants' (1983: 210).

Much relies on how the variables are assessed and coded. In order to avoid the problem of having to aggregate military capabilities, it is, for instance, common to find large and complex wars analysed as a series of dyadic disputes. The First World War may thus be considered to be either seven or eight integrated, or 26 separate, wars depending on how the writer deals with alliance structures (Weede 1980). The time lag between variables is also highly significant. By changing Diehl's approach from a three-year to a five-year gap between increasing arms expenditure and war (and by controlling for the presence of nuclear weapons as a variable with exceptionally deterring properties), Susan Sample found that 47 per cent of the disputes that had been thought not to escalate to war did in fact do so (1997). As Henk Houweling and Jan Siccama note, however, these types of study do not distinguish between arms races as reflections of broader tensions, as catalytic agents of strain in the international system and as primary causes of warfare (1981). Without an account of the mechanism of change, it is very difficult to eliminate the possibility that states perceive war to be imminent and prepare accordingly, thereby rendering arms races merely an effect of other causal factors (Diehl and Kingston 1987). Similarly, mutual military build-ups are commonly assumed to be arms races even if it cannot be demonstrated that such expenditure was directed at an opposing party or parties. As Paul Diehl and Mark Crescenzi point out, both phenomena could be 'manifestations of the enduring rivalries [between states] and thus not directly related to each other' (1998: 113).

To understand governmental strategy in this regard, it is necessary to have a clear comprehension of the intrastate dynamics that underpin arms races. Yet much of the literature overlooks such factors; as, for example, in Richardson's highly influential technical model (1960a; McGinnis 1991). Policy is, after all, 'subject to multiple decision-making processes, each one revolving around a group of relevant individuals, and then must undergo some means of aggregation to arrive at a collective outcome' (Bolks and Stoll 2000: 582–3). Accumulating human inputs in this way may be subject to a variety of factors that normally govern the treatment of crisis responses. These influences, which Robert Jervis defines as 'pressures that the actor would not admit as legitimate if he were conscious of them', will be looked at in more detail in the next section (1969: 240).

Decision-making and the Cuban missile crisis

Foreign policy in general and decision-making during crises in particular have frequently been presented as 'an intelligent rational continuum' in which leaders identify and disseminate obtainable goals, the attainment of which is only constrained by the resistance envisaged (Morrow 1985). The accuracy of this representation, however, has long been open to question, as we saw in the case of social mobilisation in Chapter 8. After all, even if individuals can be shown to be acting in rational, value-maximising ways, there can be no assurance that dyadically rational outcomes will emerge. Indeed, Table 9.2 shows that, in order to achieve collective optimality, the individual may have to act irrationally. Moreover, as there is no independent means of measuring

Table 9.2 The prisoners' dilemma

	Prisoner B	
Prisoner A	Denies charges	Confesses to charges
Denies charges	Both get 6 months	A gets 10 years, B goes free
Confesses to charges	B gets 10 years, A goes free	Both get 2 years

1 Each prisoner is interviewed separately and given the various outcomes outlined above.
2 If your partner confesses, you are better off confessing (2 rather than 10 years' imprisonment).
3 If your partner does not confess, you are much better off confessing (freedom rather than 10 years).
4 Therefore, you should confess.
5 If both prisoners act rationally, both will confess and get 2 years' imprisonment.
6 If both prisoners act irrationally and deny the charges, both will get 6 months.
7 This is the optimum outcome as the total time spent in prison for both parties is 1 year – the lowest combined sentence.

the value of the various options under consideration outside the mind of the decision-maker, to claim that a choice was made because it was preferred is a tautology that tells us little about how the decision was reached and even less about how it might be (mis)applied (Green and Shapiro 1994: 6).

As Gregory Herek and colleagues point out, 'an objectively rational approach to decision-making is never fully possible because such an approach requires complete knowledge and anticipation of the consequences that will follow from every conceivable choice' (1987: 203–4). Instead of seeking to maximise their values within a set of given constraints, decision-makers may respond to the immense complexity of rapidly changing and apparently incoherent environments by deploying a series of compromises in order to reduce individual duress and to impose a manageable degree of simplicity and order on the crisis (Janis and Mann 1977). In contrast to realist assumptions of rational dispassion, this is seen as likely to be informed by such factors as personality, ideology, emotion and prejudice either as a direct pressure on information-gathering and -processing procedures or as a form of ego defence aimed at dealing with the conflicting values brought on by the crisis (Holsti and George 1975). Irving Janis identifies seven scenarios in this regard (1989). First, potentially viable policy alternatives may be overlooked, deliberately ignored or unjustifiably dismissed. Second, the objectives of action are not retained while various decisional options are considered, leading to a disjuncture between preferred method and preferred outcome. Third, decision-makers fail to comprehend the range of possible consequences of their judgements. They may become over-sanguine by neglecting to predict costs or excessively conservative by not envisaging benefits.

Fourth, the information-gathering process may be perfunctory and deficient, resulting in an inadequate consideration of the various courses of action available. Fifth, the processing of data may be subject to selective biases. Chaim Kaufmann identifies two ways in which this might occur during crises (1994: 562–3). Information tends to be rejected if it does not conform to options already preferred, especially if an individual decision-maker has already invested significant amounts of time, resources and status in support of a particular direction. Information may also be accredited unwarranted evidentiary value on the basis of its immediate salience. First-hand experiences, vivid testimony, emotionally arousing material and sensorially exciting media may all produce an effect on decision-makers disproportionate to their actual evidential worth (Anderson 1983). Sixth, decision-makers during crises are inclined not to reconsider previously rejected alternatives in the light of new information. Instead, potentially contradictory data are rejected gratuitously on the grounds that earlier policies 'would have produced good results if accidents had not happened or enemies had not acted malevolently' (Starbuck 1985: 346). A re-evaluation is likely to occur only when it becomes less laborious than tolerating the dissonance generated by the awareness of obvious inconsistencies (Jervis 1976: 181–7). Finally, decision-making processes may fail to consider the various contingencies that emerge when instructions are implemented and monitored.

Large organisations are regarded as particularly prone to these types of influence. For John Steinbruner, collective decisions reached and executed within highly differentiated bureaucracies are not simply based on the reasons that support a particular course of action, but also on the individual and structural routines, priorities and inefficiencies of the actors involved. These are exacerbated by the inherent vagueness of implementation in three ways – what he calls the 'cognitive dimensions of political and organisational phenomena' (1974: 124). First, 'grooved thinking' is, he argues, a common feature of long-established organisations in which bureaucrats deal with a narrow range of recurring problems and increasingly produce automatic and stereotypical responses. Abstruse decision-making issues are therefore fragmented, and no single individual acts with an awareness of the wider picture. 'Uncommitted thinking', on the other hand, occurs at the very top of the organisational hierarchy and results from the difficulties in dealing with this wider picture. In extremely complex environments, leaders, faced with highly unrealistic workloads, may constantly vacillate between alternatives. Finally, a decision-maker is also subject to 'theoretical thinking', through which he 'buffer[s] himself from the impact of uncertainty' by organising his beliefs around a single value and imposing a comprehensive pattern of meaning on immediate events (Steinbruner 1974: 132). Organisational management will, it is suggested, tend to incorporate and normalise this value throughout its structure.

As an organisation's entire output cannot possibly be fully understood by a single individual, his or her responsibilities must be broken up into manageable divisions and then co-ordinated under standard operating procedures. These are generally not based upon the kinds of value-maximising objectives envisaged by rational choice models, but rather by the maintenance of acceptable-level goals through a process of, what Herb Simon calls, 'satisficing' (1958; Cyert and March 1992: 120). Moreover, because a secondary function of the imposition of standard operating procedures is to 'provide a means for indoctrinating new members into the habitual patterns of organisational behavior', it would seem probable that policy outcomes are likely to resemble previous policy outcomes (Simon 1960: 10). As the implications of every possible decision cannot be fully understood, policy tends to copy what is perceived to have been successful – or at least not disastrous – in the past. So, instead of a pattern of outcome change that shows sharp new directions, which might be expected on the basis of rational choice assumptions, organisational inertia ensures that adjustments are liable to be marginal (Lustick 1980). This is what David Braybrooke and Charles Lindblom call 'disjointed incrementalism'. Basing their work on Karl Popper's concept of 'piecemeal social engineering', they suggest that policy tends to avoid provoking 'social cleavages along ideological lines . . . [by developing a] continuing series of remedial moves on which some agreement can be developed'. They continue by citing America's decision to move from a peacetime to a wartime economy (announced in 1940 as an 'unlimited national emergency') as actually a series of small-scale measures 'through which industry was led into war production step by step, somewhat against its desires, if not against its will' (1963: 82; 1973: 213–14).

Arguably, the most important (or, to Colin Gray, 'near-sacred') analysis of decision-making during militarised international disputes is Graham Allison's 1969 study of the Cuban missile crisis – incontrovertibly the most threatening confrontation of modern times (Gray 1976: 28). In this, and in a subsequent and extended work published in 1971 and then revised with Philip Zelikow and reissued in 1999, Allison 'made analysts of policy more self-conscious about . . . the behavior of organizations, and the tugs and rivalries within bureaucracies' (Holsti 1972: 137; Bernstein 2000: 134–5). Building on the earlier work of Richard Snyder (1958), Richard Neustadt (1960), Samuel Huntington (1961) and Roger Hilsman (1967), he established two models – 'organisational process' and 'bureaucratic politics' – which, he suggested, offer a more plausible explanation of how decisions emerge during crises than accounts of rational 'actions structured in accordance with human goals and purposes' (Cornford 1974: 233; Steiner 1977: 394). He then applies these to the deliberations of the National Security Council's Executive Committee (ExCom). Convened on 16 October 1962 in response to reports that the Soviet Union was constructing six medium-range (1,100 mile reach) and three intermediate-range (2,200 mile reach) ballistic missile sites in Cuba in readiness for the arrival of around 40 nuclear weapons, the Committee was asked 'to make a prompt and intense survey of the dangers and all possible courses of action' (Horelick 1964: 366; Sorensen 1965: 675). Six possible (and non-exclusive) alternatives were put forward (probably alongside the existing objective of killing Castro): (1) do nothing, (2) exert diplomatic pressure, (3) make a secret approach to the Cuban leader Fidel Castro, (4) invade Cuba, (5) bomb Cuba and (6) blockade Cuba (Brune 1996: 43).

To understand how these options were evaluated, Allison first looked at the role of organisational customs and practices. Presuming that military planners are inclined to favour 'formulaic solutions that reduce problems to manageable terms, clarify responsibilities and calculations of capabilities vis-à-vis objectives, and maximise certainty and efficiency', he advanced four propositions: '(1) existing organizational routines limit the range of available options in a given situation; (2) organizational routines resist change; (3) existing organizational routines determine the course of implementation; and (4) organizational routines systematically induce instrumental irrationalities in state behavior' (Betts 1977: 157; Welch 1992: 120). These can, Allison suggests, lead to rigidity and an inability to revise pre-existing plans in the light of changing contemporary circumstances. As pre-crisis strategising tends to assume a conservative bias based on inferences drawn from worst-case scenarios, such inflexibility may serve to escalate disputes and thus act as an indirect cause of conflict. As Jack Levy notes, 'there is often a failure to recognise the independent role of other variables in contributing to the rigid implementation of an existing plan, which results in the exaggeration of the causal importance of the inherent rigidity of the plans themselves' (1986: 218).

Moreover, in restricting both the conceptual and the practical options available to political executives, as well as the opportunities for critical reflection, organisational path dependency may increase the efficacy of military mobilisation and the attractiveness of its commitment to value maximisation – a sequence of action that frequently commences automatically once high levels of alert are reached (George 1984: 227). The overall result is not only an over-reliance on the armed forces for the execution of decisions, but also irrational policy outcomes born of organisational habit. Standard operating procedures, or what Desmond Ball calls 'unavoidable technical reasons', meant, for instance, that the Soviet authorities did not (or were not able to) change the design of the missile silos on Cuba from those already constructed (and known to the United States – a fact of which the Politburo must have been fully aware) inside their own borders (1974: 77–8). As Allison observes, 'it was the established Soviet four-slash "signature" of excavations . . . that alerted American intelligence analysts to the Soviet deployment' in the first place (1971: 107).

The second of Allison's approaches – bureaucratic politics – has often been conflated with the organisational process model as a general constraint on rational decision-making during crisis (Wagner 1974: 488). Although, in one formulation, the latter is construed as simply an institutional limitation upon the operation of bureaucracies (Allison and Halperin 1972: 43), it proposes, in fact, quite different limitations to value maximisation (Allison 1987: 525). Analysing Allison's thesis in the light of precursory work, Robert Art identifies five propositions in this regard (1973: 468–9). First, in place of a centralised governing power, states actually consist of a series of authority centres, or fiefdoms, between which there is little interconnectivity. Second, from each of these 'quasi-sovereign powers' come individuals with different views on any given decisional issue (Schilling 1962: 22). Such opinions are drawn, at least in part, from a combination of the responsibilities over which these individuals feel accountable and their standing within the organisational sub-unit or the bureaucratic whole. Where you stand is, in other words, dependent on where you sit (Miles cited in Neustadt and May 1986: 157).

Third, policy subject to bureaucratic politics emerges from 'bargaining along regularized circuits among players positioned hierarchically within the government' (Allison 1971: 144). This is particularly likely to occur in instances in which individuals share beliefs about the causation of a crisis, but differ over which goals to pursue – especially when more collegial attempts to reconcile collective differences fail (Thompson and Tuden 1987). Fourth, as individuals lower down the bureaucratic ladder have the capacity to damage their superiors (first by achieving an informational advantage and, second, by obtaining external support from other bureaucratic sub-units as well as the media and the legislature), senior members of the executive (including the president) are obliged to consider a wide range of disparate views (Bendor and Hammond 1992: 315–16). Fifth, the outcome of such bargaining processes is that decisions do not so much reflect the rational pursuit of clearly identified objectives as the conditions under which they are taken. As Roger Hilsman puts it, the relative power of 'participating groups is as relevant to the final decisions as the cogency and wisdom of the arguments used in support of the policy adopted. Who advocates a particular policy may be as important as what he advocates' (1959: 365).

Allison then uses these two approaches – organisational processes and bureaucratic politics – to analyse ExCom's six choices (listed above). He concludes that the possibility of making a secret approach to Castro was dismissed on the grounds that he was unlikely to possess full control over the use of the missiles. An invasion of Cuba was also rejected as an initial step as it could always be included with any of the other alternatives at a later time. Early on in ExCom's deliberations, the other two non-military options were similarly discarded. Allison argues that this was largely driven by the configuration of bureaucratic interests that surrounded the president. These prompted a close association between Kennedy's position as chief executive and the types of outcomes that he favoured (regardless of their intrinsic merit), thereby narrowing the Committee's debate and, in part, determining its conclusions. Stephen Krasner summarises Allison's characterisation of the president's standpoint thus:

> failure to act decisively would undermine the confidence of members of his Administration, convince the permanent government that his Administration lacked leadership, hurt the Democrats in the forthcoming election, destroy his reputation among members of Congress, cause American allies and enemies to question American courage, invite a second Bay of Pigs [a failed invasion of 1,300 American-backed counter-revolutionaries in April 1961 personally authorised by Kennedy], and feed his [Kennedy's] own doubts about himself.
>
> (1972: 171)

ExCom's ultimate decision to opt for a naval blockade and not air strikes was, in Allison's view, also a function of intrabureaucratic wrangles. It was, he suggests, based on U-2 intelligence flights carried out after a number of delays caused by the Central Intelligence Agency and the United States Air Force being unable to reach agreement over whose responsibility the flights were. Had they been undertaken earlier, it is possible that ExCom might have favoured a less coercive option. Had the flights taken place later, then the missiles might have been in place, making a naval blockade valueless. Moreover, it is possible, Allison contends, that some of ExCom's early vacillations were a result of the Air Force having no contingency plan for such a scenario. As they did have an organisational process – a standard operating procedure in other words – for carpet-bombing Cuba in readiness for a land invasion, Air Command repeatedly referred to the need for some 500 sorties when only nine known missile sites existed, leading to considerable confusion among the members of ExCom. Indeed, a key reason for dismissing the air option was that the missiles were reported, again on the basis of standard classificatory procedures, to be mobile – a fact that turned out, shortly after the decision to impose a naval blockade had been reached, to be untrue. In accordance with Allison's predictions, the case for an air strike was not reopened. Furthermore, once the blockade was in place, ExCom had great difficulty in imposing its decisions upon the organisational echelons below it. For instance, Kennedy, hoping to give the Soviet leader Nikita Khrushchev more time to reach a decision, ordered the Navy to draw in its ships away from the approaching Soviet vessels to 500 miles off Cuban waters. However, as Krasner notes, 'the Navy being both anxious to guard its prerogatives and confronted with the difficulty of moving large numbers of ships' failed to implement the directive promptly (1972: 177–8; Smith 1980).

Conclusion

This chapter has outlined some of the key debates regarding conflict causality within international relations. It has focused on the dynamics of crises, the way they emerge and their effects on state behaviour. Here, the literature is highly fragmented with most writers preferring to undertake empirical tests of particular variables without seeking to amass a coherent body of theory. For this reason, presenting a varied account of conflict causality is a challenge. However, two aspects have been considered in more detail as possible causal elements in the onset of interstate war – alliance structures and military build-ups. Both have been analysed in terms of a range of domestic and international pressures under which political elites take on treaty obligations and initiate armament expenditure programmes.

This chapter then looked at the dynamics of crisis escalation as an explanation of how alliances and military spending may lead to polarisation and arms races. Here, competing visions of national interest are important. These include the notion of deterrence as a means of preventing war in an ostensibly hostile geopolitical environment. Leaders may thus respond to a perceived rise in national insecurity or international tension by pursuing various forms of agreement with other states or by acquiring new weaponry and/or updating their existing arsenal. Although these arrangements may be ostensibly aimed at deterring others – thereby making escalation less likely – they may threaten other states, which then respond with similar measures, leading to a spiral of negative reciprocity, bloc polarisation and arms races. This 'security dilemma' is rooted in the rational decision to forge treaty commitments and to acquire weaponry in order to feel more secure, yet results in the irrational outcome of accentuated threat perceptions and greater relational tensions.

The exact role of deterrence and the security dilemma in intensifying or defusing crises is open to considerable debate, as is the precise relationship between weapons, alliances and the causes of war. Such differing views have rendered a clear understanding of conflict causality difficult to obtain, particularly as the historical record appears to support various positions, depending on how the empirical data are treated. Much clearly relies on the bellicosity of state leaders – a factor which, in turn, depends on the way in which decisions are made by governing elites. Traditionally, analyses of this process tended to see the higher echelons of national administrations as unitary actors seeking to maximise a clearly understood set of values. However, as Graham Allison's well-known study of the Cuban missile crisis demonstrates, such a rationalist approach may not represent the actual dynamics of decision-making very accurately. As many have noted, the essential weakness here is that, without an explicit account of decisional mechanisms within states, associations between disputes and war will inevitably remain correlative rather then causal. Indeed, organisational inertia and the disparate character of bureaucratic politics may combine to restrict elites' capacity to pursue their goals, thereby producing disjointed increments rather than categorical and imminently applicable judgements.

For this reason, the second section of this chapter has focused on analyses of crises that are not limited to rationalist understandings of the state as value-maximising unitary entities. Decision-making processes that place political elites within broader organisational and bureaucratic structures were considered. The Cuban missile crisis was discussed as a pre-eminent example of how such an approach could cast new light on the connection between individual rationality, group dynamics, implemented outcomes and many of the issues looked at earlier in the chapter. It involved large states with considerable military and economic reserves, a history of conflictive relations (most recently in the abortive Bay of Pigs invasion and more generally in south-east Asia) and extensive borders potentially contiguous with members of the opposing bloc. Both Cuba and the United States perceived the crisis to involve a wide range of vital interests, concerning the homeland security of both themselves and their allies. Although there was not a significant horizontal escalation of the crisis, vertical escalation involved a high degree of magnitude and, with the deployment and testing of American ballistic missiles in Italy and Turkey continuing throughout the autumn of 1962, considerable intensity. Seeing these events in acute and precipitous terms is, however, not the only way to understand their broader implications. The contest between the Soviet Union and the United States against a backdrop of periodic confrontation and numerous proxy conflicts may be seen, instead, as part of a long-term crisis intrinsic to global leadership. Put another way, crises could, as Chapter 10 will explain, be regarded as key markers in an age-old struggle between an incumbent hegemon and its nearest rival, with each prepared to deploy sufficient armaments to provoke a global war aimed at preventing or facilitating a change of world leader.

10 Hegemony

In the previous chapter, we looked at various components of crises and their relationship with conflict and violence. For the most part, conflictive situations were assessed within timeframes not longer than a decade or so. An alternative way to regard the escalation of disputes, as well as arms races and alliance behaviour, is to focus on the level of the global system. Here, understandings of conflict and violence – especially very substantial bloodshed – have tended to be based around the contest for world leadership. As such, this chapter looks at the pursuit and maintenance of hegemony as a causal element in the initiation of conflicts in general and large-scale systemic wars in particular. It considers first the widely held view that configurations of hegemonic domination are subject to cyclical patterns of ascendancy and decline. In this regard, a number of economists writing in the nineteenth and early twentieth century have been influential in identifying the fluctuating pattern of capitalist development. By the 1960s, interest in how these variations relate to the occurrence of major wars between the foremost capitalist economies had coalesced into a large body of literature predominantly focused on cyclical shifts in power apparent from the late fifteenth century onwards. Second, this chapter examines the possible mechanisms through which such shifts may lead to conflict. Here, the effects of power parity and dissatisfaction are important – as both linear and cyclical patterns of international relations. Once the strength of a challenger, unhappy with the status quo, reaches a point of equivalence with either a global or a regional hegemon, war may result. Alternatively, the dominant Power could be expected to recognise the potential threat posed by its developing adversary and launch a war aimed at arresting that advance and preventing, or at least delaying, its own decline.

Long cycles and global war

There are many ways to understand the term 'hegemony'. It has been used to describe the means through which the global core extracts resources from the periphery (Wallerstein 1984), the ability of a single strong state to preserve international stability and order (Keohane 1984) and the role of knowledge and ideas in establishing and maintaining social structures of domination (Cox 1987). It may be considered a benign force that secures 'the emergence of open international economic systems' or a system of expropriation structured to benefit the powerful (McKeown 1983: 73). More generally, it is 'the ability of one country to shape the rules and arrangements for political and economic relations among nations' (Goldstein and Rapkin 1991: 936). For our purposes, a hegemonic power is 'a core state that commands an unrivaled position of economic and military superiority among the core states and is thus able largely to shape the operation of the international system' (Goldstein 1988: 5).

Since the emergence of the world system following a period of extended European expansion during the fifteenth century (Buzan 1993: 331), such states have prevailed in three ways (Wallerstein 1974b: 404–6). First, by mythologising, indoctrinating/educating and decentralising some actual authority, a hegemon may convince other Powers that the perpetuation of the world system under its suzerainty is in their collective and mutual interests. Second, as Joshua Goldstein notes, the hegemon ensures that the 'system is characterized economically by the unequal geographical division of labor between the core (secondary producers of manufactured goods) and the periphery (primary producers of raw materials)'. Third, it can concentrate sufficient military force to maintain its supremacy coercively. So, as Goldstein continues, the system becomes 'characterized by the systematic use of violence both to maintain and to change the power relationships in the system' (1988: 2).

Such a use of violence in pursuit or defence of hegemony is the focus of this chapter. While these efforts have tended to have been exerted at a global level (to establish global leadership rather than throughout the globe) and have therefore involved very large wars, they are, however, comparatively rare. Of 114 international conflicts involving Great Powers between 1495 and 1945, only five conglomerated wars are generally regarded to be of a sufficient scale to warrant such a definition (Levy 1983). These have lasted an average of 25 years each, have been estimated to have accounted for almost 80 per cent of all battle deaths of the period and, during the concluding stage of the most recent example (1939–45), may have absorbed as much as one-third of the world's entire economic product (Rasler and Thompson 1992).

In studying the relationship between global warfare and hegemony, it is common to 'consider some version of a "hegemonic cycle", a process of competition, challenge, hegemonic war, the emergence of hegemony, and its erosion in the face of other countries' long-term recovery and growth' (Goldstein and Rapkin 1991: 936). Indeed, it is probable that 'ever since Polybius, scholars have dreamed of discovering a regular cyclical pattern in the interactions of politics, both domestic and international' and especially at the level of global domination (Rosecrance 1987: 283). After all, highly

regularised forms of periodicity within the natural world have always imposed structured timeframes upon human endeavours as varied as farming,
oceanic navigation and energy generation. The intimate correlation between
these and economic production has long been noted and has clearly had an
impact on factors such as pricing, waged labour and supply. In the case of
modern capitalism, Christopher Chase-Dunn and Peter Grimes, building on
the work of Ernest Mandel (1975), describe this tendency thus:

> a new set of products is introduced that sells well, the market expands,
> and related employment swells, allowing for expansion of worker/
> 'consumer' spending. The market eventually becomes saturated, sales
> drop, income contracts, and workers are laid off. . . . But eventually, the
> excess inventory is sold out, production resumes, and renewed growth
> is possible.
>
> (1995: 404)

According to the French physician Clement Juglar, this process may occur approximately every 7–11 years at the point when most production
machinery is coming to end of its working life and firms are synchroni-
cally beginning to order replacements (1966). Examples of Juglar recessions
include the American economic downturns of the mid-1970s, early 1980s
and early 1990s. Simon Kuznets also traced cyclical patterns in a number
of diverse economies in Japan, Belgium and Argentina (1971). These are
between 20 and 25 years in length and have been explained in a number of
ways, including migration and generational fluctuations in housing demand.
Perhaps the most influential of the cycle economists, however, was Nikolai
Kondratieff. He noted oscillations in price indices over a period of 40 and
60 years between 1795 and 1925 that he believed may rest on the periodic
need to incorporate new technology through large-scale capital investment
(1984). This tends to take place, he maintains, initially in key industrial sectors ((1) cotton, textiles and iron (1780–1817), (2) railways, steam and steel
(1840–75), (3) electricity, industrial chemistry and the internal combustion
engine (1890–1920)) before becoming diffused throughout the economy
(Rostow 1975). Once this occurs, overall investment slowly moves away
from production and towards speculation, thereby inhibiting demand and
gradually depressing the economy as a whole (progressively compressing,
in other words, the peaks and troughs of intracyclical Juglar and Kuznets
patterns) (Berry 1991). According to Joseph Schumpeter, who revised Kondratieff's work to place a greater emphasis on innovation rather than investment, the effects of this type of cycle can be seen in the recessions of 1825,
1873 and 1930 (1934).

The relationship between these cycles and conflict is complex and has
long been subject to extensive debate. Writers such as Johan Åkerman have
suggested that, as Kondratieff booms appear to culminate in periods of military confrontation, it is the frequency of warfare that explains the apparent

periodicity of economic change (cited in Eklund 1980). This is because wars tend to increase short-term spending and demand while shifting production away from non-military goods, thereby forcing prices up rapidly and prompting a Kondratieff upswing. Once demand lessens following the conclusion of the war, limitations to production (commonly exacerbated by shortages of labour, foreign exchange, equipment and so on), push prices down, depress the economy and generate a Kondratieff downswing (Bernstein 1940: 524–7). Indeed, as Table 10.1 shows, 'there can be little doubt that wars and their associated economic disruptions do lead to price level increases', at least during those in which the United States and Great Britain have been involved (Thompson and Zuk 1982: 633).

Kondratieff himself, however, held the view that cyclical economic patterns may cause wars. He suggested that, because periods of extended commercial enlargement tend to destabilise political systems by accentuating the international competition for raw materials and markets and by intensifying domestic struggles over wealth distribution, 'the most disastrous and extensive wars and revolutions occur' during the upswing section of the cycle (1935: 111). Quincy Wright, working during the Second World War, broadly agrees. He argues that economic cycles, synchronous with Kondratieff's findings, may, in part, be a cause of warfare concentrations 'in approximately fifty-year oscillations' with especially intense periods of conflict occurring alternately (1965: 227).

This prompted Ludwig Dehio to construct a centenary cycle of global conflagration (1962). France, he argues, initiated the first challenge for supremacy in 1494 by attacking the Venetians and beginning a prolonged struggle over Italy. This benefited Spain under Charles V (who inherited the

Table 10.1 Selected British and American wars and wholesale price index fluctuations (1913 = 100)

War	War peak	Preceding 5-year mean
Great Britain		
Seven Years	93	78
American Independence	110	96
Napoleonic	201	157
Crimean	118	92
First World War	228	94
United States		
Mexican	88	80
Civil War	189	97
Spanish	69	70
First World War	188	102
Second World War	152	115

Source: Adapted from Thompson and Zuk (1982: 633).

Habsburg throne in 1515), which, led by Charles' son Philip II, succeeded in obstructing France's ascendancy by defeating Portugal in 1580 and assuming control of Venice's trade routes (de Oliveira Marques 1972). Spain's hegemony was, however, immediately qualified by England's destruction of her navy in 1588, leading to a long period of gradual decline and ending in a conclusive land battle at Rocroi in 1643. Her place was slowly taken by a resurgent France following Louis XIV's coronation in 1661. Again, England led the rest of Europe's resistance and, by combining forces with the Netherlands, eventually halted French ascendancy in 1692, before successfully preventing her from returning to power by winning the War of the Spanish Succession in 1713. This ushered in another century of stalemate before France again rose to hegemony in 1792. Abruptly deposed in 1805 at Trafalgar by Britain and then crushed in Moscow in 1812, France's authority was replaced by a century of Anglo-Russian competition, which ultimately permitted the expansion of German power – a process curtailed in 1918 (again by Britain operating in concert with a number of other Powers). In divergence from the previous pattern, however, the victorious coalition failed to take control of the international system and could not prevent a second German challenge from leading to another, even more destructive period of concentrated war (North and Thomas 1973).

Dehio's 'four-crested wave of regional power concentration and domination, with its delineation of peaks and troughs and waves of varying shapes' has been highly influential (Thompson 1992: 135). Arnold Toynbee, for instance, also structures his account of the last 500 years around the drive to achieve hegemony. His 115-year cycle of 'general war' (1494–1525, 1568–1609, 1672–1713, 1792–1815 and 1914–18) corresponds broadly with Dehio's 'drives for world domination' (Toynbee 1954). Like Dehio, he regards each cycle as initiated by an ambitious continental Power (the Spanish Habsburgs, the French twice and Germany). For Toynbee, however, this is not driven by relative expansions in military strength. Instead, hegemonic patterns of conflict and violence are a reflection of more fundamental cultural and political changes: notably, the generational transference of war fatigue as a constraint upon martial bellicosity – elements also important to Pitirim Sorokin's historiographic work (1957) and Lewis Richardson's study of international crises (1960b). 'The survivors of a generation that has been of military age during a bout of war will', Toynbee writes, 'be shy, for the rest of their lives, of bringing a repetition of this tragic experience either upon themselves or upon their children'. Therefore, he continues,

> the psychological resistance of any move towards the breaking of peace . . . is likely to be prohibitively strong until a new generation . . . has had time to grow up and come into power. On the same showing, a bout of war, once precipitated, is likely to persist until the peace-bred generation that has light-heartedly run into war has been replaced, in its turn, by a war-torn generation.
>
> (cited in Goldstein 1988: 117)

Building on this early work and in arguably the most developed account of hegemonic long cycles, George Modelski (often writing with William Thompson) puts forward an account of shifts in world leadership based on the primacy of naval power. As Table 10.2 illustrates, the importance of transoceanic navigation began long before the Portuguese explorer, Vasco da Gama, rounded the Cape of Good Hope in 1498. Once he did so, however, the Lisbon–Goa shipping lines quickly began to replace the ancient roadways of central Asia with the maritime trade of modernity. 'In the series of swift naval campaigns that followed, a string of bases was established and rival fleets were wiped off the oceans' (Modelski 1978: 218). Venice, pressured by France, was unable to come to the aid of the Egyptian and Indian fleets upon which she had hitherto based her economic strength, thereby precipitating the transformation of a previously dispersed global system that lacked 'self-maintenance and defence against interlopers' into a new order marked by 'severe conflict of global dimensions' (Modelski 1978: 219). At this time, the key quantitative measure of global power was the number of ocean-going vessels a state could muster. Almost immediately, though, Portugal found it difficult to finance a navy sufficient to maintain its commercial interests and, as early as 1508, it was obliged to relinquish its pepper monopoly to an Italian–Dutch conglomeration of traders (Diffie and Winius 1977: 414).

The failure of Spain to consolidate its usurpation of Portuguese assets at the end of the sixteenth century permitted the Netherlands to rebel and to obtain a favourable peace settlement with support from the French and British in 1609. Assisted by interest rates below 3 per cent for much of the seventeenth century, the Dutch were then able to gain control of over three-quarters of Europe's entire merchant fleet by 1660 – through which it took over much of Spain's Latin American possessions and explored new territory in southern Africa, south-east Asia and the American eastern seaboard (Tilly 1975b). Weakened by rising pressures from France, the Netherlands gave way to ascendant British trade – now supported by armoured galleons – during the early part of the eighteenth century. By deploying its new industrial might (especially in Asia) without attempting to supplant the colonial Powers of previous cycles, Britain secured her position throughout the rest of the century despite suffering setbacks in the Americas. This, combined with her enduring naval superiority, ensured that she retained the hegemonic incumbency following the global wars of the early nineteenth century. Increasingly, though, she was losing her economic pre-eminence and, although the Royal Navy remained the world's most powerful fleet right up until the turn of the next century, the industrial challenge of the United States and Germany became ever more pronounced. During the subsequent, and most recent, period of global warfare, it became clear that both the American economy and its newly acquired network of naval ports (from which an unrivalled fleet of aircraft carriers patrolled) had achieved global supremacy, a position underlined by an enduring nuclear submarine superiority (Modelski 1981).

In Modelski's model, then, each cycle is started by a period of global war driven by naval and economic competition. As it identifies the next

Table 10.2 World leadership and long cycles

Approximate timing or long cycle	World power or lead economy	Lead commodities or sectors	Primary challenger	Primary opposition to challenger	Global war period	Successor to world power or lead economy
Tenth–eleventh centuries	N. Sung, China	Printing, rice, iron				
Eleventh–twelfth centuries	S. Sung, China	Maritime trade				
Thirteenth century	Genoa	Black Sea trade				
Fourteenth–fifteenth centuries	Venice	Pepper	Portugal	France	1494–1516	
1517–1608	Portugal	Gold, spices	Spain	Netherlands	1585–1608	Netherlands
1609–1713	Netherlands	Baltic and Asian trade	France	Netherlands, Britain	1689–1713	Britain
1714–1815	Britain	Caribbean and American trade	France	Britain	1793–1815	Britain
1816–1945	Britain	Textiles, iron	Germany	Britain, United States	1914–45	United States
1946–present	United States	Steel, chemicals, electronics, oil	Germany			

Source: Adapted from Rasler and Thompson (1983); Modelski and Thompson (1996, 1988).

hegemon, it may also be considered a period of 'macrodecision'. As Table 10.3 illustrates, this is followed by three subsequent periods initially entitled 'world power', 'delegitimation' and 'deconcentration' to underline the gradual decline in hegemonic authority (1987). Later, however, he renamed these phases 'execution', 'agenda-setting' and 'coalition-building' to emphasise the enduring nature of hegemonic influence within each of the cycle's components (2000). Following a period of global warfare and macrodecision, the hegemon seeks to implement a new order more conducive to its interests and then continues by exerting a regulatory influence over the international system. 'Just as the macrodecision phase denotes great substantive changes in the system, the execution phase represents the focusing of the dominant policies' (Colaresi 2001: 574). The new hegemon leads the world economy, takes a prominent role in security issues and introduces new innovations: Portugal pioneered modern navigational techniques, the Netherlands broke the omnipotence of the Catholic Church by championing Calvinist religious reforms, Britain disseminated a wide range of industrial advances and the United States is presently leading the way in technology and weaponry. Within this period of leadership/execution, however, there appears to be resistance and dissatisfaction with the new hegemon's policies and preferences.

During the next phase – delegitimation and agenda-setting – dissent gathers greater momentum, producing fresh problems, giving rise to new challenges and obliging the hegemon to seek the support of lesser Powers. As Modelski and Thompson put it, 'old contenders are emboldened, and new contenders begin to emerge. Global problem management becomes increasingly difficult . . . because there is a tendency for post-global-war orders to be temporary' (1989: 27). Eventually, these forces can be obstructed no longer and, during a period of deconcentration and coalition-building, the hegemon's authority is openly challenged by emergent coalitions of confrontational, revisionist states. A period of macrodecision results, which has, up to now, taken the form of a global war – as a succession struggle 'over which economy will replace the incumbent as the global system's military-political centre' – but could conceivably occur in other less violent forms (Modelski 1999: 18).

Table 10.3 Components of Modelski's long cycle

Macrodecision/ global war	1494– 1516	1585– 1609	1689– 1713	1793– 1815	1914–45	2030–50
Execution/world power	1516–40	1609–40	1713–40	1815–50	1945–73	2050–
Agenda-setting/ delegitimation	1540–60	1640–60	1740–63	1850–73	1973– 2000	
Coalition-building/ deconcentration	1560–85	1660–89	1763–93	1873– 1914	2000–30	

Source: Adapted from Modelski (1987).

Clearly, this is a salient issue today. At present, we are living in a time of hegemonic decline. The United States established its authority during the first half of the twentieth century through a combination of economic output, naval advance and then the use and, in Cuba, the threatened use of its nuclear arsenal. Following humiliation in Vietnam, however, American administrations have increasingly been obliged to seek the support of lesser Powers in pursuing their foreign policy objectives. According to Modelski's timeframe, we might now expect this debilitation to prompt the formation of revisionist alliances, leading to a stage of macrodecision in approximately 25 years time. He has, however, baulked at such determinism, suggesting that American deconcentration is far from imminent – that, in other words, the period since 1973 'cannot be defined as that of a loss of position as leading economy' (1981: 80).

In viewing the current cycle as potentially different from its predecessors, three considerations may be pertinent. First, recent technological advances in communications and transportation may mean that it is now impossible for one country to dominate its rivals in the way that hegemons have done in the past. Second, it might be that the proliferation of weapons of mass destruction has rendered global warfare unwinnable. Although the time elapsed since the last global war (60 years) is not currently sufficient to support the view that the maintenance of an active nuclear deterrent can prevent large-scale wars (as Samuel Huntington claims (1986: 9)), it may be that launching a global military challenge to the hegemon can no longer act as a macrodecision. Third, the last great European conflagration may have been so severe as to leave the region no longer the determinative force in world politics that it hitherto had been, thereby making the global system less susceptible to the continent's competitive intradynamics. However, as this scenario does not preclude the possibility that other ascendant and/or unstable regions may pursue policies similar to those of the Habsburgs, the French, the British and the rest, 'we will need to see less continuity and more transformation in the next quarter-century than we have seen in the past quarter-century', if another period of global warfare is to be avoided (Rasler and Thompson 2000: 329).

Parity, transition and preventive war

Developed broadly concurrently with Modelski's model, Abramo Organski's power transition theory has been a comparable influence over the study of the relationship between the pursuit of hegemony and the occurrence of severe wars. Although not explicitly episodic, Organski's starting point – that 'shifts in the international distribution of power . . . create the conditions likely to lead to at least the most important wars' – shares a number of assumptions with long-cycle theorists (Organski and Kugler 1980: 4). For instance, the international system is seen as hierarchically – or rather pyramidally – structured with the hegemon at the top, major Powers below it, lesser Powers below them and colonies (those states without sovereignty) at the bottom. Each state is presumed to recognise its position within the world order and adjust both its foreign and domestic policy accordingly (Organski 1958). Indeed, it is the latter that, in contrast to realist orthodoxy, largely determines a state's position within the international hierarchy. As Jacek Kugler and Organski put it, changes in the world's structures of power are,

> in all significant respects, the result of the domestic developmental process. Thus, the significant data for the discussion of power relations [a]re the shifts from primary to secondary to tertiary production, variations in movement of fertility and mortality from high to low rates, the increase in the ability of the political system to mobilize resources, and difference in the social mobility of populations.
>
> (1989: 177)

Fundamentally, then, the intrastate and geopolitical arenas are intimately entwined. The rules and regulations governing international interaction – or what Organski calls 'the status quo' – reflect the distribution of power (or states' 'relative capabilities') within the system. Unsurprisingly, those near to the hegemon at the top of the pyramid tend to exhibit a stronger commitment to the status quo than weaker states. To perpetuate their predominance, major Powers establish 'self-serving patterns of interaction. Thus, a wealthy free-market dominant power will likely create a liberal economic order, [and] a democratic dominant power will likely create democratically operating international political institutions' (Kugler and Lemke 2000: 131). States near the bottom of the pyramid may be disadvantaged by, and dissatisfied with, the preferences of the powerful, leading to endemic tensions.

As policies, including the decision to embark on a conflict, are assumed to be chosen when they are perceived as potentially bringing greater domestic rewards and involving fewer domestic costs than inaction, these tensions are predicted to manifest themselves as war only when the relative capabilities of dissatisfied states begin to match those seeking to endorse the status quo. This is quite different from the two predominant (and static) notions of equilibrium drawn from realism; on the one hand, that a 50–50 balance of power acts to prevent war by maintaining uncertainty over its outcome and, on the other hand, that a preponderance of power acts as a disincentive to competitors and lessens the risk of misperception (Gulick 1955; Gilpin 1981). Instead, 'major wars are often a result of a transition in power between the dominant nation in a system and a rising challenger' (de Soysa *et al.* 1997: 511).

Relative changes in the national capabilities of both acquiescent and dissatisfied states have generally been assessed under three categories. The first considers national endowment as the set of building blocks that a country might require if it is to develop its hegemonic potential. These have usually been measured by variables such as population size, territorial mass, economic strength and the presence of natural resources. The second, national performance, is the way in which a state seeks to convert its endowment into effective forms of usable power. This looks at the levels of external pressures confronting a given country as well as 'how aware and responsive a particular state-society complex is to the new resources that must be produced if it is to develop the capability to both dominate the cycles of innovation and transform that dominance into effective hegemonic potential' (Tellis *et al.* 2000: 46–7). It thus takes in variables such as a state's infrastructural and ideational capacity to select and implement the most efficient technical, social and production policies. Together, these two categories are often referred to as a state's 'relative political capacity' (Kugler and Domke 1987).

A third means of evaluating international actors' capabilities is to quantify the strength of their military. This is often undertaken by aggregating indicators such as military expenditure, the gross size of the armed forces, the destructive force of a country's arsenal or an inventory of war-fighting competencies. In the Correlates of War Project, for instance, J. David Singer and Melvin Small calculate military personnel and spending, industrial potential (the production rates of iron and steel and overall energy consumption) as well as total and urban populations (cities with over 20,000 inhabitants) (1994). In Table 10.4, these figures have been converted into percentages of the overall major Power total for the period, added together and divided by the number of indicators assessed to give an individual average capability for each state.

The shifts in domestic power represented in this table may lead to war in several ways. First, they may produce an 'appetite in the gaining state and apprehension in the declining state', thereby increasing tensions between the two (Wayman 1996: 147). A wide variety of measurements of this appetite has been suggested. Bruce Bueno de Mesquita argues that falls in the purchasing power of a nation's currency are a key gauge of domestic levels of dissatisfaction with the international order (1990). Other indicators, discussed in greater depth in the previous chapter, include military expenditure and aggressive alliance-building (Kim 1996; Werner and Kugler 1996). Conversely, a number of studies have concluded that satisfaction with the status quo can prevent the occurrence of violent conflict even within highly acute confrontations (Ray 1995). This is particularly apparent if there is a history of amity – perhaps in the form of friendly diplomatic relations, comparable political institutions or established trading links – between the protagonists (Lemke and Reed 1996). Second, shifts in relative power may change the way in which imminent war is perceived. 'The rising state may overestimate its growth, while the declining state may underestimate its decline in power. This can create a situation where both sides believe they can win a war' (Hensel and McLaughlin 1997: 5). Indeed, a power transition between disputatious rivals may increase the likelihood of war by as much as 21 per cent

Table 10.4 The distribution of relative capabilities among major Powers 1895–1995 (percentages)

	United States	United Kingdom	France	Soviet Union/ Russia	Germany	Japan	Italy	Austria– Hungary	China
1895	23.53	20.23	9.88	15.38	14.46	4.90	4.57	7.05	
1905	24.58	14.15	8.17	22.60	14.93	6.41	3.62	5.54	
1914	24.16	15.87	9.55	15.43	18.70	4.96	3.61	8.54	
1925	33.63	13.99	10.04	17.82	11.23	7.41	5.89		
1935	25.65	10.09	7.60	26.01	14.05	7.83	8.76		
1939	24.22	12.74	5.73	20.55	23.98	9.33	4.45		
1946	60.74	12.02	1.81	23.61					1.83
1955	38.60	8.20	4.90	27.08					20.42
1965	34.25	6.67	4.97	28.69					25.42
1975	28.62	5.35	4.43	33.50					28.10
1985	26.13	4.10	3.89	35.57					30.32
1995	35.25	5.65	5.87	12.56					40.67

Source: Adapted from Danilovic (2002: 89).

(Huth and Russet 1993). If, however, the rising state is at the initiation point of its ascent, is too small ever to pose a significant threat to the authority of the hegemon or is 'so large that its dominance, once it becomes industrial, is virtually guaranteed', then war is unlikely to result (Organski 1958: 334).

Third, declines in the relative power of hegemonic states may enlarge the strategic objectives that challengers believe to be attainable from initiating a conflict, thereby increasing the range and value of the benefits expected to accrue as a result. This becomes especially probable if the advance of the contender is rapid. In such a scenario, its leaders may become overambitious (in terms of their projected place in the international order) and frustrated with the slow pace of change. The hegemon's administration may, on the other hand, underestimate its opponent's current and potential growth, leading to an excessively robust response (van Evera 1999). In obviating the possibility of an incremental diffusion of tension and a peaceful transition of power (especially in the case of very large challengers), such a reaction helps to explain why many hegemonic struggles are accompanied by severe, systemic warfare. In sum, the interaction between

> two key explanatory variables, relative power and the degree of satisfaction with the international order (or status quo) . . . [is] the primary determinant of war and peace. States that have insufficient capabilities, no matter how dissatisfied with the status quo, will be fundamentally unable to challenge the dominant power. States that are powerful but satisfied will have little motivation to challenge the dominant state for its preeminent position and the accompanying ability to shape the international order. Only the powerful and dissatisfied pose a threat.
>
> (DiCicco and Levy 1999: 682)

Indeed, statistical data tend to endorse the relevance of these factors. Stuart Bremer's study of war proneness among nations of varying relative capability, for example, finds that the second-place state has tended to be the most frequent initiator of conflict (1980). This is predicted to occur at or around the point of power parity – because it is then that a reasonable chance of success can be comfortably inferred. Consequently, the greater the power of the hegemon, the more stable the international system is likely to be (Volgy and Imwalle 1995). To return to Table 10.4's illustration of the macrodecision that ended Britain's world leadership, Germany would be expected to challenge both her and Russia/the Soviet Union firstly between 1910 and 1913 and then again around the mid-1930s. She could also have been expected to resist the United States' rise to hegemony from the early 1940s onwards. More generally, when all conflicts in which major powers have participated on opposing sides are considered, it is clear that a broader correlation between shifts in power and the occurrence of warfare exists. In a study of 119 dyadic relationships, Henk Houweling and Jan Siccama find that, out of the 26 that ended in war, 12 (or 46 per cent) had been subject to an 'overtaking' – defined as 'the passing of one major power by the other nation one or more times during a test period' (one of eight 20-year blocks between 1816 and 1975). This leads them to conclude that 'differential growth rates and specifically power transitions among great powers are indeed a potent predictor of consecutive outbreak [sic] of war' (1988: 99–101).

This may be true regionally as well as globally. Localised hierarchies and transitions of power can, it has been suggested, operate in ways comparable to worldwide patterns of international relations. Regional hegemons atop their own hierarchic structures (and conceivably contented with the overall international order) establish and maintain delimited areas of authority – what Douglas Lemke calls 'relevant neighbourhoods' – which are subject to pressures from rising challengers and constant encroachments from the global leader (2002). Satisfaction with the status quo, Lemke goes on to hypothesise, may be more influenced by local issues such as transportation routes, border disputes and cultural differences than broader geopolitical concerns (1996). Empirically, there appears to be some support for such a contention, despite the obvious difficulties in excluding the influence of global Powers and the generally low number of wars that have occurred without their input. In South America, for instance, Lemke and Suzanne Werner find that, of the 119 contending dyads that did not end in war, 110 attained neither power parity nor a joint commitment to change the status quo (1996: 256).

Is, however, the attainment of power parity a necessary prerequisite for the commencement of a challenge – regional or global? Are Douglas Lemke and Jacek Kugler correct to conclude that 'the closer to parity a dyad is, the greater the threat of war' (1996: 12)? Is it not more credible to assume that the dominant Power would initiate 'preventive action to block the rising challenger while the latter is still too weak to mount a serious threat' (Levy 1987: 84)? Indeed, such a motive has frequently been cited as an explanation for the causes of European conflicts during the second half of the nineteenth century. As A. J. P. Taylor writes, the war of '1866, like the war of 1859 before it and the wars of 1870 and 1914 after it, was launched by the conservative Power, the Power standing on the defensive, which, baited beyond endurance, broke out on its tormentors' (1954: 166).

Undertaking this kind of pre-emptive action may be driven by a perception that a state's power is declining relative to an ascending adversary: it remains, in other words, a policy option for governments presiding over endogenous growth if development is slower than that of an opponent's. To fight now is thus seen to be preferable to fighting later under less favourable circumstances. As Jack Levy points out, 'if the expected values of inaction and preventive war are at all comparable, leaders may be tempted to fight a preventive war in the hope of avoiding the losses that are the inevitable by-product of continued decline' (2000: 204). Moreover, as victory declines in likelihood monotonically as the challenger's power increases, it is rational for dominant states to mobilise quickly, particularly if the challenger's growth is rapid (Tammen *et al.* 2000). Such a strategy might also offer tactical advantages, for no government, regardless of its feelings towards a forthcoming and inevitable war, 'would be so foolish as to leave to the enemy the choice of time and occasion and to wait for the moment which is most convenient for the enemy' (Otto von Bismarck quoted in Fischer 1975: 461).

Although Organski did originally acknowledge the possibility of such a war ('to destroy a competitor before it became strong enough to upset the existing international order' (1958: 371)), most power transition models rest on the assumption that, because defeating a challenger brings no new benefits (beyond a simple perpetuation of the status quo), the dominant state 'has little incentive' to proceed (Kugler and Organski 1989: 187). This leaves the precise point at which war can be expected from shifts in relative power under-theorised. Such a lack of clarity is a substantial deficiency given the wide range of statistical evidence available on the matter. Woosang Kim and James Morrow, for instance, use a modified means of calculating relative capabilities and dissatisfaction to review Houweling and Siccama's findings over the same 160-year period. While they see some support for the causal importance of the rising state's dissatisfaction levels, its growth rate and the point at which it reaches parity with the dominant Power were both found to be insignificant predictors of war initiation. 'Power transitions', they surmise, 'therefore cannot be the cause of major wars. . . . The anticipation of the long war that would result [from approaching or achieved power parity] should suffice to deter that war' (1992: 918). The fact that such wars do occur is, they continue, better explained as an unexpected outcome resulting from the pursuit of more limited international objectives. Such an inference receives some support from Daniel Geller, who, having looked at a similar set of contending dyads, concludes that 'war and dispute initiators are as likely to be inferior to their opponents as they are to be superior in the static balance of relative capabilities' (1996: 138).

Charles Doran also finds that parity points are not the most reliable correlates of impending war. For him, the weakness in the power transition model is a lack of explicit cyclicity. 'The notion that the differential growth of state power is causally related to systemic structure and stability requires', he writes, 'a theoretical formulation of the full dynamic, as attempted in power cycle theory, to attain analytical maturity'. Major war, he continues, 'is an outgrowth of certain traumatic changes in a nation's relative power and associated role and security perceptions' (1989a: 84). In keeping with the power transition school, however, his measurement of a state's proclivity for war rests upon calculations of relative capability and foreign policy interests. Using a dataset of warfare similar to that of Modelski, he plots the cyclical rise and decline of major Powers since around 1500 (illustrated in Figure 10.1). He identifies four moments at which their governments 'are most vulnerable to overreaction, misperception, or aggravated use of force which may generate massive war' (Doran and Parsons 1980: 949). These are each cycle's peak, its trough and the two inflection points at which the established trajectory of the state diverges from a predictable course. During the first two periods, both the dominant actor and the challenger suddenly realise that the former's level of relative capability has fundamentally changed from growth to recession or vice versa. Similarly, at each of the inflection points, it becomes clear to political elites that a seemingly eternal rate of ascendance or decline is, in reality, subject to abrupt changes, thereby undermining their medium- to long-term plans.

The tendency of forecasters to base their outlook on perpetual linearity prevents them from perceiving both the presence, and imminent arrival, of critical moments in a country's power trajectory, rendering their analyses 'incontrovertibly wrong at the very points where being wrong is most threatening to [their state's] continued role and security position' (Doran 1989a: 104). As such, the more far-sighted the policy planning, the greater the disparity between the projected and real futures is likely to be. This reveals the state's future security projections as dangerously misguided, leading to anxiety, belligerence and overreaction. Major war, therefore, 'grows out of a government's unsuccessful struggle to adjust to a sudden, massive change in its projected future ability to exercise leadership and implement statecraft within the international system' (Doran 1989b: 374). It occurs not at the point of dyad parity, but when confrontations overlap with the incidence of critical changes in the power trajectory of one or both the disputatious states. Using this method, then, war between Germany and both the Soviet Union and the United Kingdom could be expected rather later than the point of power parity (see Figure 10.1). Indeed, in his study of 11 warring dyads covering the five major wars from the Crimea to Korea, Doran finds that at least 90 per cent involved a 'critical point' state (1989b: 384).

Questions arise, nevertheless, as to whether a cyclical pattern of behaviour can be linked satisfactorily to the occurrence of major wars given the inevitable rise and fall of inventories of economic strength and political will. To distinguish between an inter-relationship and a discernible cycle,

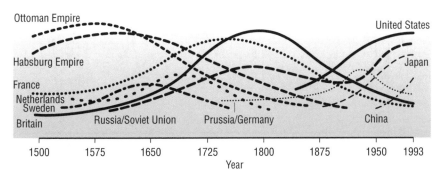

Figure 10.1 Charles Doran's power cycle structure 1500–1993. Source: Redrawn from Doran (2003: 24).

a considerable amount of data is clearly required but, with only four cycles said to be completed, a small number of warring dyads to analyse and the great rarity of hegemonic transitions, the veracity of statistical claims is likely to be open to interrogation. Simply identifying what appears to be a semi-regularised pattern of ups and downs cannot be evidence of a cycle per se. This is because any dataset will tend to show a wandering pattern around its mean. As Figure 10.2 illustrates, even randomly generated static data can take the form of a cycle and thus could be used 'to generate what looks like a plausible base dating scheme. [Merely] . . . the appearance of a "long wave" of "varying period" tells us nothing. [It] . . . may simply be an artefact of a mathematical property of stationary series' (Beck 1991: 460).

This may help to explain the vagueness of the relationship between big wars and ostensibly periodic shifts in hegemony. As Richard Rosecrance notes of Modelski's work, Portugal presided over almost constant war between the Habsburg and Valois kings and the Thirty Years' War (1618–48) happened near the start of the Netherlands' supremacy (1987). The need to achieve a fit between demonstrable historiography and explicit periodicity means that much of the literature concerning hegemony and war tends to be quite Eurocentric. For instance, Ottoman land forces as well as the Ming dynasty (which, between 1368 and 1644, developed a vast navy of four-masted ships displacing 1,500 tons, an economy producing over 100,000 tons of iron per year and a standing army said to be in excess of 3 million troops) are largely ignored (Temple 2002: 3).

Despite these obvious problems, however, understanding historical patterns of hegemonic transfer and global warfare still has considerable value, as well as real implications for the contemporary world. Indeed, if the lack of precise periodicity and a truly global focus within these studies permits us to reject Organski and Kugler's insistence that the underlying shifts in geopolitical power configurations are 'not manipulable in response to foreign-policy

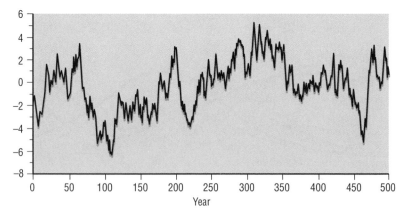

Figure 10.2 Randomly generated stationary data. Source: Redrawn from Beck (1991: 460).

needs' (1980: 63), then it may be possible to prevent – or at least – delay the next phase of world war. After all, it may be that the 'great wars of the system were not a consequence of its normal operation' and thus the current international order is not 'a system which will inevitably generate hegemonic wars' (Holsti 1985: 682, 684).

Kugler and Lemke point to four such preventative measures. First, as China will soon be in a position to challenge the United States' hegemony, efforts must be made to ensure that she is satisfied with, and therefore a supporter of, the status quo. Second, because the historical record suggests that wars are fought between hegemonic contenders despite the costs being extremely high, efforts to restrain the proliferation of weapons of mass destruction should be redoubled. Third, the North Atlantic Treaty Organisation should be enlarged to include eastern European states in the short term and then eventually Russia and China. This would expand the number of satisfied states within the international system and produce a bloc too powerful to be challenged by a rising contender. Fourth, in order to prevent regional hierarchies from leading to major wars, greater multilateralism should be promoted as a means of generating consensual support over the status quo and predicting possible flashpoints in the future (2000: 158–9).

Conclusion

This chapter has presented a consideration of the big picture – the centennial rise and fall of hegemonic Powers since the emergence of the modern world system in the fifteenth century. It has looked at the relationship between hegemony and the incidence of conflicts in general and large-scale warfare in particular. It has reviewed the ways in which changes in economic and military power have influenced the course of international relations over the last five centuries. Here, conflicts are caused either by incumbent hegemons protecting their standing in a preventative war against an ascendant Power or by rising challengers initiating a confrontation in order to achieve the status of world leader. As the benefits of such a position are vast, each is predicted to be prepared to suffer considerable losses. Resultant conflicts are therefore typically pursued on a colossal scale; a fact that renders them comparatively uncommon. Indeed, in plotting the incidence of these rare conflagrations, analysts, drawing on economists' work on the periodisation of boom and recession, frequently propose that a pattern of cyclical perio- dicity is apparent. Here, fluctuating levels of naval capability are often seen as especially important in determining the succession of hegemonic powers and the accompanying occurrence of severe periods of conflict.

Associated with the study of these shifts in coercive strength are expla- nations of warfare based on power transitions – broadly the focus of this chapter's second section. These generally concentrate on linear patterns of capability assessed by variables such as military strength, differential econom- ic growth rates and satisfaction with the regional or global status quo. Many predict that war is most likely to begin when the relative might of two or more disputatious Powers is approximately equal. It is at the point of power parity that a rising challenger might expect to secure victory. An alternative way of analysing a similar process is to assume that the dominant Power or Powers will act to arrest the challenger's ascendancy before it becomes an imminent threat. These approaches and long-cycle theories both tend to focus on the determinative properties of states' internal characteristics. As such, they offer something of a challenge to the assumptions of classical realism, which hold that global conflict tends to be a consequence of three inter-related features of the system itself – the inherently uneven and chaotic nature of geopolitics, the changing objectives of national interest and states' constantly shifting relative power to project their military force abroad.

Nonetheless, there is little agreement among writers in this field over both the precise timings of shifts in the international balance of power and the identity of the variables that drive such fluctuations in state capabilities. This widespread divergence of opinion is due, in part, to questions over the very existence of cyclical periodicity. It has been noted, for instance, that attempting to draw inferences from the historical record is inevitably epistemologically weak – the fact that something can be demonstrated to have happened regularly in the past is not, by itself, an assurance that it will continue to happen in the future. Such reservations notwithstanding, however, the issues at stake in the investigation of the causes of global warfare are of such magnitude as to ensure that these approaches remain an important area in the study of international politics in general and conflict in particular. Indeed, it is particularly pertinent today when globalised changes to the world order now mean that 'few, if any, issue areas . . . remain effectively closed off from system dynamics' (Marshall 1999: 7).

Most writers are, for instance, agreed that the weight of the past does not make another world war inevitable at a given point in the future. Globalisation, the unprecedented scale of the last great conflict and the uniquely deterrent properties of nuclear weapons may all combine to make the hegemony of the United States different from earlier periods of leadership. To prevent a new hegemon from emerging amid the customary bloodshed, it may, for instance, be necessary to make certain that the next great challenger remains content with the status quo, that mass destruction armaments do not fall into the hands of the dissatisfied and that more egalitarian forms of multilateralism are promoted. After all, to fail in these regards and to permit the world to pass through another calamitous period of hegemonic change could have uniquely fateful consequences. As George Modelski and Patrick Morgan put it, should a systemic war 'occur again amidst a plethora of nuclear weapons it will mean destruction on a scale endangering the existence of civilisation and the human species' (1985: 394).

11 Conclusion

This chapter will present a review of the overarching themes of the book. Extending the work of Paul Rogers and Oliver Ramsbotham (1999), it focuses on seven overlapping centres of debate. These concern, first, the transformation of conflictive situations. Here, important problems relate to the definition of conflict and the role of the researcher. Second, an attempt to connect analyses of conflict and violence with broader debates across disciplinary boundaries generates a number of issues of coherence within the literature. These relate to matters of both principle and empirical measurements. Third, the implied or explicit association between studies of conflict and the achievement of peace raises important questions regarding the nature of change and the utility of violence. Fourth, the use of multi-levels of analysis presents debates over the applicability of theoretical models and the relationship between the domestic and international social spheres. Fifth, an aspiration to incorporate approaches from various cultural traditions into the analysis of conflict and violence has valuable implications for both research and policy. Sixth, a tension between empirical and normative elements of research provokes notable debates over the relationship between values and analysis, particularly in the areas of methodology and epistemology. Finally, the issue of the practical or policy implications of research prompts a number of significant ethical considerations, not least in what precisely theory should seek to cover, how academics should relate to decision-makers and the degree to which researchers become complicit in policy outcomes. Each of these areas will be looked at in turn with the aim of reflecting on the main findings of the book.

Transformation, levels of interdisciplinarity and peace

The first area of debate relevant to the focus of this book concerns attempts by many conflict analysts and peace researchers 'to address the root causes of direct violence and to explore ways of overcoming structural inequalities and of promoting equitable and cooperative relations between and within human collectivities' (Rogers and Ramsbotham 1999: 741). Superficially, such a sentiment appears to be an uncomplicated assertion of a normative position to which most would ascribe. Many aid agencies, for instance, have abandoned the premises of neutrality, impartiality and independence discussed in Chapter 1 and altered their programmes to not only address 'immediate needs but also tackle the causes of vulnerability and insecurity, even though these are likely to be political in character' (Vaux 2006: 242). Few, however, get beyond these types of vague allusion to the difficulties that such aims portend. Andy Storey, for instance, concludes that assistance to conflict-affected countries ought not to fall into the hands of an 'abusive authority' (1997: 392), while others suggest that the reconstruction of defective states 'should be seized on as a tool to promote peace and justice' (Fox 2001: 277). Such consequentialist reasoning is clearly an important departure from the previously pre-eminent need to remain detached from local politics. Moreover, because it attempts neither to define what form an 'abusive authority' might take nor to distinguish peace from pacification, it is not, by itself, an autonomous political position. So, without an indication of how the three objectives highlighted by Rogers and Ramsbotham – an effort to prevent violence, to work towards a more egalitarian world and to promote greater levels of social or cultural reciprocity and understanding – are to be pursued, the problem of definition, as outlined in Chapters 2 and 3, is left unresolved, leading to a number of key problems.

The first emerges from adopting a subjectivist approach to identifying the causes of conflict, measuring inequality and specifying the meaning of cooperative relations. By relying on participatory approaches, the self-expressed perceptions of subjects may be used to define the conflictive situation. Because, as Chapter 3 highlighted, these will probably be influenced by, and therefore tend to replicate, existing power relations (particularly, as discussed in Chapter 6, along the lines of gender, race and class), a third party's analysis using this method will tend to produce conservative rather than progressive outcomes. This leads on to a second problem: because subjects are likely to specify their immediate needs rather than an account of potential root causes, third-party action may be conservative and 'minimalist' (Goodhand and Atkinson 2001). The consequence of this is that those intervening in conflictive situations may abdicate moral responsibility not only for what is going on around them, but also for the consequences of their own actions. An oft-cited example of the former was the refusal of the Red Cross to allow its operatives to be called as witnesses to the International Criminal Tribunal for the former Yugoslavia in 1999 despite its unparalleled access to instances of human rights abuse – a decision derided as 'cautious, lawyerly' and suggestive of a 'complicity with war crimes' (Ignatieff 1999: 204; 1998: 124; Berman 2005). A similarly controversial example of the latter is said to have occurred in the Goma refugee camps of the Democratic Republic of the Congo where relief agencies, responding to the 'minimal' and immediate needs of the displaced, were alleged to have been unwittingly aiding Hutu war criminals (Cooley and Ron 2002).

By objectifying aid recipients' interests in this way, a third problem emerges – that ignoring subjects' perceptions undermines the third party's claim of objectivity or greater perspicaciousness. While such a position has the potential to overcome existing power relations by revealing the contingent and immanently constructed nature of the conflictive situation, it does not explain how the observer's judgement is protected from the misperceptions ascribed to the subject's social environment. Associated with this is a fourth problem – namely that, by objectifying the conflictive situation, power is relocated from the protagonists to those seeking to effect an intervention. The 'maximalist' agenda of many non-governmental organisations (NGOs) today has thus proved an attractive vehicle for the promotion of Great Power interests. Major bilateral donors have, for instance, increasingly pressured the growing NGO sector to bear more of the material and ethical responsibility for international action. To do this, aid levels have risen from $2.1 billion in 1990 to $5.9 billion in 2000, of which the United States has contributed between 20 and 30 per cent of the annual allocation. Simultaneously, there has been a sharp decline in the funds allocated to multilateral agencies in favour of explicitly earmarked bilateral aid (Randel and German 2002). In 1988, for instance, the United Nations received 45 per cent of the global humanitarian budget, compared with below 25 per cent today. This has had 'a significant impact on the discretion available to humanitarian organisations' with the consequence that 'state interests, rather than the humanitarian principle of relief based on need, drives [sic] funding decisions' (Barnett 2005: 11).

The second area of debate relates to 'the realization that an interdisciplinary response [is needed] . . . to supplement an international relations approach with insights from the other political and social sciences, as well as from social psychology, anthropology and other disciplines' (Rogers and Ramsbotham 1999: 741). At one level, this aspiration to 'an intersubjective, conversed and cooperative approach' is (as the preceding chapters have sought to demonstrate) a considerable strength (Muñoz 2005: 9). Understandings of conflict, violence and, by extension, peace have long been informed by a wide range of disciplinary traditions. As indicated by the progression of the book chapters above, these stretch from theories of definition, structural violence, relative deprivation, diversions and functions, crises, social learning and constructivism drawn from politics, sociology, psychology and international relations to economic, theological, socio-biological and historiographic commentaries on greed, inherency and hegemony. Indeed, few topics have been discussed in publications as diverse as the *Western Criminology Review*, the *Australian and New Zealand Journal of Family Therapy* and *Poultry Science*.

While such enrichment has militated against the emergence of a spurious 'magic formula, which, mechanically applied, will produce the desired result and thus substitute for the uncertainties and risks of political action' (Morgenthau 1946: 95), it has, in failing to convert multidisciplinarity into cross-disciplinarity, also produced a splintered and inchoate field of study. In attempting to gain an understanding of warfare at the abstract level, for instance, a 'theoretical deficit' (Cusak 1995: 191) has been identified in which

> there is no consensus as to what the causes of war are, what methodologies are most useful for discovering and validating those causes, what general theories of world politics and human behavior a theory of war might be subsumed within, what criteria are appropriate for evaluating competing theories, or even whether it is possible to generalize about anything as complex and contextually dependent as war.
>
> (Levy 1998: 140)

The result is that the study of 'armed conflict and war remains fragmented between disciplinary boundaries, which produce conflicting and often mutually exclusive theories' (Porto 2002: 1).

Similarly, at the empirical level, a proliferation of datasets proceeding from varying definitional bases, using competing indicators and adhering to contrasting coding conventions has generated considerable confusion over even rudimentary measurements such as conflict frequencies, battlefield intensities and mortality rates. The study of international warfare is, for instance, a field largely made up of discrete topics. As Dina Zinnes has commented, everybody 'loves their variable; nobody [i]s willing to stand up and say, "I give up my variable"' (quoted in Brecher *et al.* 2000: 37). At the level of civil war, similar problems exist. In reviewing the current literature, Nicholas Sambanis points to nine major categories of concern: 'poverty and slow economic growth', 'ethnic diversity and polarization', 'natural resources', 'ethnic diversity', 'geographical dispersion, rough terrain, and security dilemmas', 'democracy: level and change', 'ethnic vs. revolutionary wars', 'external intervention in civil wars' and 'post-war peacebuilding and war recurrence' (2002). The presence of such an 'enormous diversity of theoretical, methodological, and epistemological perspectives' on the study of conflict, violence and peace acutely 'complicates the task of providing a concise assessment of the field' (Levy 1998: 140). This is a major problem for, as Muñoz notes, 'one of the greatest obstacles' in converting these perspectives into a 'commonly recognised theoretical field [is the absence of a] . . . system of organising and articulating the information at our disposal on the subject' (2005: 2). Clearly,

> order [must] be imposed on this explanatory chaos. We need theoretical templates to test against the burgeoning descriptive material lest it remain raw data. We need syntheses of findings, to show where approaches may agree, and to clarify where they do not.
>
> (Ferguson 1990: 27)

A primary purpose of this book, as Chapter 1 set out, has therefore been to try to respond to this inconsonance while retaining some of the field's immense richness. As such, it has attempted to escape what João Gomes Porto calls 'the tyranny of the single-cause' by presenting a wide-ranging review of the key theories involved in the explanation of the causes of conflict and violence (2002). In ordering these into loose categories, the book's aim has been, first, to address the fragmentary nature of writing on this topic and, second, to offer the reader a means of comparing various factors and mechanisms. Each chapter has thus identified and approached an important sample of research that shares a rudimentary basis of similar assumptions. By looking at common analytical themes in this way, this book has, it is hoped, not only highlighted significant areas of congruousness, but also solidified a somewhat nebulous literature, thereby allowing the reader to develop a clearer understanding of the current landscape of conflict studies.

The third of Rogers and Ramsbotham's categories overlaps closely with the first: it is 'a search for peaceful ways to settle disputes and for non-violent transformations of potentially or actually violent situations . . . [without] endorsing the status quo' (1999: 741). Although, like the first area of debate, this appears to represent a general good, the coverage of this book does, again like the earlier element, reveal a number of important questions surrounding how such an aspiration may be realised. The first is the problem of development. Working from the assumption that violence is a response to deprivation and pointing to the high correlation between low growth rates and the incidence of civil war, the provision of socio-economic support to poor countries is frequently presented as just such a means of non-violently transforming situations with high levels of latent or suppressed conflict (Collier 2007). As we saw in Chapters 7 and 8, however, the process of development may, itself, be a cause of violence or may offer enhanced outlets for pre-existing tensions. This can happen in a number of ways – the efficacy of ethnic affiliation may be intensified by urbanisation, greater labour flexibility or democratisation, grievances may be created or exacerbated by growing social stratification and social groups may be mobilised more easily by a drop in forgone income, the availability of rewards (such as natural resource rents) and a rise in transborder interaction (Congleton 1995). Indeed, the suggestion here is that, even if development occurs in a broadly beneficial way, the reduction of inequality and the creation of affluence can provide a more facilitative political environment for violent conflict than a process of impoverishment (Newman 1991).

A second issue raised by this book (particularly in Chapters 5 and 8) pertinent to the transformation of conflictive situations is the possibility that violence is not an aberration that requires remedial redress, but 'a normal response to commonplace conditions' born of the fact that 'the fundamental disposition of individuals ([or] groups) in politics is to maximize influence, or power, over decisions' (Eckstein 1980: 143). Moreover, if this tendency is ultimately derived from our evolutionary heritage, from determinative cultural–historical legacies or from self-centred assessments of cost and benefit, then violence requires little, if any, explanation. It may be that effecting change through social measures can do little to alter the human condition, to reform ancient cultural patterns or to lessen avarice, and that any potential future is likely to include some degree of inequality, frustration and cultural variation. If this is true, then attempting to develop the type of transformative measures implied by the topics looked at in Chapters 3, 6 and 7 is broadly futile. Instead, peace may emerge from the successful repression of 'human nature'. A programme of defensive securitisation, including the judicious use of coercion on a utilitarian basis, may be a more reliable way to settle disputes and to reduce the incidence of, or potential for, violence. Using this reasoning, it is, in order to protect the comparatively pacific polities of the West, necessary to see the 'Caribbean Rim, virtually all of Africa, the Balkans, the Caucasus, central Asia, the Middle East and Southwest Asia, and much of Southeast Asia' as a 'strategic threat environment' against which we must, concludes Thomas Barnett (formerly at the United States' Department of Defense), 'firewall the Core [the West]' (Barnett 2003: 174–5; 2004).

The fourth area of debate relates to the potential merit of a multi-level analysis 'to overcome the institutionalized dichotomy between studies of "internal" and "external" dimensions, [which are now] seen to be inadequate for the analysis of prevailing patterns of conflict' (Rogers and Ramsbotham 1999: 741). Throughout this book, there has been an acknowledgement that, although some topics and research questions (such as those dealt with in Chapters 9 and 10) lend themselves to a particular level of analysis, most models of conflict and violence can be applied to a wide range of actors. Individuals may be affected by structural violence, rewarded by conflict, learn to be aggressive and motivated by egoistic deprivation, avarice or the chance to free-ride. Groups may suffer from ethnocentric structural violence, be cohered by the occurrence of conflict, be conditioned to act aggressively and be mobilised by fraternal deprivation or the availability of resources. States and dyads may be similarly influenced by the distribution of resources, the decisions of their leaders and the presence of grievances, while, at the systemic level, structural violence and gradual shifts in the global balance of power may play a subliminal and non-agential role.

In a number of ways, adopting such an approach to analysing conflict and violence has the potential to ameliorate some of the problems of interdisciplinary diversity referred to earlier. Dennis Sandole, for instance, uses 'a multi-level map and pre-theory of variables operative at the trans-societal, societal and decision-making levels that may be relevant to the initiation and escalation of violent conflict and war' as a response to what he considers the 'fragmented, bivariate nature of quantitative studies of war' (1999: 178). Conceptually, too, it is important, if a fuller understanding of conflict and violence is to be achieved, to transcend what Edward Azar identified as the tendency for sociologists, anthropologists and psychologists to restrict their interests to 'civil wars, insurgencies, revolts, coups, protests, riots, [and] re-bellion' while leaving experts on international relations to work on 'interstate wars, crises, invasions, border conflicts, [and] blockades' (1990: 6). In this way, a major advantage of deploying a multi-level analysis is 'the theoretical purchase it provides to attempts to integrate the effects of internal politics and environmental pressures on foreign policies' (Ray 2001: 384).

This is important as it has the potential to break down the 'internal/ex-ternal conceptual straitjacket' of realism's response to domestic unrest and civil wars (Rogers and Ramsbotham 1999: 752). As Steven David observes, assuming that internal conflict stems from domestic anarchy comparable to that which realists ascribe to the international arena, concentrating on the level of the state tends to limit analyses to a focus upon the imposition of order (1997). If this does not prove possible, then the same logic of ir-redeemable differences leads writers to advocate the break up of the state into ethnically homogeneous independent countries that can then form the basis of a balance of power, again akin to the international system (Lind 1994). Studies of domestic conflict have thus arguably been constrained by a 'Hobbesian/Machiavellian preoccupation with *raison d'état*, the survival of the regime, and the equivocation of the extant regime with the legitimate state' (Marshall 1999: 127). Whatever forms civil wars take, then, realism is, for writers such as Andrew Mack, 'largely irrelevant to their explanation' and even less helpful in proposing the resolution of their underlying causes (2002: 516).

Culture, norms and practice

A fifth area of debate relates to 'the adoption of a global and multi-cultural approach, which would locate sources of violence globally and regionally as well as locally, and draw on conceptions of peace and non-violent so-cial transformation from all cultures' (Rogers and Ramsbotham 1999: 741). Indeed, as this book highlights, the study of conflict and violence has a di-verse international history. At the level of the individual, Johan Galtung's work has, for instance, been significantly influenced by Indian traditions of non-violence and the *dependencia* theorists of South America. Similarly, an-thropologists, and some others, have long attempted to include situational analyses from conflict participants as a means of overcoming the tenden-cy of third parties to impose an artificial division between a passive target and an active perpetrator (Nordstrom 1997). As Stathis Kalyvas notes, the 'flawed perception that victimhood and guilt are mutually exclusive catego-ries . . . [overlooks] those who partake in the process of violence in a variety of ways without, however, being directly involved in its outcome' (2006: 21). Women, for instance, may be frequent subjects of violence and conflict, while also being soldiers, denouncers and bureaucratic officers (Joshi 2002). It is, however, difficult to say for sure as gender is frequently overlooked as an analytical category in a discipline which is, as the reference section of this book demonstrates, overwhelmingly staffed by men (Taylor and Beinstein Miller 1994).

Indeed, perhaps most marginal of all to state-level discourses on conflict and violence are women (and, to a lesser degree, men) from rural areas. The fact that academia is located mainly in urban centres has produced a 'systematic slippage between political ideas as understood in the city and as practised in the village' (Scott 1977: 4). The lives, motives and struggles of peasants, illiterates and rural itinerants have frequently been ignored, dismissed or obscured by more accessible, vocal and articulate groups – a primary consequence of which is the clouding of data and, given the great number of statistical studies later found to be inaccurate, the undermining of the types of quantitative work examined in Chapter 8 (Wood 2003). An urban bias also tends to lead not only to pejorative views of agrarian primitivism, but also, in some cases, to a romanticising discourse on the 'noble savage' fighting to defend a 'natural' way of life against the encroachment of modernity (Starn 1998). Both are forms of reification which, influenced by the standpoint of the researcher, frequently present an 'epistemic bias . . . in favour of the assumption that all (or most) participants in conflicts are motivated by ideological concerns' (Kalyvas 2006: 44). While such partiality may be a particular problem for grievance theorists (looked at in Chapter 7), an over-emphasis on ideology can additionally cause the researcher to objectify cultural categories in ways unjustifiably exogenous to the conflict itself. Homogenised and immutable identities may, in other words, be ascribed to protagonists and then used to infer motivations, even though these could equally be a contingent and dynamic product of the conflict and not the types of 'ancient hatreds' discussed in Chapter 5 (Bayly 2000).

Comparable problems of representation exist at the global level. For most of the postwar era, stereotypes of the 'other' Superpower have persisted as conflict analysts have expended 'little effort to get inside the culture of the cold war', resulting in limited contact between Western and Eastern social science (Pitt 1989: xiv). Ignorance frequently produces fear and, as it is the job of military elites to prevent opponents from gaining an upper hand, a mutual need to exaggerate the nature of the threat – leading to the kinds of diversionary politics talked about in Chapter 4 (Brasset 1989: 44). Such tensions have also dampened efforts to understand the causes of conflict and violence outside the two blocs, thereby acutely limiting the impact of insights from the global South and its academic traditions. As Holsti puts it, 'both Western and communist analysts ignored local dynamics and local problems. Wars in the peripheries, they believed, were inevitably caused by the machinations of the adversary'. Indeed, the fact that, after 1989, 'American and European analysts suddenly discovered "ethnic wars," and argued that a new . . . periphery of violence and chaos were appearing' in areas previously secured by Superpower beneficence suggests, Holsti continues, a continued exclusion of 'spokespersons from the peripheries' amid a perpetuation of 'Western conceits and post-imperial perspectives' (1999: 286, 291–2). Such continuities mean that 'our modern, sophisticated theories and understandings do not fit Third World facts very well, often rendering analysis and policy prescriptions ineffective, counter-productive, or exacerbative [sic]' (Marshall 1999: 1).

Part of the reason for this can be found at the policy level. Despite a small army of personnel employed in developing countries by aid agencies, there is, in many cases, little effort to heed cultural and religious sensitivities (Minear and Weiss 1993). This is reinforced by the menial nature of local staff appointments, differentiated pay and conditions between those recruited in-country and overseas and the generalist and temporary nature of most expatriate appointments (Barakat *et al.* 2003). A study carried out among the 240 international NGOs in Bosnia, for instance, found that 'virtually all donor grant mechanisms had a time frame of one year or less . . . [and s]ome were for six months or even three' (Smillie and Todorovic 2001: 31). The utility of gaining a specialised understanding of local conditions is thus rejected. Instead, 'the only useful form of knowledge is that which translates easily into a series of technical solutions' to the problems encountered by organisations when implementing their own projects and programmes (Duffield 1999: 32). By characterising violent conflicts as grounded upon 'irrational acts stemming from a development malaise', aid agencies working in conflict-affected contexts commonly treat their programmes as 'closed systems' isolated from the social setting in which they function (Fowler 1995; Uphoff 1995; Duffield 1999: 33). Consequently, most 'have surprisingly little to say, by way of concrete analysis, about the nature of the alternative political structures that are emerging in protracted crises' (Duffield 1998b: 181).

A sixth area of debate relates to the fact that much of what we have looked at in this book may be thought of as 'both an analytic and a normative enterprise'. Many writers have attempted to ground their work in 'quantitative research and comparative empirical study, but, in anti-positivistic vein', Rogers and Ramsbotham contend, most are also motivated 'by ethical concerns and commitments' (1999: 741–2). This tension between values and empirics has given rise to a number of important contradictions. The first concerns the functionality of violence. Whereas researchers may propound a wish to see alternative responses to conflict, violence can be demonstrated empirically to offer important benefits to both participants and bystanders. Chapters 2 and 4 showed that this may involve individuals from every stratum of society, as well as groups and larger social groupings. Moreover, as peace may be seen as resulting from security and/or from equality, any attempt to understand the causes of violence cannot arbitrarily dismiss the pursuit of peace as a cause of violence. A second problem concerns the unit of analysis. Because, as Chapter 3 highlighted, greater violence is exerted non-behaviourally than directly, the researcher is perhaps obliged to focus upon structural inequalities rather than warfare and the like. Indeed, even if the rather nebulous character of structural influences renders direct mani-festations of violence a more rewarding focus for research, the primacy of collective conflicts remains difficult to justify in empirical terms given that women being assaulted by their partners is believed to be the most common form of violence worldwide (Pettman 1998: 155).

A third consideration is the relationship between analysis and values. At one level, this is a tension between the need to develop accurate, numeric treatments of conflict variables and to elucidate critical insights into their de-terminant contexts, diachronic variance and cultural specificity. Acclaiming the professional value of working in a 'hard' science freed from the vagaries of theoretical evaluation, the former position holds that it is vital that theory and data remain separate in order to demonstrate general applicability. It is also an important way to avoid what Stathis Kalyvas calls 'partisan bias' (2006: 35). This is the tendency to consent to a particular version of events, thereby excluding other counterfactual or potentially important accounts, impairing the process of research and rendering a dual commitment to ana-lytical rigour and normative argumentation untenable. Typically, it may entail the uncritical acceptance of victims' testimonies, the exaggeration of actors' comparative brutality and the attribution of credence to the persuasive over the inarticulate. Instead, studies of conflict should, Gerald Steinberg insists, be solely grounded upon 'careful and value-free academic discourse'. To see moral judgements as preconditions to research rather than outcomes is, he continues, at the root of the discipline's failure 'to provide empirically use-ful analysis and prescriptions for resolving to managing protracted ethno-national conflicts' (2004: 14, 15).

An alternative way to see the interaction between analysis and value is as determined by 'a kind of "as if" positivism: . . . that facts are only interpret-able, and can only be grouped into sociologically-significant categories, in terms of meaning systems' (Mann 1994: 42). In this sense, an empirical measurement of conflict and violence does not, in itself, suggest a particular course of action. The facts cannot simply speak for themselves. In order to form the basis for an analysis, they require explicit connections to con-cepts by a researcher unavoidably driven not only by the quality of the data, but also by his/her own values. As unobservables, such as gender, class and markets, cannot be fully excluded as either causal elements or sources of bias, theory may be more usefully generated through a process of reciprocal evaluation with data (Somers 1999). Rather than being derived from some overarching paradigm, causality perhaps more plausibly emerges not from discrete individual motives (of the type looked at in Chapter 8), but through the relational pathways of contingent and variable 'situational mechanisms' (Stinchcombe 1995). In this way, empirical material's 'very form is dictated by theoretical concepts operationalised as variables using linguistic catego-ries which may themselves impose specific cultural understandings' (Hart 1994: 22).

If, however, these cultural understandings are, themselves, determined by socially constructed power relations – or what Max Horkheimer calls 'the false consciousness of the bourgeois savant' – then the production of knowledge is likely to endorse these same power relations (1972: 197). Rather than pursuing 'inquiry according to the dictates of the unfettered theoretical imagination', the theorist must 'respond to the practical concerns of those whose support or mere tolerance makes it possible in the first place' (Nardin 1980: 477). For some post-modernist writing, this also means that the notion of a value–fact separation, which undermines empirical research's claim to truth, must be similarly contingent. It is implied, in other words, that analyses of conflict and violence are contextually defined narratives (rather than depictions of events and processes) which reveal as much about the power of language and intertextual relations as traditions of scholastic endeavour. In order to sustain the claim that such a position represents an illuminating alternative to bland positivism and to prevent it from undermining its own claim to knowledge, however, critical thought must also, in the view of Horkheimer and others in the Frankfurt School, include a commitment to action or 'praxis' (Alker 1988; Østerud 1996; Smith 1997).

This brings us to Rogers and Ramsbotham's final area of debate: that a 'close relationship between theory and practice' has meant that many analysts working on conflict and violence 'have been more concerned with the policy implications of their research than with its reception among fellow academics' (1999: 742). This aims to overcome what, as early as the mid-1970s, John Vasquez recognised as a 'two cultures' problem in conveying academics' understanding of the cause of war/conditions of peace to political elites (1976). Since then, there has been, for many writers, little evidence that, despite becoming a substantial industry, research into conflict and violence has had much impact on the policy community (Lopez 1985; Mack 2002: 516). An important reason for this may be that there is a tendency among writers to produce research purporting to be a conscientious response to a social problem that is nevertheless so esoteric as to be comprehensible only to those initiated into the intricacies of the subject matter. If such a disposition should become a reason for academia to decline engagement with a broader audience on an issue such as violent conflict, it may be considered inexcusable. As Anna Simons notes, 'from the perspective of those who might die, our unwillingness to reason with those who control the means of destruction might seem unconscionable' (1999: 75).

If, as Andrew Mack suggests, 'the scholarly and policy communities communicate badly', though, it is hoped that this book cannot easily be placed as an example of 'the former rarely seeking to make their work more accessible to the latter' (2002: 515). Rather, it has aimed to challenge the current inclination of 'policy communities' to discard explanation in favour of descriptive accounts that tend to see conflict and violence in apolitical and atheoretical terms. It has sought to get beyond the characterisation of contemporary warfare as marked by ill-defined and variable battlefield objectives that have 'little to no ennobling purpose or outcome' (Shaw 2000:

172). Within these studies of so-called 'new wars', political functions are not acknowledged and recruitment is said to be driven by spurious ethnic or religious affiliations (through which 'elites reproduce their power') that mask the actual intention of participation, which is asset seizure, the looting and control of markets and trade routes and the extraction of protection money from local people and aid agencies (Snow 1996: 57). Attempting to explain the causes of such phenomena is largely avoided, or simply ascribed to the mere utility of violence in the expression of avarice. Such motives are assumed to be endemic to all societies, so explanation rests solely on the idea that the state in which the civil unrest has occurred is a 'failure', 'weak', 'collapsed' and so on, thus permitting the emergence of circular patterns of low tax revenue, poor infrastructure and high public disorder – ultimately producing 'violent war economies' (Jung 2003: 2; Chojnacki 2006: 31).

Such ideas have had a profound impact on policy making. In 1999, for instance, the World Bank committed a special edition of its journal *Development Outreach* – which it describes as 'a flagship magazine in the field of global knowledge for development which reflects the learning programs of the World Bank' – to the 'new wars'. Despite this, though, the 'success' of the new wars thesis arguably does not represent the establishment of a mutually interactive connection between the work of academics and policy makers. Rather, such a reaffirmation of realism's vision of an amoral and self-seeking world in which the systematic and strategic use of murder, rape, mass expulsion, land-mining and demolition are an inevitable result of a decrease in Superpower authority exhibits, to many, the summation of conflict analysts' failure to effect significant changes in the orientation of policy formation processes. Instead of generating nuanced and sophisticated responses to the rise in civil wars, it would seem that academics' contribution to political elites' 'understanding of the new wars emphasises the reappearance of ancient tribal hatreds and other forms of biocultural determinism' (Duffield 2001: 18). Edward Newman, for instance, concludes his review of the new war thesis by suggesting that, 'while it was once politically difficult to even raise the idea of trusteeships for regions that defy sovereign responsibility, today the idea may be unavoidable. Research on violent conflict should be approached within this normative context' (2004: 187). As Alex Callinicos points out, these are attractive to the West because they represent conflict in a way that does not implicate outside forces and thus tend to offer support to those advocating interventional action and the imposition of a political transformation project (Callinicos 2004).

It would appear, then, that influence is, in fact, from the 'policy community' to academics, whose production of knowledge may be incorporated into what Robert Cooper (a senior aide to Tony Blair and recently Director-General for External Affairs at the European Union) describes as 'a new kind of imperialism' needed today to deal 'with more old-fashioned kinds of states'. This includes, he continues, 'revert[ing] to rougher methods of an earlier age – force, pre-emptive attack, deception, whatever is necessary to deal with those who still live in the 19th century' (2002: 16–18). In this way, 'academic opinion is brought in according to its utility in furthering established policy aims. A "good" academic is a technocrat, who does practical, problem-serving work, not the "value orientated" scholar who questions basic policy premises' (Ferguson 1989: 155, partly quoting Chomsky 1982: 89). Practical research thus frequently concentrates on the mechanisms of organising an intervention into a conflict-affected state, while neither addressing the normative underpinnings of such an enterprise nor seeking to investigate the causes of the conflict beyond a single-factor precept of acquisitiveness (Cilliers 2000; Kothari 2005). The result, Roland Paris notes, is that much of the current range of academic literature 'is too limited in the scope of its inquiry and devotes too much attention to "policy relevance," or the goal of offering advice and recommendations to decisionmakers' (2000: 27). Surely, if there is to be an active interface between researchers attempting to explain the causes of conflict and violence, it is, Heikki Patomäki notes, 'without prejudice, to help understand war and peace in a more realistic and able manner'. The policy relevance of conflict analyses for those purporting to pursue peace must, in other words, be prefigured by academic autonomy. Indeed, as Patomäki (after Galtung) continues, once scholarly endeavour becomes 'a faithful tool supporting the basic ideology of some international organization, foreign ministry or peace organization . . . it has ceased to be science and research' (2001: 730).

References

Aberle, D. (1962) 'A note on relative deprivation theory', in S. Thrupp (ed.) *Millennial Dreams in Action: Essays in Comparative Study*, The Hague: Mouton.

Abernethy, V. (1978) 'Female hierarchy: an evolutionary perspective', in L. Tiger and H. Fowler (eds) *Female Hierarchies*, Chicago: Beresford Book Service.

Abrahamian, E. (2005) 'The US media, Huntington and September 11', *Third World Quarterly* 24: 529–44.

Africa Rights (1994) *Rwanda: Death, Despair and Defiance*, London: Africa Rights.

Ahorsu, K. E. (2004) 'The political economy of civil wars in Sub-Saharan Africa – a conceptual framework', paper presented to the WIDER Conference on Making Peace Work, Helsinki, June. Available online: http://www.wider.unu.edu/conference/conference-2004-1/conference%202004-1-papers/Ahorsu-1905.pdf (accessed 15 November 2006).

Ainsworth, M., Bleher, M., Waters, E. and Wall, S. (1978) *Patterns of Attachment: A Psychological Study of the Strange Situation*, Hillsdale, NJ: Erlbaum.

Ajami, F. (1993) 'The summoning', *Foreign Affairs* 72: 2–9.

Akbar, M. (2002) *The Shade of the Sword: Jihad and the Conflict between Islam and Christianity*, London: Routledge.

Akers, R. (1998) *Social Learning and Social Structure: A General Theory of Crime and Deviance*, Boston, MA: Northeastern University Press.

Alesina, A. and Perotti, R. (1996) 'Income distribution, political instability and investment', *European Economic Review* 40: 1203–28.

Alexander, R. and Borgia, G. (1978) 'Group selection, altruism, and the levels of organization of life', *Annual Review of Ecological Systems* 9: 449–74.

Ali, R. (1984) 'Holier than thou: the Iran–Iraq War', *Middle East Review* 17: 50–7.

Alker, H. (1988) 'Emancipatory empiricism: towards the renewal of empirical peace research', in P. Wallensteen (ed.) *Peace Research: Achievements and Challenges*, Boulder, CO: Westview.

Alkire, S. (2002) 'Dimensions of human development', *World Development* 30: 181–206.

Allen, E. and the Sociobiology Study Group (1976) 'Sociobiology: another biological determinism', *BioScience* 26: 182–6.

Allison, G. (1969) 'Conceptual models and the Cuban Missile Crisis', *American Political Science Review* 63: 689–718.

—— (1971) *Essence of Decision: Explaining the Cuban Missile Crisis*, Boston, MA: Little Brown.

—— (1987) 'Book review: *The Politics of Policy Making in Defense and Foreign Affairs: Conceptual Models and Bureaucratic Politics*, by Roger Hilsman (Englewood Cliffs, NJ: Prentice-Hall)', *Political Science Quarterly* 102: 524–5.

Allison, G. and Halperin, M. (1972) 'Bureaucratic politics: a paradigm and some policy implications', in R. Tanter and R. Ullman (eds) *Theory and Policy in International Relations*, Princeton, NJ: Princeton University Press.

Allison, G. and Zelikow, P. (1999) *Essence of Decision: Explaining the Cuban Missile Crisis*, 2nd edn, New York: Longman.

Altemeyer, B. (1998) 'The other "authoritarian personality"', *Advances in Experimental Social Psychology* 30: 47–92.

Altfeld, M. (1983) 'Arms races? And escalation? A comment on Wallace', *International Studies Quarterly* 27: 225–31.

Anderson, C. (1983) 'Abstract and concrete data in the perseverance of social theories: when weak data lead to unshakeable beliefs', *Journal of Personality and Social Psychology* 19: 93–108.

Angell, N. (1910) *The Great Illusion*, New York: Putnam.

Ardrey, R. (1966) *The Territorial Imperative*, New York: Atheneum.

—— (1970) *The Social Contract*, New York: Atheneum.

Arendt, H. (1963) *On Revolution*, New York: The Viking Press.

Arrighi, E. (1972) *Unequal Exchange: A Study of the Imperialism of Trade*, New York: Monthly Review Press.

Art, R. (1973) 'Bureaucratic politics and American foreign policy: a critique', *Policy Sciences* 467–90.

Asch, S. (1951) 'Opinions and social pressure', *Scientific American* 193: 31–5.

Atkinson, J. (1982) 'Old and new conceptions of how expected consequences influence actions', in N. Feather (ed.) *Expectations and Actions: Expectancy Value Models in Psychology*, Hillsdale, NJ: Erlbaum.

Attinà, F. (2004) 'State aggregation in defense pacts: systemic explanations', Catania: Jean Monnet Working Papers in Comparative and International Politics 56. Available online: http://www.fscpo.unict.it/EuroMed/jmwp56.pdf (accessed 12 February 2006).

Aya, R. (1979) 'Theories of revolution reconsidered: contrasting models of collective violence', *Theory and Society* 8: 39–99.

Azam, J.-P. (2001) 'The redistributive state and conflicts in Africa', *Journal of Peace Research* 37: 429–44.

Azar, E. (1990) *The Management of Protracted Social Conflict: Theory and Cases*, Aldershot: Dartmouth.

Baldwin, D. (1979) 'Power analysis and world politics: new trends versus old techniques', *World Politics* 31: 161–94.

Ball, D. (1974) 'The blind men and the elephant: a critique of bureaucratic politics theory', *Australian Outlook* 28: 71–92.

Ballentine, K. and Nitzschke, H. (2003) 'Beyond greed and grievance: policy lessons from studies in the political economy of armed conflict', New York: International Peace Academy Policy Report. Available online: http://www.ipacademy.org/PDF_Reports/BGG_rpt.pdf (accessed 26 January 2006).

Ballentine, K. and Sherman, J. (2003) 'Introduction', in K. Ballentine and J. Sherman (eds) *The Political Economy of Armed Conflict: Beyond Greed and Grievance*, Boulder, CO: Lynne Rienner.

Bandura, A. (1973) *Aggression: A Social Learning Analysis*, Englewood Cliffs, NJ: Prentice-Hall.

—— (1976) 'On social learning and aggression', in E. Hollander and R. Hunt (eds) *Current Perspectives in Social Psychology*, 4th edn, Oxford: Oxford University Press.

Bandura, A. and Walters, R. (1963) *Social Learning and Personality Development*, New York: Holt, Rinehart and Winston.

Bandura, A., Ross, D. and Ross, S. (1961) 'Transmission of aggression through imitation of aggressive models', *Journal of Abnormal Social Psychology* 63: 575–82.

Barakat, S., Jacoby, T. and Kapisazovic, Z. (2003) 'International organizations and local staff: the case of Sarajevo', in E. Date-Bah (ed.) *Jobs after War: A Critical Challenge in the Peace and Reconstruction Puzzle*, Geneva: ILO Books.

Barash, D. (1977) *Sociobiology and Behaviour*, New York: Elsevier.

—— (1980) *Sociobiology: The Whisperings Within*, London: Souvenir Press.

Barash, D. and Webel, C. (2002) *Peace and Conflict Studies*, London: Sage.

Bardhan, P. (1997) 'Method in the madness? A political-economy analysis of ethnic conflicts in less developed countries', *World Development* 25: 1381–98.

Barnett, M. (2005) 'Can humanitarianism save itself?', Social Science Research Council, Emergencies and Humanitarian Action Programme. Available online: http://www.ssrc.org/programs/emergencies/publications/barnett_paper.pdf (accessed 1 May 2005).

Barnett, T. (2003) 'The Pentagon's new map: it explains why we're going to war and why we'll keep going to war', *Esquire* March: 174–6.

—— (2004) *The Pentagon's New Map: War and Peace in the Twenty-First Century*, New York: Putnam.

Bateson, P. (1989) 'Is aggression instinctive?', in J. Groebel and R. Hinde (eds) *Aggression and War: Their Biological and Social Bases*, Cambridge: Cambridge University Press.

Bayly, C. (2000) 'Rallying around the subaltern', in V. Chaturvedi (ed.) *Mapping Subaltern Studies and the Postcolonial*, London: Verso.

Beck, N. (1991) 'The illusion of cycles in international relations', *International Studies Quarterly* 35: 455–76.

Bee, H. (1997) *The Developing Child*, New York: Addison-Wesley Longman.

Bendix, R. (1967) 'Tradition and modernity reconsidered', *Comparative Studies in Society and History* 9: 292–346.

Bendor, J. and Hammond, T. (1992) 'Rethinking Allison's models', *American Political Science Review* 86: 301–22.

van Benthem van den Bergh, G. (1972) 'Some critical notes on Johan Galtung's "A structural theory of imperialism"', *Journal of Peace Research* 9: 77–85.

Berdal, M. (2005) 'Beyond greed and grievance – and not too soon . . . a review essay', *Review of International Studies* 31: 687–98.

Berdal, M. and Keen, D. (1997) 'Violence and economic agendas in civil wars: some policy implications for outside intervention', *Millennium: Journal of International Studies* 26: 795–818.

Berdal, M. and Malone, D. (2000) 'Introduction', in M. Berdal and D. Malone (eds) *Greed and Grievance: Economic Agendas in Civil Wars*, Boulder, CO: Lynne Rienner.

Berkowitz, L. (1962) *Aggression: A Social-Psychological Analysis*, New York: McGraw-Hill.

—— (1965) 'The concept of aggressive drive: some additional considerations', *Advances in Experimental Social Psychology* 2: 301–29.

—— (1990) 'Biological roots: are humans inherently violent?', in B. Glad (ed.) *Psychological Dimensions of War*, London: Sage.

Berman, E. (2005) 'In pursuit of accountability: the Red Cross, war correspondents, and evidentiary privileges in international criminal tribunals', *New York University Law Review* 80: 241–77.

Bernstein, B. (2000) 'Understanding decisionmaking, U.S. foreign policy, and the Cuban Missile Crisis: a review essay', *International Security* 25: 134–64.

Bernstein, D. (1984) 'Conflict and protest in Israeli society', *Youth and Society* 16: 129–52.

Bernstein, E. (1940) 'War and the pattern of business cycles', *American Economic Review* 30: 524–35.

Berry, B. (1991) *Long Wave Rhythms in Economic Development and Political Behavior*, Baltimore, MD: Johns Hopkins University Press.

Betts, P. (1977) *Soldiers, Statesmen, and Cold War Crisis*, Cambridge, MA: Harvard University Press.

Bilig, M. (1995) *Banal Nationalism*, London: Sage.

Birrell, D. (1972) 'Relative deprivation as a factor in conflict in Northern Ireland', *The Sociological Review* 20: 317–43.

Björkqvist, K. (1997a) 'The inevitability of conflict but not of violence: theoretical considerations on conflict and aggression', in D. Fry and K. Björkqvist (eds) *Cultural Variation in Conflict Resolution to Violence*, Mahwah, NJ: Erlbaum.

—— (1997b) 'Learning aggression from models: from a social learning to a cognitive theory of modeling', in S. Feshbach and J. Zagrodzka (eds) *Aggression: Biological, Developmental and Social Perspectives*, New York: Plenum Press.

Blainey, G. (1973) *The Causes of War*, New York: The Free Press.

Blalock, H. (1984) *Basic Dilemmas in the Social Sciences*, London: Sage.

Blass, T. (2004) *The Man who Shocked the World: The Life and Legacy of Stanley Milgram*, New York: Basic Books.

Blechman, B. and Kaplan, S. (1978) *Force Without War*, Washington, DC: Brookings.

Bloom, W. (1990) *Personal Identity, National Identity, and International Relations*, Cambridge: Cambridge University Press.

Blum, W. (2003) *Killing Hope: US Military and CIA Interventions since World War II*, London: Zed.

Bolks, S. and Stoll, R. (2000) 'The arms acquisition process: the effect of internal and external constraints on arms race dynamics', *Journal of Conflict Resolution* 44: 580–603.

Booth, J. (1991) 'Socioeconomic and political roots of national revolts in Central America', *Latin American Research Review* 26: 33–73.

Booth, K. (1990) 'The concept of strategic culture affirmed', in C. Jacobsen (ed.) *Strategic Power: USA/USSR*, Basingstoke: Macmillan.

Boring, E., Langfeld, H. and Weld, H. (1939) *Introduction to Psychology*, New York: Wiley.

Boulding, K. (1962) *Conflict and Defense*, New York: Harper.

—— (1977) 'Twelve friendly quarrels with Johan Galtung', *Journal of Peace Research* 14: 75–86.

—— (1982) 'Limits or boundaries of peace research', in G. Pardesi (ed.) *Contemporary Peace Research*, Brighton: Harvester.

Boutros-Ghali, B. (1992) *An Agenda for Peace: Preventive Diplomacy, Peacemaking and Peace-Keeping*, New York: United Nations.

Bowen, D., Bowen, E., Galoiser, S. and Masotti, L. (1968) 'Deprivation, mobility and orientation toward protest of the urban poor', *American Behavioral Scientist* 11: 20–4.

Brass, P. (1997) *Theft of an Idol: Text and Context in the Representation of Collective Violence*, Princeton, NJ: Princeton University Press.

Brasset, D. (1989) 'U.S. military elites: perceptions and values', in P. Turner and D. Pitt (eds) *The Anthropology of War and Peace: Perspectives on the Nuclear Age*, Granby, MA: Bergin and Garvey.

Braybrooke, D. and Lindblom, C. (1963) *Strategy of Decision Evaluation as a Social Process*, New York: The Free Press.

—— (1973) 'Types of decision making', in J. Rosenau (ed.) *International Politics and Foreign Policy: A Reader in Research and Theory*, New York: The Free Press

Brecher, M. and Wilkenfeld, J. (1982) 'Crises in world politics', *World Politics* 34: 380–417.

Brecher, M., James, P. and Wilkenfeld, J. (2000) 'Escalation and war in the twentieth century: findings from the International Crisis Behavior Project', in J. Vasquez (ed.) *What Do We Know about War?*, Lanham, MD: Rowman and Littlefield.

Bremer, S. (1980) 'National capabilities and war proneness', in J. D. Singer (ed.) *The Correlates of War II: Testing some Realpolitik Models*, New York: The Free Press.

—— (1992) 'Dangerous dyads: conditions affecting the likelihood of interstate war, 1816–1965', *Journal of Conflict Resolution* 36: 309–41.

Brockett, C. (1988) *Land, Power and Poverty: Agrarian Transformation and Political Conflict in Central America*, Boston, MA: Unwin Hyman.

Brown, C. (1981) 'Galtung and the Marxists on imperialism: answers vs. questions', *Millennium: Journal of International Studies* 10: 220–8.

Brown, R. (1965) *Social Psychology*, New York: The Free Press.

Brophy, I. (1945) 'The luxury of anti-negro prejudices', *Public Opinion Quarterly* 9: 456–66.

Brune, L. (1996) *The Missile Crisis of October 1962: A Review of Issues and References*, Claremont, CA: Regina Books.

Brzezinski, Z. (1997) *The Grand Chessboard: American Primacy and its Geostrategic Imperatives*, New York: Basic Books.

Buechler, S. (1999) *Social Movements in Advanced Capitalism*, Oxford: Oxford University Press.

Bueno de Mesquita, B. (1978) 'Systemic polarization and the occurrence and duration of war', *Journal of Conflict Resolution* 22: 241–67.

—— (1981) *The War Trap*, New Haven, CT: Yale University Press.

—— (1990) 'Pride of place: the origins of German hegemony', *World Politics* 43: 28–52.

Bueno de Mesquita, B. and Siverson, R. (1995) 'War and the survival of political leaders', *American Political Science Review* 89: 841–55.

Burkhalter, H. (1995) 'The question of genocide', *World Policy Journal* 11: 44–54.

Burton, J. and Dukes, F. (1990) *Conflict: Practices in Management Settlement and Resolution*, New York: St. Martin's Press.

Buzan, B. (1993) 'From international system to international society: structural realism and regime theory meet the English School', *International Organization* 47: 327–52.

Byrne, B. (1996) 'Towards a gendered understanding of conflict', *IDS Bulletin* 27: 31–40.

Callinicos, A. (2003) *An Anti-Capitalist Manifesto*, Cambridge: Polity.

—— (2004) *The New Mandarins of American Power*, Cambridge: Polity.

Calvin, J. (1949) *Institutes of the Christian Religion, Vol. I* (trans. John Allen), Grand Rapids, MI: Eerdmans.

Campbell, D. (1975) 'On the conflict between biological and social evolution and between psychology and moral tradition', *American Psychologist* 30: 1103–26.

—— (1998) *National Deconstruction: Violence, Identity, and Justice in Bosnia*, Minneapolis, MN: University of Minneapolis Press.

Cantril, H. (1965) *The Pattern of Human Concerns*, New Brunswick, NJ: Rutgers University Press.

Caprioli, M. (2000) 'Gendered conflict', *Journal of Peace Research* 37: 53–68.

Carroll, B. and Welling-Hall, B. (1993) 'Feminist perspectives on women and the use of force', in R. H. Howes and M. R. Stevenson (eds) *Women and the Use of Military Force*, Boulder, CO: Lynne Rienner.

Carter, W. (2001) *Matthew and Empire*, Harrisburg, PA: Trinity Press International.

Cater, C. (2003) 'The political economy of conflict and UN intervention: rethinking the critical cases of Africa', in K. Ballentine and J. Sherman (eds) *The Political Economy of Armed Conflict: Beyond Greed and Grievance*, Boulder, CO: Lynne Rienner.

Charnov, E. and Krebs, D. (1974) 'The evolution of alarm calls: altruism or manipulation?', *American Naturalist* 109: 107–12.

Chase-Dunn, C. and Grimes, P. (1995) 'World-systems analysis', *Annual Review of Sociology* 21: 387–417.

Chojnacki, S. (2006) 'Anything new or more of the same? Wars and military interventions in the international system, 1946–2003', *Global Society* 20: 25–46.

Chomsky, N. (1982) *Towards a New Cold War: Essays on the Current Crisis and How We Got There*, New York: Pantheon.

Chopp, R. (1986) *The Praxis of Suffering: An Interpretation of Liberation and Political Theologies*, Maryknoll, NY: Orbis Books.

Cilliers, J. (2000) 'Resource wars – a new type of insurgency', in J. Cilliers and C. Dietrich (eds) *Angola's War Economy: The Role of Oil and Diamonds*, Pretoria: Institute for Security Studies.

Císař, O. (2003) 'The transnationalisation of political conflict: beyond rationalism and constructivism', *Journal of International Relations and Development* 6: 6–22.

von Clausewitz, C. (1993) *On War* (trans. M. Howard and P. Paret), London: Everyman.

Cohn, I. and Goodwin-Gill, G. (1994) *Child Soldiers: The Role of Children in Armed Conflict*, Oxford: Clarendon Press.

Cohn, N. (1961). *The Pursuit of the Millennium: Revolutionary Millenarians and Mystical Anarchists of the Middle Ages*, Oxford: Oxford University Press.

Colaresi, M. (2001) 'Shocks to the system: Great Power rivalry and the leadership long cycle', *Journal of Conflict Resolution* 45: 569–93.

Coleman, J. (1990) *Foundations of Social Theory*, Cambridge, MA: Harvard University Press.

Collier, P. (2000a) 'Economic causes of civil conflict and their implications for policy', Washington, DC: The World Bank. Available online: http://www.worldbank.org/research/conflict/papers/civilconflict.pdf (accessed 24 January 2006).

—— (2000b) 'Doing well out of war: an economic perspective', in M. Berdal and D. Malone (eds) *Greed and Grievance: Economic Agendas in Civil Wars*, Boulder, CO: Lynne Rienner.

—— (2000c) 'Rebellion as a quasi-criminal activity', *Journal of Conflict Resolution* 44: 839–53.

—— (2001a) 'Economic causes of civil conflict and their implications for policy', in C. Crocker, F. O. Hampson and P. Aall (eds) *Turbulent Peace: The Challenges of Managing International Conflict*, Washington, DC: United States Institute of Peace.

—— (2001b) 'Ethnic diversity: an economic analysis of its implications', *Economic Policy* 32: 129–66.

—— (2007) *The Bottom Billion: Why the Poorest Countries are Failing and What Can Be Done about It*, Oxford: Oxford University Press.

Collier, P. and Hoeffler, A. (1998) 'On the economic causes of civil war', *Oxford Economic Papers* 50: 563–73.

—— (2001) 'Greed and grievance in civil war', Washington, DC: The World Bank. Available online: http://www.worldbank.org/research/conflict/papers/greedgrievance_23oct.pdf (accessed 25 January 2006).

Collier, P., Elliot, L., Hegre, H., Hoeffler, A., Reynal-Querol, M. and Sambanis, N. (2003) *Breaking the Conflict Trap: Civil War and Development Policy*, Washington, DC: The World Bank.

Congleton, R. (1995) 'Ethnic clubs, ethnic conflict, and the rise of ethnic nationalism', in A. Breton, G. Galeotti, P. Salmon and R. Wintrobe (eds) *Nationalism and Rationality*, Cambridge: Cambridge University Press.

Conover, P. J. and Shapiro, V. (1993) 'Gender, feminist consciousness, and war', *American Journal of Political Science* 37: 1079–99.

Cooley, A. and Ron, J. (2002) 'The NGO scramble: organizational insecurity and the political economy of transnational action', *International Security* 27: 5–39.

Cooper, N. (2005) 'Picking out the pieces of the liberal peaces: representations of conflict economies and the implications for policy', *Security Dialogue* 36: 463–78.

Cooper, R. (2002) 'The post-modern state', in M. Leonard (ed.) *Re-Ordering the World: The Long-Term Implications of September 11th*, London: The Foreign Policy Centre.

Cornford, J. (1974) 'The illusion of decision', *British Journal of Political Science* 4: 231–43.

Corning, P. (1971) 'The biological bases of behaviour and some implications for political science', *World Politics* 23: 321–70.

Corporate Engagement Project (2003) 'Issue paper: internal reward systems', Cambridge, MA: Collaborative For Development Action Inc. Available online: http://www.cdainc.com/publications/cep/issuepapers/cepIssuePaperRewards.pdf (accessed 26 December 2006).

Coser, L. (1956) *The Functions of Social Conflict*, New York: The Free Press.

Cotton, T. (1986) 'War and American democracy', *Journal of Conflict Resolution* 30: 616–35.

Cox, R. (1987) *Production, Power, and World Order: Social Forces in the Making of History*, New Haven, CT: Yale University Press.
—— (1996) *Approaches to World Order*, Cambridge: Cambridge University Press.
Cramer, C. (2002) 'Homo economicus goes to war: methodological individualism, rational choice and the political economy of war', *World Development* 30: 1845–64.
—— (2003) 'Does inequality cause conflict?', *Journal of International Development* 15: 397–412
Crawford, C. (1987) 'Sociobiology: of what value to psychology?', in C. Crawford, M. Smith and D. Krebs (eds) *Sociobiology and Psychology: Ideas, Issues and Applications*, Hillsdale, NJ: Erlbaum.
van Creveld, M. (2000a) 'A woman's place: reflections on the origins of violence', *Social Research* 67: 825–47.
—— (2000b) 'The great illusion: women in the military', *Millennium: Journal of International Studies* 29: 429–42.
Crooks, D. (1995) 'American children at risk: poverty and its consequences for children's health, growth and school achievement', *Yearbook of Physical Anthropology* 38: 57–86.
Cunningham, A., Jaffe, P., Baker, L., Dick, T., Malla, S., Mazaheri, N. and Poisson, S. (1998) *Theory-Derived Explanations of Male Violence against Female Partners: Literature Update and Related Implications for Treatment and Evaluation*, London: London Family Court Clinic.
Curle, A. (1971) *Making Peace*, London: Tavistock.
Cusak, T. (1995) 'On the theoretical deficit in the study of war', in S. Bremer and T. Cusak (eds) *The Process of War: Advancing the Scientific Study of War*, Amsterdam: Gordon and Breach.
Cyert, R. and March, J. (1992) *A Behavioural Theory of the Firm*, London: Blackwell.
Dahrendorf, R. (1959) *Class and Class Conflict in Industrial Society*, Stanford, CA: Stanford University Press.
Danilovic, V. (2002) *When the Stakes are High: Deterrence and Conflict among Major Powers*, Ann Arbor, MI: University of Michigan Press.
Darwin, C. (1859) *On the Origin of Species by Means of Natural Selection, or the Preservation of Favoured Races in the Struggle for Life*, London: Murray.
—— (1871) *The Descent of Man and Selection in Relation to Sex*, London: Murray.
David, P. and Wright, G. (1997) 'Increasing returns and the genesis of American resource abundance', *Industrial and Corporate Change* 6: 203–45.
David, S. (1997) 'Internal war: causes and cures', *World Politics* 49: 552–76.
Davies, J. C. (1962) 'Toward a theory of revolution', *American Sociological Review* 27: 5–18.
—— (1970) 'The J-curve of rising and declining satisfactions as a cause of some great revolutions and a contained rebellion', in H. Graham and T. Gurr (eds) *The History of Violence in America*, New York: Bantam Books.
—— (1980) 'Biological perspectives on human conflict', in T. Gurr (ed.) *Handbook of Political Conflict*, New York: The Free Press.
Defronzo, J. (1991) *Revolutions and Revolutionary Movements*, Boulder, CO: Westview Press.
Dehio, L. (1962) *The Precarious Balance: Four Centuries of the European Power Struggle*, 2nd edn, New York: Vintage Books.

Deininger, K. and Squire, L. (1998) 'New ways of looking at old issues: inequality and growth', *Journal of Development Economics* 57: 219–87.

Dencik, L. (1982) 'Peace research: pacification or revolution?', in G. Pardesi (ed.) *Contemporary Peace Research*, Brighton: Harvester.

van der Dennen, J. M. G. (2005) 'Aggression as learned behavior', University of Groningen Faculty of Law Working Papers. Available online: http://rechten. eldoc.ub.rug.nl/FILES/departments/Algemeen/DennenJMGvander/A-LEARN/ A-LEARN.pdf (accessed 13 July 2005).

Denitch, B. (1994) *The Tragic Death of Yugoslavia*, Minneapolis, MN: University of Minnesota Press.

Des Forges, A. (1999) *Leave None to tell the Story: Genocide in Rwanda*, New York: Human Rights Watch.

Deutsch, M. (1969) 'Conflict: productive and destructive', *Journal of Social Issues* 25: 7–42.

DiCicco, J. and Levy, J. (1999) 'Power shifts and problem shifts: the evolution of the power transition research program', *Journal of Conflict Resolution* 43: 675–704.

Diehl, P. (1983) 'Arms races and escalation: a closer look', *Journal of Peace Research* 20: 205–12.

Diehl, P. and Crescenzi, M. (1998) 'Reconfiguring the arms race–war debate', *Journal of Peace Research* 35: 111–18.

Diehl, P. and Kingston, J. (1987) 'Messenger or message? Military build-ups and the initiation of conflict', *The Journal of Politics* 49: 801–13.

Diffie, B. and Winius, G. (1977) *Foundations of the Portuguese Empire 1415–1580*, Minneapolis, MN: University of Minnesota Press.

Dion, K. (1986) 'Responses to perceived discrimination and relative deprivation', in J. Olson, C. Herman and M. Zanna (eds) *Relative Deprivation and Social Comparison: The Ontario Symposium*, Hillsdale, NJ: Erlbaum.

Dixon, D. (2005) *Never Come to Peace Again: Pontiac's Uprising and the Fate of the British Empire in North America*, Norman, OK: University of Oklahoma Press.

Dobash, R, Dobash, R., Cavanagh, K. and Lewis, J. (1996) *Research Evaluation of Programmes for Violent Men*, Edinburgh: The Scottish Office.

Dollard, J., Miller, N. Doob, L., Mowrer, O. and Sears, R. (1939) *Frustration and Aggression*, London: Kegan Paul, Trench, Trubner and Co.

Doran, C. (1989a) 'Power cycle theory of systems structure and stability: commonalities and complementarities', in M. Midlarsky (ed.) *Handbook of War Studies*, Boston, MA: Unwin Hyman.

—— (1989b) 'Systemic disequilibrium, foreign policy role, and the power cycle', *Journal of Conflict Resolution* 33: 371–401.

—— (2003) 'Economics, philosophy of history, and the "single dynamic" of power cycle theory: expectations, competition, and statecraft', *International Political Science Review* 24: 13–49.

Doran, C. and Parsons, W. (1980) 'War and the cycle of relative power', *American Political Science Review* 74: 947–65.

Dos Santos, T. (1970) 'The structure of dependence', *American Economic Review* 60: 235–46.

Downs, G. and Rocke, D. (1995) *Optimal Imperfection? Domestic Uncertainty and Institutions in International Relations*, Princeton, NJ: Princeton University Press.

Duckitt, J. (2000) 'Culture, personality and prejudice', in S. Renshon and J. Duckitt, (eds) *Political Psychology: Cultural and Crosscultural Foundations*, London: Macmillan.

Duffield, M. (1998a) 'Post-modern conflict: warlords, post-adjustment states and private protection', *Civil Wars* 1: 65–102.

—— (1998b) 'The symphony of the damned: racial discourse, complex political emergencies and humanitarian aid', *Disasters* 20: 173–93.

—— (1999) 'Globalization and war economies: promoting order or the return of history?', *Fletcher Forum of World Affairs* 23: 21–38.

—— (2000) 'Globalization, transborder trade, and war economies', in M. Berdal and D. Malone (eds) *Greed and Grievance: Economic Agendas in Civil Wars*, Boulder, CO: Lynne Rienner.

—— (2001) *Global Governance and the New Wars: The Merging of Development and Security*, London: Zed.

Duncan, B. (2003) 'The struggle to develop a just war tradition in the West', Melbourne: Yarra Theological Union. Available online: http://www.socialjustice. catholic.org.au/Content/pdf/the_struggle_to_develop_a_just_war_tradition_in_ the_west.pdf (accessed 28 November 2006).

Dunn, D. (1978) 'Peace research', in T. Taylor (ed.) *Approaches and Theory in International Relations*, London: Longman.

Durakovic, A. (2003) 'Health consequences of radiological warfare', Paper presented to the House of Councillors, Tokyo, November.

Durant, W. (1980) *The Story of Civilization, Vol. 4: The Age of Faith*, New York: Simon and Schuster.

Dworkin, A. (1981) *Pornography. Men Possessing Women*, London: The Women's Press.

Dyer, G. (1985) *War*, London: Guild Publishing.

East, M. (1973) 'Size and foreign policy behavior: a test of two models', *World Politics* 25: 556–76.

East, M. and Hermann, C. (1974) 'Do nation-types account for foreign policy behavior?', in J. Rosenau (ed.) *Comparing Foreign Policies: Theories, Findings and Methods*, New York: John Wiley.

Eckhardt, W. and Young, C. (1974) 'Civil conflict, imperialism and inequality', *Journal of Contemporary Revolution* 6: 76–95.

Eckstein, H. (1980) 'Theoretical approaches to explaining collective violence', in T. Gurr (ed.) *Handbook of Political Conflict*, New York: The Free Press.

Ehrenreich, B. (1997) *Blood Rites: Origins and History of the Passions of War*, New York: Metropolitan.

Eibl-Eibesfeldt, I. and Wickler, W. (1968) 'Ethology', in D. Sills (ed.) *International Encyclopaedia of the Social Sciences, Vol. IV*, New York: The Free Press.

Eisinger, P. (1973) 'The conditions of protest behavior in American cities', *American Political Science Review* 68: 11–28.

Eitzen, E. and Takafuji, E. (1997) 'Historical overview of biological warfare', in R. Zajtchuk (ed.) *Medical Aspects of Chemical and Biological Warfare*, Washington, DC: Office of The Surgeon General.

Eklund, K. (1980) 'Long waves in the development of capitalism?', *Kyklos* 33: 383–419.

Ellina, M. and Moore, W. (1990) 'Discrimination and political violence: a cross-national study with two time periods', *Western Political Quarterly* 43: 267–78.

Ellis, J. (1993) *World War II: A Statistical Survey*, New York: Facts on File.

Elshtain, J. B. (1985) 'Reflections on war and political discourse: realism, just war and feminism in a nuclear age', *Political Theory* 13: 39–57.

—— (2000) 'Shooting at the wrong target: a response to van Creveld', *Millennium: Journal of International Studies* 29: 443–8.

Enloe, C. (1988) *Does Khaki Become You? The Militarization of Women's Lives*, 2nd edn, London: Pandora Press.

—— (2000) *Manoeuvres: The International Politics of Militarizing Women's Lives*, Berkeley, CA: University of California Press.

Erickson, J. (1999) *The Road to Stalingrad: Stalin's War with Germany, Vol. I*, New Haven, CT: Yale University Press.

Eron, L., Gentry, J. and Schlegel, P. (eds) (1994) *Reason to Hope: A Psychosocial Perspective on Violence and Youth*, Washington, DC: American Psychological Association.

Esteban, J.-M. and Ray, D. (1994) 'On the measurement of polarization', *Econometrica* 62: 819–51.

Etounga-Manguelle, D. (2000) 'Does Africa need a cultural adjustment program?', in L. Harrison and S. Huntington (eds) *Culture Matters: How Values Shape Human Progress*, New York: Basic Books.

Etzioni, A. (1968) *The Active Society*, New York: The Free Press.

van Evera, S. (1994) 'Hypotheses on nationalism and war', *International Security* 18: 5–39.

—— (1999) *Causes of War: Structures of Power and the Roots of International Conflict*, Ithaca, NY: Cornell University Press.

Everitt, A. (2001) *Cicero: The Life and Times of Rome's Greatest Politician*, New York: Random House.

Farmer, P. (1996) 'On suffering and structural violence: a view from below', *Daedalus* 125: 261–83.

—— (2003) *Pathologies of Power: Health, Human Rights, and the New War on the Poor*, Berkeley, CA: University of California Press.

Fearon, J. and Laitin, D. (2000) 'Violence and the social construction of ethnic identity', *International Organization* 54: 845–77.

—— (2003) 'Ethnicity, insurgency, and civil war', *American Political Science Review* 97: 75–91.

Feierabend, I. and Feierabend, R. (1966) 'Aggressive behaviors within polities 1948–1962: a cross-national study', *Journal of Conflict Resolution* 10: 249–71.

—— (1972) 'Systemic conditions of political aggression: an application of frustration–aggression theory', in I. Feierabend, R. Feierabend and T. Gurr (eds) *Anger, Violence, and Politics: Theories and Research*, Englewood Cliffs, NJ: Prentice-Hall.

Feierabend, I. Nesvold, B. and Feierabend, R. (1970) 'Political coerciveness and turmoil', *Law and Society Review* 5: 93–118.

Feierabend, I., Feierabend, R. and Nesvold, B. (1973) 'The comparative study of revolution and violence', *Comparative Politics* 5: 393–424.

Felson, R. (1996) 'Mass media effects on violent behaviour', *Annual Review of Sociology* 22: 103–28.

Ferguson, R. B. (1989) 'Anthropology and war', in P. Turner and D. Pitt (eds) *The Anthropology of War and Peace: Perspectives on the Nuclear Age*, Granby, MA: Bergin and Garvey.

—— (1990) 'Explaining war', in J. Hass (ed.) *The Anthropology of War*, Cambridge: Cambridge University Press.

Ferguson, Y. and Mansbach, R. (1996) *Politics, Authority, Identities, and Change*, Columbia, SC: University of South Carolina Press.

Ferrell, V. (1996) *The Wonders of Nature, Vol. II*, Altamont, TN: Harvestime Books.

Feshbach, S. (1964) 'The function of aggression and the regulation of aggressive drive', *Psychological Review* 71: 257–72.

Fine, B. (2001) 'Economics imperialism and intellectual progress: the present as history of economic thought?', *History of Economics Review* 32: 10–36.

Finkel, S., Muller, E. and Opp, K.-D. (1989) 'Personal influence, collective rationality, and mass political action', *American Political Science Review* 83: 885–903.

Finney, P. (2002) 'On memory, identity and war', *Rethinking History* 6: 1–13.

Fischer, F. (1975) *War of Illusions: German Policies from 1911 to 1914*, New York: Norton.

Fleming, D. (1969) 'On living in a biological revolution', *Atlantic* 223: 64–70.

Floud, R., Wachter, K. and Gregory, A. (1990) *Height, Health and History: Nutritional Status in the United Kingdom, 1750–1980*, Cambridge: Cambridge University Press.

Foreman, R. (1963) 'Resignation as a collective behaviour response', *American Journal of Sociology* 69: 285–90.

Fowler A. (1995) 'Assessing NGO performance: difficulties, dilemmas and a way ahead', in M. Edwards and D. Hulme (eds) *Non-Governmental Organisation: Performance and Accountability – Beyond the Magic Bullet*, London: Earthscan.

Fox, C. and Boulton, M. J. (2003) 'Evaluating the effectiveness of a social skills training (SST) programme for victims of bullying', *Educational Research* 45: 231–47.

Fox, F. (2001) 'New humanitarianism: does it provide a moral banner for the 21st century?', *Disasters* 25: 275–89.

Frank, R. (1985) *Choosing the Right Pond: Human Behaviour and the Search for Status*, Oxford: Oxford University Press.

Freedman, J., Levy, A., Buchanan, R. and Price, J. (1972) 'Crowding and human aggression', *Journal of Experimental Social Psychology* 8: 528–48.

Freeman, J. (1979) 'Resource mobilization and strategy', in M. Zald and J. McCarthy (eds) *The Dynamics of Social Movements: Resource Mobilization, Social Control and Tactics*, Cambridge, MA: Winthrop.

Frost, M. (2004) 'Ethics and war: beyond just war theory', Paper presented to Fifth Pan-European International Relations Conference, The Hague, September 2004. Available online: http://www.sgir.org/conference2004/papers/Frost%20-%20Ethics%20and%20War%20Beyond%20Just%20War%20Theory.pdf (accessed 26 November 2006).

Fukuyama, F. (1998) 'Women and the evolution of world politics', *Foreign Affairs* 77: 24–40.

Fuller, J. (1992) *The Conduct of War 1789–1961: A Study of the Impact of the French, Industrial, and Russian Revolutions on War and its Conduct*, Cambridge, MA: Da Capo Press.

Gagnon, V. (1995) 'Ethnic nationalism and international conflict: the case of Serbia', *International Security* 19: 130–66.

Galtung, J. (1969) 'Violence, peace, and peace research', *Journal of Peace Research* 6: 167–91.

—— (1971) 'A structural theory of imperialism', *Journal of Peace Research* 8: 81–117.

—— (1975) *Essays in Peace Research, Vol. I*, Copenhagen: Christian Ejlers.

—— (1980) 'A structural theory of imperialism – ten years later', *Millennium: Journal of International Studies* 9: 181–96.

—— (1990) 'Cultural violence', *Journal of Peace Research* 27: 291–305.

Galtung, J. and Høivik, T. (1971) 'Structural and direct violence: a note on operationalization', *Journal of Peace Research* 8: 73–6.

Galtung, J., Guha, A., Wirak, A., Sjlie, S., Cifuentes, M. and Goldstein, H. (1975) 'Measuring world development', *Alternatives* 1: 131–58.

Gamba, V. and Cornwell, R. (2000) 'Arms, elites, and resources in the Angolan civil war', in M. Berdal and D. Malone (eds) *Greed and Grievance: Economic Agendas in Civil Wars*, Boulder, CO: Lynne Rienner.

Gamson, W. (1975) *The Strategy of Social Protest*, Homewood, IL: Dorsey.

Garver, N. (1968) 'What violence is', *The Nation* 209: 819–22.

Gates, S. (2002) 'Recruitment and allegiance: the microfoundations of rebellion', *Journal of Conflict Resolution* 46: 111–30.

Gati, C. (1992) 'From Sarajevo to Sarajevo', *Foreign Affairs* 71: 64–78.

Geller, D. (1992) 'Power transition and conflict initiation', *Conflict Management and Peace Science* 12: 1–16.

—— (1996) 'Relative power, rationality, and international conflict', in J. Kugler and D. Lemke (eds) *Parity and war: Evaluations and Extensions of "The War Ledger"*, Ann Arbor MI: University of Michigan Press.

—— (2000) 'Material capabilities: power and international conflict', in J. Vasquez (ed.) *What Do We Know about War?*, Lanham, MD: Rowman and Littlefield.

Geller, D. and Singer, J. D. (1998) *Nations at War: A Scientific Study of International Conflict*, Cambridge: Cambridge University Press.

Gelpi, C. (1997) 'Democratic diversions – governmental structure and the externalization of domestic conflict', *Journal of Conflict Resolution* 41: 255–82.

George, A. (1971) 'Primary groups, organizations, and military performance', in R. Little (ed.) *Handbook of Military Institutions*, Beverly Hills, CA: Sage.

—— (1984) 'Crisis management: the interaction of political and military considerations', *Survival* 26: 223–34.

Giddens, A. (1984) *The Constitution of Society*, Cambridge: Polity.

Gilbert, M. (1994) *The First World War: A Complete History*, New York: Henry Holt.

Giles, L. (1910) *Sun Tzu the Art of War: The Oldest Military Treatise in the World*. Available online: http://www.geocities.com/tijeloum/virtualbook/suntzu.pdf (accessed 3 April 2006).

Gilligan, C. (1993) *In a Different Voice: Psychological Theory and Women's Development*, Cambridge, MA: Harvard University Press.

Gilpin, R. (1981) *War and Change in World Politics*, Cambridge: Cambridge University Press.

Gissinger, R. and Gleditsch, N. P. (1999) 'Globalization and conflict: welfare distribution, and political unrest', *Journal of World-Systems Research* 5: 327–65.

Gochman, C. and Leng, R. (1983) 'Realpolitik and the road to war: an analysis of attributes and behavior', *International Studies Quarterly* 27: 97–120.

Goldsmith, R. (1946) 'The power of victory: munitions output in World War II', *Military Affairs* 10: 69–80.

Goldstein, J. H. (1989) 'Beliefs about human aggression', in J. Groebel and R. Hinde (eds) *Aggression and War: Their Biological and Social Bases*, Cambridge: Cambridge University Press.

Goldstein, J. S. (1988) *Long Cycles: Prosperity and War in the Modern Age*, New Haven, CT: Yale University Press.

—— (2001) *War and Gender: How Gender Shapes the War System and Vice Versa*, Cambridge: Cambridge University Press.

Goldstein, J. S. and Rapkin, D. (1991) 'After insularity: hegemony and the future world order', *Futures* 23: 935–59.

Goldstein, M. (1984) 'The war between Iran and Iraq', *Middle East Review* 17: 41–9.

Goldstone, J. (1994) 'Is revolution individually rational? Groups and individuals in revolutionary collective action', *Rationality and Society* 6: 139–66.

Goodhand, J. (2001) 'Violent conflict, poverty and chronic poverty', Manchester: Chronic Poverty Research Centre Working Paper Number 6. Available online: http://www.chronicpoverty.org/pdfs/06Goodhand.pdf (accessed 27 January 2006).

—— (2003) 'Enduring disorder and persistent poverty: a review of the linkages between war and chromic poverty', *World Development* 31: 629–46.

Goodhand, J. and Atkinson, P. (2001) *Conflict and Aid: Enhancing the Peacebuilding Impact of International Engagement – a Synthesis of Findings from Afghanistan, Liberia and Sri Lanka*, London: International Alert.

Gottschalk, P. and Smeeding, T. (2000) 'Empirical evidence on income inequality in industrialized countries', in A. Atkinson and F. Bourguignon (eds) *Handbook of Income Distribution*, Amsterdam: North-Holland.

Gould, S. (1981) *The Mismeasure of Man*, New York: Norton.

Gourevitch, P. (1998) *We Wish to Inform You That Tomorrow We Will Be Killed with Our Families: Stories from Rwanda*, New York: Farrar, Straus and Giroux.

Gray, C. (1976) *The Soviet–American Arms Race*, Farnborough: Saxon House.

—— (1981) *The MX ICBM and National Security*, New York: Praeger.

—— (1999) *Modern Strategy*, Oxford: Oxford University Press.

Green, D. and Shapiro, I. (1994) *Pathologies of Rational Choice Theory: A Critique of Applications in Political Science*, New Haven, CT: Yale University Press.

Griffin, K. and Gurley, J. (1985) 'Radical analysis of imperialism, the Third World, and the transition to socialism: a survey article', *Journal of Economic Literature* 23: 1089–143.

Grimmett, R. (2001) *Conventional Arms Transfers to Developing Nations, 1993–2000*, Washington, DC: Congressional Research Service.

Groom, A. J. R. (1988) 'Paradigms in conflict: the strategist, the conflict researcher and the peace researcher', *Review of International Studies* 14: 97–115.

—— (1992) 'Approaches to conflict and cooperation in international relations: lessons from theory for practice', Canterbury: University of Kent. Available online: http://www.ukc.uk/politics/publications/journals/kentpapers/groom1.html (accessed 28 November 2006).

Grossman, D. (1996) *On Killing: The Psychological Cost of Learning to Kill in War and Society*, Boston, MA: Little, Brown and Co.

Grossman, H. (1991) 'A general equilibrium model of insurrections', *American Economic Review* 81: 912–21.

Grummon, S. (1982) *The Iran–Iraq War: Islam Embattled*, New York: Praeger.

Guáqueta, A. (2003) 'The Colombian conflict: political and economic dimensions', in K. Ballentine and J. Sherman (eds) *The Political Economy of Armed Conflict: Beyond Greed and Grievance*, Boulder, CO: Lynne Rienner.

Guhl, A., Craig, J. and Mueller, C. (1960) 'Selectiveness breeding for aggressiveness in chickens', *Poultry Science* 39: 970–80.

Gulick, E. (1955) *Europe's Classic Balance of Power*, Ithaca, NY: Cornell University Press.

Gurney, J. and Tierney, K. (1982) 'Relative deprivation and social movements: a critical look at twenty years of theory and research', *The Sociological Quarterly* 23: 33–47.

Gurr, T. (1968) 'Psychological factors in civil violence', *World Politics* 20: 245–78.

—— (1973) 'The revolution–social-change nexus: some old theories and new hypotheses', *Comparative Politics* 5: 359–92.

—— (1974) *Why Men Rebel*, 4th edn, Princeton, NJ: Princeton University Press.

—— (1994) 'Peoples against states: ethnopolitical conflict and the changing world system', *International Studies Quarterly* 38: 347–78.

Gurr, T. and Goldstone, J. (1991) 'Comparisons and policy implications', in J. Goldstone, T. Gurr and F. Moshiri (eds) *Revolutions of the Late Twentieth Century*, Boulder, CO: Westview Press.

Haas, E. (1961) 'International integration: the European and the universal process', *International Organization* 15: 366–92.

Haber, L. (1986) *The Poisonous Cloud: Chemical Warfare in the First World War*, Oxford: Oxford University Press.

Habermas, J. (1971) *Toward a Rational Society: Student Protest, Science and Politics* (trans. J. Shapiro), London: Heinemann.

Hables Gray, C. (1997) *Postmodern War: The New Politics of Conflict*, London: Routledge.

Hall, R. (1999) *National Collective Identity: Social Constructs and International Systems*, New York: Columbia University Press.

Hamilton, W. (1964) 'The genetic evolution of social behaviour: I and II', *Journal of Theoretical Biology* 7: 1–52.

Harbom, L. and Wallensteen, P. (2005) 'Armed conflict and its international dimensions, 1946–2004', *Journal of Peace Research* 42: 623–35.

Hardin, R. (1995) *One for All: The Logic of Group Conflict*, Princeton, NJ: Princeton University Press.

Harlow, H. and Harlow, C. (eds) (1986) *From Learning to Love: The Selected Papers of H. F. Harlow*, New York: Praeger.

Harrington, E. (2004) 'The social psychology of hatred', *Journal of Hate Studies* 3: 49–82.

Harrison, L. (2000) 'Promoting progressive cultural change', in L. Harrison and S. Huntington (eds) *Culture Matters: How Values Shape Human Progress*, New York: Basic Books.

Hart, N. (1994) 'John Goldthorpe and the relics of sociology', *British Journal of Sociology* 45: 21–30.

Hartup, W. (1983) 'Peer relations', in P. Mussen and E. M. Hetherington (eds) *Handbook of Child Psychology, Vol. IV: Socialization, Personality, and Social Development*, New York: Wiley.

Hastings, M. and Jenkins, S. (1984) *The Battle for the Falklands*, London: Norton.

Havighurst, A. (1979) *Britain in Transition: The Twentieth Century*, Chicago, IL: University of Chicago Press.

von Hayek, F. (1991) *The Fatal Conceit: The Errors of Socialism* (ed. W. Bartley), Chicago, IL: University of Chicago Press.

Hechter, M. (1987) *Principles of Group Solidarity*, Berkeley, CA: University of California Press.

Hegre, H., Ellingsen, T., Gates, S. and Gleditsch, N. P. (2001) 'Toward a democratic civil peace? Democracy, political change, and civil war', *American Political Science Review* 95: 33–48.

Held, D., Goldblatt, D., McGrew, A. and Perraton, J. (1997) 'The globalisation of economic activity', *New Political Economy* 2: 257–77.

Hensel, P. (2000) 'Territory: theory and evidence on geography and conflict', in J. Vasquez (ed.) *What Do We Know about War?*, Lanham, MD: Rowman and Littlefield.

Hensel, P. and McLaughlin, S. (1997) 'Power transitions and dispute escalation in evolving interstate rivalries', Department of Political Science, Florida State University. Available online: http://garnet.acns.fsu.edu/~phensel/Research/apsa96.pdf (accessed 18 March 2006).

Herbst, J. (2000a) 'Economic incentives, natural resources and conflict in Africa', *Journal of African Economies* 9: 270–94.

—— (2000b) *States and Power in Africa: Comparative Lessons in Authority and Control*, Princeton, NJ: Princeton University Press.

Herek, G., Janis, I. and Huth, P. (1987) 'Decision making during international crises: is quality of process related to outcome?', *Journal of Conflict Resolution* 31: 203–26.

Hibbs, D. (1973) *Mass Political Violence*, New York: Wiley.

Hilsman, R. (1959) 'The foreign-policy consensus: an interim report', *Journal of Conflict Resolution* 3: 361–82.

—— (1967) *To Move a Nation: The Politics of Foreign Policy in the Administration of John F. Kennedy*, Garden City, NJ: Doubleday.

Hinde, R. (1993) 'Aggression and war: individuals, groups and states', in P. Tetlock, J. Husbands and R. Jervis (eds) *Behaviour, Society and International Conflict, Vol. III*, Oxford: Oxford University Press.

Hobsbawm, E. (1990) *Nations and Nationalism since 1780*, Cambridge: Cambridge University Press.

—— (1997) *On History*, London: Abacus.

Hoffman, M. (1987) 'Critical theory and the inter-paradigm debate', *Millennium: Journal of International Studies* 16: 231–49.

Hogenraad, R. (2005) 'What the words of war can tell us about the risk of war', *Peace and Conflict: Journal of Peace Psychology* 11: 137–51.

Høivik, T. (1977) 'The demography of structural violence', *Journal of Peace Research* 14: 59–73.

Holbrooke, R. (1999) *To End a War*, New York: Modern Library.

Holmes, R. (1985) *Acts of War: The Behavior of Men in Battle*, New York: The Free Press.

Holsti, K. (1985) 'The necrologists of international relations', *Canadian Journal of Political Science* 18: 675–95.

—— (1991) *Peace and War: Armed Conflicts and International Order 1648–1989*, Cambridge: Cambridge University Press.

—— (1999) 'The coming chaos? Armed conflict in the world's periphery', in T. Paul and J. Hall (eds) *International Order and the Future of World Politics*, Cambridge: Cambridge University Press.

—— (2000) 'Political causes of humanitarian emergencies', in E. Nafziger, F. Stewart and R. Väyrynen (eds) *War, Hunger and Displacement: The Origins of Humanitarian Emergencies*, Oxford: Oxford University Press.

Holsti, O. (1972) 'Book review: *Essence of Decision: Explaining the Cuban Missile Crisis*, by Graham Allison (Boston, MA: Little Brown)', *Western Political Quarterly* 25: 136–40.

Holsti, O. and George, A. (1975) 'The effects of stress on the performance of foreign policy-makers', in C. Cotter (ed.) *Political Science Annual, Vol. VI*, Indianapolis, IN: Bobbs-Merrill.

Holsti, O., North, R. and Brody, R. (1968) 'Perception and action in the 1914 crisis', in J. D. Singer (ed.) *Quantitative International Politics*, New York: The Free Press.

Hopf, T. (1998) 'The promise of constructivism in international relations theory', *International Security* 23: 171–200.

Hopmann, P. T. (1967) 'International conflict and cohesion in the communist system', *International Studies Quarterly* 17: 212–36.

Horelick, A. (1964) 'The Cuban Missile Crisis: an analysis of Soviet calculations and behavior', *World Politics* 16: 363–89.

Horkheimer, M. (1972) *Critical Theory*, New York: Herder and Herder.

Hough, R., Kelly, J., Miller, S., Derossier, R., Mann, F. and Seligson, M. (1982) 'Land and labor in Guatemala: an assessment', Washington, DC: USAID. Available online: http://sitemason.vanderbilt.edu/files/jE1LYA/Land%20and%20Labor%20in%20Guatemala%20An%20Assessment.pdf (accessed 9 December 2005).

Houweling, H. and Siccama, J. (1981) 'The arms race–war relationship: why serious disputes matter', *Arms Control* 2: 157–97.

—— (1988) 'Power transitions as a cause of war', *Journal of Conflict Resolution* 32: 87–102.

Hudson, K. (2005) *CND – Now More than Ever: The Story of a Peace Movement*, London: Vision.

Human Rights Watch (1995) *Playing the 'Communal Card': Communal Violence and Human Rights*, New York: Human Rights Watch.

Humphreys, M. (2005) 'Natural resources, conflict, and conflict resolution: uncovering the mechanisms', *Journal of Conflict Resolution* 49: 508–37.

Huntington, S. (1961) *The Common Defense: Strategic Programs in National Politics*, New York: Columbia University Press.

—— (1968) *Political Order in Changing Societies*, New Haven, CT: Yale University Press.

—— (1986) 'Playing to win', *The National Interest* 2: 8–16.

—— (1993) 'The clash of civilizations?', *Foreign Affairs* 72: 22–49.

—— (1996) *The Clash of Civilizations and the Remaking of World Order*, New York: Simon and Schuster.

Hussain, J. (2003) *Islam: Its Law and Society*, 2nd edn, Annandale, NSW: Federation Press.

Hutchinson, E. (1965) *The Ecological Theatre and the Evolutionary Play*, New Haven, CT: Yale University Press.

Huth, P. (2000) 'Territory: why are territorial disputes between states a central cause of international conflict', in J. Vasquez (ed.) *What Do We Know about War?*, Lanham, MD: Rowman and Littlefield.

Huth, P. and Russett, B. (1988) 'Deterrence failure and crisis escalation', *International Studies Quarterly* 32: 29–45.

—— (1993) 'General deterrence between enduring rivals: testing three competing models', *American Political Science Review* 87: 61–73.

Ignatieff, M. (1998) *The Warrior's Honour: Ethnic War and the Modern Conscience*, London: Chatto and Windus.

—— (1999) 'The International Committee of the Red Cross', in R. Gutman and D. Rieff (eds) *Crimes of War: What People Should Know*, New York: Norton.

Iklé, F. (2005) *Every War Must End*, New York: Columbia University Press.

International Fund for Agricultural Development (1992) *Report and Recommendations to the Executive Board on a Proposed Loan to the Rwandese Republic for the Byumba Agricultural Development Project – Phase II*, Rome: International Fund for Agricultural Development.

Ingram, D. (1987) *Habermas and the Dialectic of Reason*, New Haven, CT: Yale University Press.

Ismael, Y. (1982) *Iraq and Iran: Roots of Conflict*, Syracuse, NY: Syracuse University Press.

Jabri, V. (1996) *Discourse on Violence: Conflict Analysis Reconsidered*, Manchester: Manchester University Press.

Jackson, L. and Johnson, W. (1974) *Protest by the Poor*, Lexington, MA: Heath.

Jacobs, D. and O'Brien, R. (1998) 'The determinants of deadly force: a structural analysis of police violence', *American Journal of Sociology* 103: 837–62.

Jacobs, P., Brunton, M., Melville, M., Britain, R. and McClemont, W. (1965) 'Aggressive behaviour, mental sub-normality and the XYY male', *Nature* 208: 1351–2.

Jacobsen, T. (1970) *Towards the Image of Tammuz and other Essays in Mesopotamian History and Culture*, Cambridge, MA: Harvard University Press.

Jacoby, T. (2004a) 'Method, narrative and historiography in Michael Mann's sociology of state development', *The Sociological Review* 52: 404–21.

—— (2004b) 'Nietzsche, historiography and Yugoslav nationalism', *Politics* 24: 65–71.

—— (2005) 'Cultural determinism, western hegemony and the efficacy of defective states', *Review of African Political Economy* 105: 215–33.

Jaggers, K. and Gurr, T. (1995) 'Tracking democracy's third wave with the Polity III data', *Journal of Peace Research* 32: 469–82.

James, K. (1996) 'Truth or fiction: men as victims of domestic assault', *Australian and New Zealand Journal of Family Therapy* 19: 121–5.

James, P. and Oneal, J. (1991) 'The influence of domestic and international politics on the president's use of force', *Journal of Conflict Resolution* 35: 307–32.

Janis, I. (1989) *Crucial Decisions: Leadership in Policy Making and Crisis*, New York: The Free Press.

Janis, I. and Mann, L. (1977) *Decision Making: A Psychological Analysis of Conflict, Choice and Commitment*, New York: The Free Press.

Jaspers, W. (2005) 'Sudden death? Conflict de-escalation as government strategy in Nigeria's Niger Delta region', Universiteit Utrecht. Available online: http://asterix.library.uu.nl/files/scrol/d1/r199/W.Jaspers_0060720_scriptie.doc (accessed 16 February 2006).

Jenkins, J. C. (1983) 'Resource mobilization theory and the study of social movements', *Annual Review of Sociology* 9: 527–53.

Jenkins, J. C. and Perrow, C. (1977) 'Insurgency of the powerless: farm worker movements', *American Sociological Review* 42: 249–68.

Jeong, H. W. (2000) *Peace and Conflict Studies: An Introduction*, Aldershot: Ashgate.

Jervis, R. (1969) 'Hypotheses on misconception', in J. Rosenau (ed.) *International Politics and Foreign Policy: A Reader in Research and Theory*, New York: The Free Press.

—— (1976) *Perception and Misperception in International Politics*, Princeton, NJ: Princeton University Press.

—— (1978) 'Cooperation under the security dilemma', *World Politics* 30: 167–214.

—— (1988) 'War and misperception', *Journal of Interdisciplinary History* 18: 675–700.

Johnson, J. (1987) *The Quest for Peace: Three Moral Traditions in Western Cultural History*, Princeton, NJ: Princeton University Press.

Johnston, A. (1995) 'Thinking about strategic culture', *International Security* 19: 32–64.

Jolly, A. (1985) *The Evolution of Primate Behaviour*, Basingstoke: Macmillan.

Jones, D. (1990) 'Soviet strategic culture', in C. Jacobsen (ed.) *Strategic Power: USA/USSR*, Basingstoke: Macmillan.

Jones, D. E. (1997) *Women Warriors: A History*, Washington, DC: Brassey's.

Jones, G. (1980) *Social Darwinism and English Thought: The Interaction between Biological and Social Theory*, Brighton: Harvester.

Jones, H. (1915) 'Philosophical landmarks: being a survey of the recent gains and the present problems of reflective thought', *The Rice Institute Pamphlet* 1: 195–255.

Joshi, V. (2002) 'The "private" becomes the "public": wives as denouncers in the Third Reich', *Journal of Contemporary History* 37: 419–35.

Judah, T. (1997) 'The Serbs: the sweet and rotten smell of history', *Daedalus* 126: 23–45.

Juglar, C. (1966) *A Brief History of Panics and their Periodical Occurrence in the United States*, 3rd edn (trans. D. Thom), New York: A. W. Kelly.

Jung, D. (2003) 'Towards global civil war?', in D. Jung (ed.) *Shadow Globalization, Ethnic Conflicts and New Wars: A Political Economy of Intra-State War*, London: Routledge.

Kaldor, M. (1990) *The Imaginary War: Understanding the East–West Conflict*, London: Blackwell.

—— (1999) *New and Old Wars: Organised Violence in a Global Era*, Cambridge: Polity.

—— (2001) 'Wanted: global politics', *The Nation*, 5 November. Available online: http://www.thenation.com/doc/20011105/kaldor/2 (accessed 8 April 2006).

Kalimtzis, K. (2000) *Aristotle on Political Enmity and Disease. An Inquiry into Stasis*, Albany, NY: State University of New York Press.

Kalyvas, S. (1999) 'Wanton and senseless? The logic of massacres in Algeria', *Rationality and Society* 11: 243–85.

—— (2006) *The Logic of Violence in Civil War*, Cambridge: Cambridge University Press.

Kapferer, B. (1988) *Legends of People/Myths of State: Violence, Intolerance, and Po-

litical Culture in Sri Lanka and Australia, Washington, DC: Smithsonian Institution Press.

Kaplan, M. (1957) *System and Process in International Politics*, New York: John Wiley.

Kaplan, R. (1991) 'History's cauldron', *Atlantic Monthly* 267: 93–104.

—— (1993) *Balkan Ghosts: A Journey through History*, New York: Random House.

—— (1994) 'The coming anarchy: how scarcity, crime, overpopulation and disease are rapidly destroying the social fabric of our planet', *Atlantic Monthly* 273: 44–76.

—— (2000) *The Coming of Anarchy: Shattering the Dreams of the Post Cold War*, New York: Random House.

Kaufmann, C. (1994) 'Out of the lab and into the archives: a method for testing psychological explanation of political decision making', *International Studies Quarterly* 38: 557–86.

Kaye, H. (1997) *The Social Meaning of Modern Biology: From Social Darwinism to Sociobiology*, New Brunswick, NJ: Transaction.

Keen, D. (1997) 'A rational kind of madness', *Oxford Development Studies* 25: 67–76.

—— (1998) 'The economic functions of violence in civil wars', *Adelphi Paper* 320, Oxford: Oxford University Press.

—— (2000a) 'War, crime and access to resources', in E. Nafziger, F. Stewart and R. Väyrynen (eds) *War, Hunger and Displacement: The Origins of Humanitarian Emergencies*, Oxford: Oxford University Press.

—— (2000b) 'Incentives and disincentives for violence', in M. Berdal and D. Malone (eds) *Greed and Grievance: Economic Agendas in Civil Wars*, Boulder, CO: Lynne Rienner.

Kegley, C. (1991) 'Explaining Great-Power peace: the sources of prolonged postwar stability', in C. Kegley (ed.) *The Long Postwar Peace: Contending Explanations and Projections*, New York: Harper Collins.

Kellaghan, T. (1994) 'Family and schooling', in T. Husen and T. Postlewaite (eds) *The International Encyclopaedia of Education*, Tarrytown, NY: Elsevier.

Kellett, A. (1990) 'The soldier in battle: motivational and behavioral aspects of the combat experience', in B. Glad (ed.) *Psychological Dimensions of War*, London: Sage.

Kelly, D. (2001) 'The assault on civilization', *Navigator* 4: 1–4.

Kennan, G. (1982) *The Nuclear Delusion: Soviet–American Relations in the Atomic Age*, New York: Pantheon.

—— (1996) *At a Century's Ending: Reflections 1982–1995*, New York: Norton.

Kennett, L. (1997) *G.I.: The American Soldier in World War II*, Norman, OK: University of Oklahoma Press.

Kent, G. (1999) 'Structural violence against children', *Nexus* 1: 27–50.

Kent, S. (1982) 'Relative deprivation and resource mobilization: a study of early Quakerism', *The British Journal of Sociology* 33: 529–44.

Keohane, R. (1984) *After Hegemony: Cooperation and Discord in the World Political Economy*, Princeton, NJ: Princeton University Press.

Khan, R. (1978) 'Violence and socio-economic development', *International Social Science Journal* 30: 834–57.

Kim, W. (1996) 'Power parity, alliance, and war from 1648 to 1975', in J. Kugler and

D. Lemke (eds) *Parity and War: Evaluations and Extensions of The War Ledger*, Ann Arbor, MI: University of Michigan Press.

Kim, W. and Morrow, J. (1992) 'When do power shifts lead to war?', *American Journal of Political Science* 36: 896–922.

Kindleberger, C. (1977) 'U.S. foreign economic policy, 1776–1976', *Foreign Affairs* 55: 395–417.

Kitschelt, H. (1986) 'Political opportunity structures and political protest: anti-nuclear movements in four democracies', *British Journal of Political Science* 16: 57–85.

Klandermans, B. (1984) 'Mobilization and participation: social-psychological expansions of resource mobilization theory', *American Sociological Review* 49: 583–600.

—— (1989) 'Does happiness soothe political protest? The complex relation between discontent and political unrest', in R. Veenhoven (ed.) *How Harmful is Happiness? Consequences of Enjoying Life or Not*, Rotterdam: Universitaire Pers Rotterdam.

Kling, M. (1956) 'Toward a theory of power and political instability in Latin America', *Western Political Quarterly* 9: 21–35.

Köhler, G. and Alcock, N. (1976) 'An empirical table of structural violence', *Journal of Peace Research* 13: 343–56.

Kondratieff, N. (1935) 'The long waves in economic life' (trans. F. Stolper), *Review of Economic Statistics* 17: 105–15.

—— (1984) *The Long Wave Cycle* (trans. G. Daniels), New York: Richardson and Snyder.

Korpi, W. (1974) 'Conflict, power and relative deprivation', *American Political Science Review* 68: 1569–78.

Kostelny, K. and Garbarino, J. (2001) 'The war close to home: children and violence in the United States', in D. Christie, R. Wagner and D. Winter (eds) *Peace, Conflict and Violence: Peace Psychology for the 21st Century*, Upper Saddle River, NJ: Prentice-Hall.

Kothari, U. (2005) 'Authority and expertise: the professionalisation of international development and the ordering of dissent', *Antipode* 37: 425–46.

Krasner, S. (1972) 'Are bureaucracies important? (or Allison wonderland)', *Foreign Policy* 7: 159–79.

Krebs, D. (1987) 'The challenge of altruism in biology and psychology', in C. Crawford, M. Smith and D. Krebs (eds) *Sociobiology and Psychology: Ideas, Issues and Applications*, Hillsdale, NJ: Erlbaum.

Kriesberg, L. (1998) *Constructive Conflicts: From Escalation to Resolution*, Lanham, MD: Rowman and Littlefield.

Kronlid, D. (2003) *Ecofeminism and Environmental Ethics: An Analysis of Ecofeminist Ethical Theory*, Uppsala: Uppsala University Press.

Kugler, J. and Domke, W. (1987) 'Comparing the strength of nations', *Comparative Political Studies* 19: 39–69.

Kugler, J. and Lemke, D. (2000) 'The power transition research programme: assessing theoretical and empirical advances', in M. Midlarsky (ed.) *Handbook of War Studies II*, Ann Arbor, MI: University of Michigan Press.

Kugler, J. and Organski, A. (1989) 'The power transition: a retrospective and prospective evaluation', in M. Midlarsky (ed.) *Handbook of War Studies*, Boston, MA: Unwin Hyman.

Kull, S. (1990) 'War and the attraction to destruction', in B. Glad (ed.) *Psychological Dimensions of War*, London: Sage.

Kuznets, S. (1971) *Economic Growth of Nations: Total Output and Production Structure*, Cambridge, MA: Harvard University Press.

Lagerspetz, K. (1989) 'Media and the social environment', in J. Groebel and R. Hinde (eds) *Aggression and War: Their Biological and Social Bases*, Cambridge: Cambridge University Press.

Lake, M. and Damousi, J. (1995) 'Warfare, history and gender', in J. Damousi and M. Lake (eds) *Gender and War: Australians at War in the Twentieth Century*, Cambridge: Cambridge University Press.

Lam, R. and Wantchekon, L. (2004) 'Political Dutch disease', Paper presented to the Northeast Universities Development Consortium Conference, Montréal, October. Available online: http://www.hec.ca/neudc2004/fp/wantchekon_leonard_avril_16.pdf (accessed 26 January 2006).

Lawler, P. (1995) *A Question of Values: Johan Galtung's Peace Research*, Boulder, CO: Lynne Rienner.

Lawrence, P. (1997) *Modernity and War: The Creed of Absolute Violence*, London: Macmillan.

Leaky, R. and Lewin, R. (1977) *Origins*, New York: Dutton.

Learner, D. (1958) *The Passing of Traditional Society*, Glencoe, IL: The Free Press.

Le Billon, P. (2001) 'The political ecology of war: natural resources and armed conflicts', *Political Geography* 20: 561–84.

Lebow, N. (1981) *Between Peace and War*, Baltimore, MD: Johns Hopkins University Press.

Lee, G., Akers, R. and Borg, M. (2004) 'Social learning and structural factors in adolescent substance use', *Western Criminology Review* 5: 17–34.

Leeds, B. (2003) 'Do alliances deter aggression? The influence of military alliances on the initiation of militarized interstate disputes', *American Journal of Political Science* 47: 427–39.

Leeds, B., Long, A. and McLaughlin Mitchell, S. (2000) 'Reevaluating alliance reliability: specific threat, specific promises', *Journal of Conflict Resolution* 44: 686–99.

Leites, N. and Wolf, C. (1970) *Rebellion and Authority*, Chicago, IL: Markham.

Lemke, D. (1996) 'Small states and war: an expansion of the power transition theory', in J. Kugler and D. Lemke (eds) *Parity and War: Evaluations and Extensions of The War Ledger*, Ann Arbor, MI: University of Michigan Press.

—— (2002) *Regions of War and Peace*, Cambridge: Cambridge University Press.

Lemke, D. and Kugler, J. (1996) 'The evolution of the power transition perspective', in J. Kugler and D. Lemke (eds) *Parity and War: Evaluations and Extensions of The War Ledger*, Ann Arbor, MI: University of Michigan Press.

Lemke, D. and Reed, W. (1996) 'Regime types and status quo evaluations: power transition theory and the democratic peace', *International Interactions* 22: 143–64.

Lemke, D. and Werner, S. (1996) 'Power parity, commitment to change, and war', *International Studies Quarterly* 40: 235–60.

Leng, R. (1983) 'When will they ever learn? Coercive bargaining in recurrent crises', *Journal of Conflict Resolution* 27: 379–419.

—— (2000) 'Escalation: crisis behavior and war', in J. Vasquez (ed.) *What Do We Know about War?*, Lanham, MD: Rowman and Littlefield.

Lenski, G. (1988) 'Rethinking macrosociological theory', *American Sociological Review* 53: 163–71.

Leonard, E. (1994) *Yankee Women: Gender Battles in the Civil War*, New York: Norton.

Levy, J. (1981) 'Alliance formation and war behavior: an analysis of the Great Powers, 1495–1975', *Journal of Conflict Resolution* 25: 581–613.

—— (1983) *War in the Modern Great Power System 1495–1975*, Lexington, KY: University of Kentucky Press.

—— (1986) 'Organizational routines and the causes of war', *International Studies Quarterly* 30: 193–222.

—— (1987) 'Declining power and the preventive motive for war', *World Politics* 40: 82–107.

—— (1988) 'Domestic politics and war', *Journal of Interdisciplinary History* 18: 653–73.

—— (1993) 'The diversionary theory of war: a critique', in M. Midlarsky (ed.) *Handbook of War Studies*, 2nd edn, Ann Arbor, MI: Michigan University Press.

—— (1996) 'Contending theories of international conflict: a levels of analysis approach', in C. Crocker, F. Hampson and P. Aall (eds) *Managing Global Chaos: Sources of and Responses to International Conflict*, Washington, DC: United States Institute of Peace.

—— (1998) 'The causes of war and the conditions of peace', *Annual Review of Political Science* 1: 139–65.

—— (2000) 'Loss aversion, framing effects, and international conflict: perspective from prospect theory', in M. Midlarsky (ed.) *Handbook of War Studies II*, Ann Arbor, MI: Michigan University Press.

Levy, J. and Morgan, C. (1984) 'The frequency and seriousness of war: an inverse relationship', *Journal of Conflict Resolution* 28: 731–49.

Levy, J., Walker, T. and Edwards, M. (2004) 'Continuity and change in the evolution of warfare', in Z. Maoz and A. Gat (eds) *War in a Changing World*, Ann Arbor, MI: Michigan University Press.

Lewis, W. (1961) 'Feuding and social change in Morocco', *Journal of Conflict Resolution* 5: 43–54.

Lichbach, M. I. (1989) 'An evaluation of "does economic inequality breed political conflict?" studies', *World Politics* 41: 431–70.

—— (1994a) 'What makes rational peasants revolutionary? Dilemma, paradox, and irony in peasant collective action', *World Politics* 46: 383–418.

—— (1994b) 'Rethinking rationality and rebellion: theories of collective action and problems of collective dissent', *Rationality and Society* 6: 8–39.

Lind, M. (1994) 'In defense of liberal nationalism', *Foreign Affairs* 73: 87–99.

Liska, G. (1962) *Nations in Alliance: The Limits of Interdependence*, Baltimore, MD: Johns Hopkins University Press.

Lloyd, E. and Feldman, M. (2002) 'Evolutionary psychology: a view from evolutionary biology', *Psychological Inquiry* 13: 150–6.

Locher, B. and Prügl, E. (2001a) 'Feminism and constructivism: worlds apart or sharing the middle ground?', *International Studies Quarterly* 42: 111–29.

—— (2001b) 'Feminism: constructivism's other pedigree', in K. Fierke and K. Jørgensen (eds) *Constructing International Relations: Toward a New Generation*, Armonk, NY: M. E. Sharpe.

Lopez, G. (1985) 'A university peace studies curriculum for the 1990s', *Journal of Peace Research* 22: 117–28.

—— (1989) 'Trends in college curricula and programs', *Annals of the American Academy of Political and Social Science* 504: 61–71.

Lord, F. (1976) *Civil War Collector's Encyclopedia*, Harrisburg, PA: The Stackpole Company.

Lorenz, K. (1966) *On Aggression*, New York: Harcourt, Brace and World.

Lumsden, C. and Wilson, E. (1981) *Genes, Mind, and Culture: The Coevolutionary Process*, Cambridge, MA: Harvard University Press.

Lupsha, P. (1971) 'Explanation of political violence: some psychological theories versus indignation', *Politics and Society* 2: 89–104.

Lustick, I. (1980) 'Explaining the variable utility of disjointed incrementalism: four propositions', *American Political Science Review* 74: 342–53.

McAdam, D., McCarthy, J. and Zald, M. (1988) 'Social movements', in N. Smelser (ed.) *Handbook of Sociology*, Beverly Hills, CA: Sage.

McCarthy, J and Zald, M. (1973) *The Trend of Social Movements*, Morristown, NJ: General Learning.

—— (1977) 'Resource mobilization and social movements: a partial theory', *American Journal of Sociology* 82: 1212–41.

Maccoby, E. (1998) *The Two Sexes: Growing Up Apart, Coming Together*, Cambridge, MA: Harvard University Press.

McCord, W., McCord, J., and Zola, I. (1959) *Origins of Crime: A New Evaluation of the Cambridge-Somerville Youth Study*, Cambridge: Cambridge University Press.

McGinnis, M. (1991) 'Richardson, rationality, and restrictive models of arms races', *Journal of Conflict Resolution* 35: 443–73.

MacGinty, R. (2006) *No War, No Peace: The Rejuvenation of Stalled Peace Processes and Peace Accords*, Basingstoke: Palgrave Macmillan.

McGregor, S. (2003) 'Consumerism as a source of structural violence', Kappa Omicron Nu Leadership Society Human Sciences Working Paper Archive. Available online: http://www.kon.org/hswp/archive/consumerism.pdf (accessed 9 June 2005).

Mack, A. (2002) 'Civil war: academic research and the policy community', *Journal of Peace Research* 39: 515–25.

Mack, R. (1965) 'The components of social conflict', *Social Problems* 12: 388–97.

McKeown, T. (1983) 'Hegemonic stability theory and nineteenth-century tariff levels in Europe', *International Organization* 37: 73–91.

MacLean, P. (1967) 'The brain in relation to empathy and medical education', *Journal of Nervous and Mental Disease* 144: 374–82.

McLoyd, V. and Wilson, L. (1991) 'The strain of living poor: parenting social support and child mental health', in A. Huston (ed.) *Children in Poverty: Child Development and Public Policy*, Cambridge: Cambridge University Press.

McNeill, W. (1984) *The Pursuit of Power*, Chicago, IL: University of Chicago Press.

Mahdavy, H. (1970) 'The rentier state, the case of Iran', in M. Cook (ed.) *Studies in the Economic History of the Middle East*, Oxford: Oxford University Press.

Maier, N. (1942) 'The role of frustration in social movements', *Psychological Review* 49: 586–99.

—— (1949) *Frustration: The Study of Behavior without a Goal*, New York: McGraw-Hill.

Malthus, T. (1798) *An Essay on the Principle of Population, as it affects the Future*

Improvement of Society, with Remarks on the Speculations of Mr Godwin, M. Condorcet and Other Writers, London: Joseph Johnson.

Mandel, E. (1975) *Late Capitalism*, London: New Left Books.

Mann, M. (1986) *The Sources of Social Power, Vol. I*, Cambridge: Cambridge University Press.

—— (1993) *The Sources of Social Power, Vol. II*, Cambridge: Cambridge University Press.

—— (1994) 'In praise of macro-sociology: a reply to Goldthorpe', *British Journal of Sociology* 45: 37–54.

Manning, A. (1989) 'The genetic bases of aggression', in J. Groebel and R. Hinde (eds) *Aggression and War: Their Biological and Social Bases*, Cambridge: Cambridge University Press.

Maoz, Z. (1990) *Paradoxes of War: On the Art of National Self-Entrapment*, Boston, MA: Unwin Hyman.

—— (2000) 'Alliances: the street gangs of world politics – their origins, management, and consequences 1816–1986', in J. Vasquez (ed.) *What Do We Know about War?*, Lanham, MD: Rowman and Littlefield.

Marshall, M. (1999) *Third World War: System, Process, and Conflict Dynamics*, Lanham, MD: Rowman and Littlefield.

Marshall, S. (1947) *Men against Fire: The Problem of Battlefield Command in Future War*, Washington, DC: William Morrow.

Maslow, A. (1943) 'A theory of human motivation', *Psychological Review* 50: 370–96.

Maxson, S., Ginsborg, B. and Trattner, A. (1979) 'Interaction of Y-chromosomal and autosomal gene(s) in the development of intermale aggression in mice', *Behavior Genetics* 9: 219–26.

Mazurana, D. and McKay, S. (2001) 'Women, girls and structural violence: a global analysis', in D. Christie, R. Wagner and D. Winter (eds) *Peace Conflict and Violence: Peace Psychology for the 21st Century*, Upper Saddle River, NJ: Prentice-Hall.

Mehler, B. (1978) 'Sources in the study of eugenics #2: the bureau of social hygiene papers', *The Mendel Newsletter* 16. Archival Resources for the History of Genetics and Allied Sciences. Available online: http://www.ferris.edu/isar/archives/sources/bsh.htm (accessed 19 June 2005).

Melotti, U. (1987) 'In-group/out-group relations and the issues of group selection', in V. Reynolds, V. Falger and I. Vine (eds) *The Sociobiology of Ethnocentrism: Evolutionary Dimensions of Xenophobia, Discrimination, Racism and Nationalism*, London: Croom Helm.

Menkhaus, K. (2004) 'Vicious circles and the security–development nexus in Somalia', *Conflict Security and Development* 4: 149–65.

Merton, R. and Kitt, A. (1950) 'Contributions to the theory of reference group behavior', in R. Merton and A. Kitt (eds) *Continuities in Social Research: Studies in the Scope and Method of the American Soldier*, Glencoe, IL: The Free Press.

Midlarsky, M. (1998) 'Democracy and Islam: implications for civilizational conflict and the democratic peace', *International Studies Quarterly* 42: 485–511.

Milgram, S. (1963) 'Behavioral study of obedience', *Journal of Abnormal Social Psychology* 67: 371–8.

—— (1974) *Obedience to Authority: An Experimental View*, New York: Harper and Row.

Miller, A. (1986) *The Obedience Experiments*, New York: Praeger.

Miller, A., Bolce, L. and Halligan, M. (1977) 'The J-curve theory and the black urban riots: an empirical test of progressive relative deprivation theory', *American Political Science Review* 71: 964–82.

Miller, N., Sears, R., Mowrer, O., Doob, L. and Dollard, J. (1941) 'The frustration–aggression hypothesis', *Psychological Review* 48: 337–42.

Miller, R. (1999) 'Regime type, strategic interaction, and the diversionary use of force', *Journal of Conflict Resolution* 43: 388–402.

Minear L. and Weiss T. (1993) *Humanitarian Action in Times of War: A Handbook for Practitioners*, Boulder, CO: Lynne Rienner.

Mitchell, B. (1998) *Women in the Military: Flirting with Disaster*, Washington, DC: Regnery.

Mitchell, C. (1980) 'Evaluating conflict', *Journal of Peace Research* 17: 61–75.

—— (1981a) *The Structure of International Conflict*, Basingstoke: Macmillan.

—— (1981b) *Peacemaking and the Consultant's Role*, Farnborough: Gower.

Mitchell, E. (1968) 'Inequality and insurgency: a statistical summary of South Vietnam', *World Politics* 20: 421–38.

Modelski, G. (1978) 'The long cycle of global politics and the nation-state', *Comparative Studies in Society and History* 20: 214–38.

—— (1981) 'Long cycles, Kondratieffs and alternating innovations: implications for U.S. foreign policy', in C. Kegley and P. McGowan (eds) *The Political Economy of Foreign Policy Behavior*, Beverly Hills, CA: Sage.

—— (1987) *Long Cycles in World Politics*, Seattle, WA: University of Washington Press.

—— (1999) 'From leadership to organization: the evolution of global politics', in V. Bornschier and C. Chase-Dunn (eds) *The Future of Global Conflict*, London: Sage.

—— (2000) 'World system evolution', in R. Denemark, J. Friedman, B. Gills and G. Modelski (eds) *World System History: The Social Science of Long-Term Change*, London: Routledge.

Modelski, G. and Morgan, P. (1985) 'Understanding global war', *Journal of Conflict Resolution* 29: 391–417.

Modelski, G. and Thompson, W. (1988) *Seapower and Global Politics 1994–1993*, Basingstoke: Macmillan.

—— (1989) 'Long cycles and global war', in M. Midlarsky (ed.) *Handbook of War Studies*, Boston, MA: Unwin Hyman.

—— (1996) *Leading Sectors and World Powers: The Coevolution of Global Economics and Politics*, Columbia, SC: University of South Carolina Press.

Moe, T. (1980) *The Organization of Interests: Incentives and Internal Dynamics of Political Interest Groups*, Chicago, IL: University of Chicago Press.

van der Molen, P. (1990) 'The biological instability of social equilibria', in J. van der Dennen and V. Falger (eds) *Sociobiology and Conflict*, London: Chapman and Hall.

Moore, D. and Aweiss, S. (2003) 'Outcome expectations in prolonged conflicts: perceptions of sense of control and relative deprivation', *Sociological Inquiry* 73: 190–211.

Moore, J. (1979) *The Post-Darwinian Controversies*, Cambridge: Cambridge University Press.

Moore, M. (2004) 'Revenues, state formation and the quality of governance in developing countries', *International Political Science Review* 25: 297–319.

Moore, W. (1995) 'Rational rebels: overcoming the free-rider problem', *Political Research Quarterly* 48: 417–54.

Moore, W. and Jaggers, K. (1990) 'Deprivation, mobilization and the state: a synthetic model of rebellion', *Journal of Developing Societies* 6: 17–36.

Morgan, C. and Anderson, C. (1999) 'Domestic support and diversionary external conflict in Great Britain, 1950–1992,' *Journal of Politics* 61: 799–814.

Morgan, C. and Bickers, K. (1992) 'Domestic discontent and the external use of force', *Journal of Conflict Resolution* 36: 25–52.

Morgenthau, H. (1946) *Scientific Man vs. Power Politics*, Chicago, IL: University of Chicago Press.

—— (1948) *Politics among Nations: The Struggle for Power and Peace*, New York: Alfred A. Knopf.

—— (1960) *The Purpose of American Politics*, New York: Alfred A. Knopf.

Morgenthau, H. and Thompson, K. (1985) *Politics among Nations: The Struggle for Power and Peace*, 6th edn, New York: Random House.

Morris, D. (1977) *Manwatching: A Field Guide to Human Behavior*, New York: Abrams.

Morrison, D. (1971) 'Some notes toward theory on relative deprivation, social movements and social change', *American Behavioral Scientist* 14: 675–90.

Morrison, D. and Steeves, A. (1967) 'Deprivation, discontent, and social movement participation: evidence on a contemporary farmers' movement, the NFO', *Rural Sociology* 32: 414–34.

Morrow, J. (1985) 'A continuous-outcome expected utility theory of war', *Journal of Conflict Resolution* 29: 473–502.

Mottahedeh, R. (1995) 'Clash of civilizations? An Islamicist's critique', *Harvard Middle Eastern and Islamic Review* 2: 1–26.

Mueller, J. (1973) *War, Presidents and Public Opinion*, New York: Wiley.

—— (2000) 'The banality of "ethnic war"', *International Security* 25: 42–70.

Muller, E. (1985) 'Income inequality, regime repressiveness, and political violence', *American Sociological Review* 50: 47–61.

Muller, E. and Opp, K.-D. (1986) 'Rational choice and rebellious collective action', *American Political Science Review* 80: 471–87.

Muller, E. and Weede, E. (1990) 'Cross-national variation in political violence: a rational choice approach', *Journal of Conflict Resolution* 34: 624–51.

—— (1994) 'Theories of rebellion: relative deprivation and power contention', *Rationality and Society* 6: 40–57.

Muñoz, F. (2005) 'Imperfect peace', Instituto de la Paz y los Conflictos, Universidad de Granada. Available online: http://www.ugr.es/%7Efmunoz/documentos/imperfectpeace.pdf (accessed 7 January 2007).

Murphy, R. (1957) 'Intergroup hostility and social cohesion', *American Anthropologist* 59: 1018–35.

Murshed, S. M. and Gates, S. (2003) 'Spatial-horizontal inequality and the Maoist insurgency in Nepal', Paper presented to the UNU/WIDER Project Conference on Spatial Inequality in Asia, Tokyo, March. Available online: http://www.wider.unu.edu/conference/conference-2003-1/conference-2003-1-papers/s%20mansoob%20murshed%20-%20scott%20gates.pdf (accessed 15 December 2005).

Nafziger, E. W. and Auvinen, J. (2002) 'Economic development, inequality, war, and state violence', *World Development* 30: 153–63.

Nardin, T. (1980) 'Theory and practice in conflict research', in T. Gurr (ed.) *Handbook of Political Conflict*, New York: The Free Press.

Nelson, S. (1974) 'Nature/nurture revisited I: a review of the biological bases of conflict', *Journal of Conflict Resolution* 18: 285–335.

Neustadt, R. (1960) *Presidential Power: The Politics of Leadership*, New York: John Wiley.

Neustadt, R. and May, E. (1986) *Thinking in Time: The Uses of History for Decision-Makers*, New York: The Free Press.

Newman, E. (2004) 'The "new wars" debate: a historical perspective is needed', *Security Dialogue* 35: 173–89.

Newman, S. (1991) 'Does modernization breed ethnic conflict?', *World Politics* 43: 451–78.

Newsome, B. (2003) 'The myth of intrinsic combat motivation', *The Journal of Strategic Studies* 26: 24–46.

Nincic, M. and Nincic, D. (2002) 'Race, gender and war', *Journal of Peace Research* 39: 547–68.

Nordstrom, C. (1997) *A Different Kind of War Story*, Philadelphia, PA: University of Pennsylvania Press.

Norpoth, H. (1987a) 'The Falklands War and government popularity in Britain: rally without consequence or surge without decline?', *Electoral Studies* 6: 3–16.

—— (1987b) 'Guns and butter and government popularity in Britain', *American Political Science Review* 81: 949–59.

Norris, P. and Inglehart, R. (2002) 'Islam and the West: testing the "clash of civilizations" thesis', Harvard MA: John F. Kennedy School of Government, Faculty Research Working Paper Series. Available online: http://ksgnotes1.harvard.edu/Research/wpaper.nsf/rwp/RWP020–15/$File/rwp02_015_norris_rev1.pdf (accessed 30 June 2005).

Norton, A. (1988) *Reflections on Political Identity*, Baltimore, MD: Johns Hopkins University Press.

North, D. and Thomas, R. (1973) *The Rise of the Western World: A New Economic History*, Cambridge: Cambridge University Press.

Novak, M. (2001) 'Rediscovering culture', *Journal of Democracy* 12: 168–72.

O'Beirne, K. (1998) 'The war machine as child minder', in G. Frost (ed.) *Not Fit to Fight: The Cultural Subversion of the Armed Forces*, London: Social Affairs Unit.

Oberschall, A. (1969) 'Rising expectations and political turmoil', *Journal of Development Studies* 6: 5–22.

—— (1973) *Social Conflict and Social Movements*, Englewood Cliffs, NJ: Prentice-Hall.

—— (1978) 'Theories of social conflict', *Annual Review of Sociology* 4: 291–315.

—— (1979) 'Protracted conflict', in M. Zald and J. McCarthy (eds) *The Dynamics of Social Movements: Resource Mobilization, Social Control and Tactics*, Cambridge, MA: Winthrop.

—— (1994) 'Rational choice in collective protests', *Rationality and Society* 6: 79–100.

O'Gorman, E. (1999) 'Writing women's wars: Foucauldian strategies of engagement', in V. Jabri and E. O'Gorman (eds) *Women, Culture and International Relations*, Boulder, CO: Lynne Rienner.

Ohlin, G. (1966) *Foreign Aid Policies Reconsidered*, Paris: OECD.

Okin, S. M. (1990) 'Thinking like a woman', in D. Rhode (ed.) *Theoretical Perspectives on Sexual Difference*, New Haven, CT: Yale University Press.

de Oliveira Marques, A. (1972) *History of Portugal*, New York: Columbia University Press.

Olson, M. (1971) *The Logic of Collective Action: Public Goods and the Theory of Groups*, Cambridge, MA: Harvard University Press.

Onuf, N. (1989) *World of Our Making: Rules and Rule in Social Theory and International Relations*, Columbia, SC: University of South Carolina Press.

Organski, A. (1958) *World Politics*, New York: Alfred A. Knopf.

Organski, A. and Kugler, J. (1980) *The War Ledger*, Chicago, IL: University of Chicago Press.

Osgood, J. (2006) *Caesar's Legacy: Civil War and the Emergence of the Roman Empire*, Cambridge: Cambridge University Press.

Osgood, R. (1967) 'The expansion of force', in R. Osgood and R. Tucker (eds) *Force, Order and Justice*, Baltimore, MD: Johns Hopkins University Press.

Østerud, Ø. (1996) 'Antinomies of postmodernism in international relations', *Journal of Peace Research* 33: 385–90.

Ostrom, C. and Hoole, F. (1978) 'Alliances and wars revisited: a research note', *International Studies Quarterly* 22: 215–36.

Ostrom, C. and Job, B. (1986) 'The president and the political use of force', *American Political Science Review* 80: 541–66.

Ostrom, E. (1990) *Governing the Commons: The Evolution of Institutions for Collective Action*, Cambridge, MA: Harvard University Press.

Otterbein, K. (1994) *Feuding and Warfare*, Langhorne, PA: Gordon and Breach.

Outram, Q. (2001) 'The socio-economic relations of warfare and the military mortality crises of the Thirty Years' War', *Medical History* 45: 151–84.

Overy, R. (1995) *Why the Allies Won*, New York: Norton.

Page, B. and Shapiro, R. (1992) *The Rational Public: Fifty Years of Trends in Americans' Policy Preferences*, Chicago, IL: University of Chicago Press.

Paley, W. (1986) *Natural Theology: or Evidences of the Existence and Attributes of the Deity, Collected from the Appearances of Nature*, 12th edn, Charlottesville, VA: Lincoln-Rembrandt.

Paris, R. (2000) 'Broadening the study of peace operations', *International Studies Review* 2: 27–44.

Parker, G. (1988) *The Military Revolution: Military Innovation and the Rise of the West*, Cambridge: Cambridge University Press.

Parsons, T. (1951) *The Social System*, New York: The Free Press.

Pastore, N. (1949) *The Nature–Nurture Controversy*, New York: King's Crown Press.

Patel, S. (1992) 'In tribute to the golden age of the South's development', *World Development* 20: 767–77.

Patomäki, H. (2001) 'The challenge of critical theories: peace research at the start of the new century', *Journal of Peace Research* 38: 723–37.

Pesic, V. (1996) *Serbian Nationalism and the Origins of the Yugoslav Crisis*, Washington, DC: United States Institute of Peace.

Peter, K. and Petryszak, N. (1980) 'Sociobiology versus biosociology', in A. Montagu (ed.) *Sociobiology Examined*, Oxford: Oxford University Press.

Peterson, S. and Runyan, A. (1993) *Global Gender Issues: Dilemmas in World Politics*, Boulder, CO: Westview.

Pettman, J. (1998) 'Nationalism and after', *Review of International Studies* 24: 149–64.

Pinard, M. and Hamilton, R. (1986) 'Motivational dimensions in the Quebec independent movement: a test of a new model', in L. Kriesberg (ed.) *Research in Social Movements Conflicts and Change*, Greenwich, CT: JAI Press.

Pipes, R. (1977) 'Why the Soviet Union thinks it could fight and win a nuclear war', *Commentary* 64: 21–34.

Pisano, R. and Taylor, S. P. (1971) 'Reduction of physical aggression: the effects of four strategies', *Journal of Personality and Social Psychology* 19: 237–42.

Pitt, D. (1989) 'Introduction', in P. Turner and D. Pitt (eds) *The Anthropology of War and Peace: Perspectives on the Nuclear Age*, Granby, MA: Bergin and Garvey.

Portes, A. (1971) 'On the logic of post-factum explanations: the hypothesis of lower-class frustrations as the cause of leftist radicalism', *Social Forces* 50: 26–44.

Porto, J. G. (2002) 'Contemporary conflict analysis in perspective', in J. Lind and K. Sturman (eds) *Scarcity and Surfeit: The Ecology of Africa's Conflicts*, Pretoria: Institute of Security Studies.

Post, J. (1993) 'The defining moment of Saddam's life: a political psychology perspective on the leadership and decision making of Saddam Hussein during the gulf crisis', in S. Renshon (ed.) *The Political Psychology of the Gulf War: Leaders, Publics and the Process of Conflict*, Pittsburgh, PA: University of Pittsburgh Press.

—— (2004) *Leaders and their Followers in a Dangerous World: The Psychology of Political Behavior*, Ithaca, NY: Cornell University Press.

Preti, A. (2002) 'Guatemala: violence in peacetime – a critical analysis of the armed conflict and the peace process', *Disaster* 26: 99–119.

Price, J. (2001) *Thucydides and Internal War*, Cambridge: Cambridge University Press.

Prunier, G. (1995) *The Rwandan Crisis: History of a Genocide*, New York: Columbia University Press.

Pugh, M. Cooper, N. and Goodhand, J. (2004) *War Economies in a Regional Context: Challenges of Transformation*, Boulder, CO: Lynne Rienner.

Qoma, K. (2004) 'Africa can curb arms proliferation', Pretoria: Institute for Security Studies. Available online: http://www.smallarmsnet.org/issues/themes/armsprol.htm (accessed 15 November 2006).

Randel, J. and German, T. (2002) 'Trends in the financing of humanitarian assistance', in J. Macrae (ed.) *The New Humanitarianism: A Review of Trends in Global Humanitarian Action*, London: Overseas Development Institute.

Rasler, K. and Thompson, W. (1983) 'Global wars, public debts, and the long cycle', *World Politics* 35: 489–516.

—— (1992) 'War making and state making: governmental expenditures, tax revenues, and global wars', in J. Vasquez and M. Henehan (eds) *The Scientific Study of Peace and War: A Text Reader*, Cambridge, MA: Lexington.

—— (2000) 'Global war and the political economy of structural change', in M. Midlarsky (ed.) *Handbook of War Studies II*, Ann Arbor, MI: University of Michigan Press.

Ray, J. E. (1995) *Democracy and International Conflict: An Evaluation of the Democratic Peace Proposition*, Columbia, SC: University of South Carolina Press.

—— (2001) 'Integrating levels of analysis in world politics', *Journal of Theoretical Politics* 13: 355–88.

Regan, P. and Norton, D. (2005) 'Greed, grievance and mobilization in civil wars', *Journal of Conflict Resolution* 49: 319–36.

Reichberg, G. (2002) 'Just war or perpetual peace?', *Journal of Military Ethics* 1: 16–35.

Reno, W. (2000a) 'Shadow states and the political economy of civil wars', in M. Berdal and D. Malone (eds) *Greed and Grievance: Economic Agendas in Civil Wars*, Boulder, CO: Lynne Rienner.

—— (2000b) 'Clandestine economies, violence and states in Africa', *Journal of International Affairs* 53: 433–59.

—— (2000c) 'Liberia and Sierra Leone: the competition for patronage in resource-rich economies', in E. Nafziger, F. Stewart and R. Väyrynen (eds) *War, Hunger and Displacement: The Origins of Humanitarian Emergencies*, Oxford: Oxford University Press.

de Reuck, A. (1984) 'The logic of conflict', in M. Banks (ed.) *Conflict in World Society*, Brighton: Wheatsheaf.

Rhodes, R. (1995) *Dark Sun: The Making of the Hydrogen Bomb*, New York: Simon and Schuster.

Richards, D., Morgan, C., Wilson, R., Schwebach, V. and Young, G. (1993) 'Good times, bad times and the diversionary use of force: a tale of some not-so-free agents', *Journal of Conflict Resolution* 37: 504–35.

Richardson, L. (1960a) *Arms and Insecurity: A Mathematical Study of the Causes and Origins of War* (eds N. Rashevsky and E. Trucco), Pittsburgh, PA: Boxwood Press.

—— (1960b) *Statistics of Deadly Quarrels* (eds Q. Wright and C. Lienau), Pittsburgh, PA: Boxwood Press.

Richman-Loo, N. and Weber, R. (1996) 'Gender and weapons design', in J. Stiehm (ed.) *It's Our Military, Too!*, Philadelphia, PA: Temple University Press.

Ridker, R. (1962) 'Discontent and economic growth', *Economic Development and Cultural Change* 11: 1–15.

Rizman, R. (1999) 'Radical right politics in Slovenia', in S. Ramet (ed.) *The Radical Right in Central and Eastern Europe since 1989*, Philadelphia, PA: Pennsylvania University Press.

Rogers, C. (1993) 'Military revolutions of the Hundred Years' War', *Journal of Military History* 57: 241–78.

Rogers, P. and Ramsbotham, O. (1999) 'Then and now: peace research – past and future', *Political Studies* 47: 740–54.

Rogowski, R. (1985) 'Causes and varieties of nationalism: a rationalist account', in E. Tiryakian and R. Rogowski (eds) *New Nationalisms of the Developed West: Toward Explanation*, Boston, MA: Allen and Unwin.

Rosecrance, R. (1987) 'Long cycle theory and international relations', *International Organization* 41: 283–301.

Rosen, S. (1995) 'Military effectiveness: why society matters', *International Security* 19: 5–31.

Rosenblatt, P. (1964) 'Origins and effects of group ethnocentrism and nationalism', *Journal of Conflict Resolution* 8: 131–46.

Ross, M. (2000) 'Culture and ethnic conflict', in S. Renshon, and J. Duckitt (eds) *Political Psychology: Cultural and Crosscultural Foundations*, London: Macmillan.

—— (2003) 'Oil, drugs and diamonds: the varying roles of natural resources in civil war', in K. Ballentine and J. Sherman (eds) *The Political Economy of Armed Conflict: Beyond Greed and Grievance*, Boulder, CO: Lynne Rienner.

—— (2004) 'How does natural resource wealth influence civil wars? Evidence from thirteen cases', *International Organization* 58: 35–67.

Rostow, W. (1953) *The Process of Economic Growth*, Oxford: Clarendon Press.

—— (1975) 'Kondratieff, Schumpeter and Kuznets: trend periods revisited', *Journal of Economic History* 35: 719–53.

Rouhana, N. (1997) *Palestinian Citizens in an Ethnic Jewish State: Identities in Conflict*, New Haven, CT: Yale University Press.

Ruby, C. (2002) 'Are terrorists mentally deranged?', *Analyses of Social Issues and Public Policy* 2: 15–26.

Ruddick, S. (1989) *Maternal Thinking: Towards a Politics of Peace*, Boston, MA: Beacon Press.

Rummel, R. (1963) 'Dimensions of conflict behaviour within and between nations', *General Systems* 8: 1–50.

—— (1968) 'The relationship between national attributes and foreign conflict behavior', in J. D. Singer (ed.) *Quantitative International Politics: Insights and Evidence*, New York: The Free Press.

—— (1994) *Death by Government*, London: Transaction.

Runciman, W. G. (1966) *Relative Deprivation and Social Justice*, Berkeley, CA: University of California Press.

Runyan, A. (1994) 'Radical feminism: alternative futures', in P. Beckman and F. D'Amico (eds) *Women, Gender and World Politics: Perspectives, Policies, and Prospects*, Westport, CT: Bergin and Garvey.

Rushton, J., Fulker, D., Neale, M., Nias, D. and Eysenck, H. (1985) 'Altruism and aggression: individual differences are substantially heritable', *Journal of Personality and Social Psychology* 50: 1192–8.

Russett, B. (1964) 'Inequality and instability: the relation of land tenure to politics', *World Politics* 16: 442–54.

—— (1989) 'Democracy, public opinion, and nuclear weapons', in P. Tetlock, J. Husbands, R. Jervis, P. Stern and C. Tilly (eds) *Behaviour, Society, and Nuclear War, Vol. I*, Oxford: Oxford University Press.

—— (2002) 'Violence and disease: trade as suppressor of conflict when suppressors matter', in E. Mansfield and B. Pollins (eds) *Economic Interdependence and International Conflict: New Perspectives on an Enduring Debate*, Ann Arbor, MI: University of Michigan Press.

Sabrosky, A. (1980) 'Interstate alliances: their reliability and the expansion of war', in J. D. Singer (ed.) *The Correlates of War II: Testing some Realpolitik Models*, New York: The Free Press.

Sahlins, M. (1977) *The Use and Abuse of Biology*, London: Tavistock.

Sambanis, N. (2002) 'A review of recent advances and future direction in the quantitative literature on civil war', *Defence and Peace Economics* 13: 215–43.

Sample, S. (1997) 'Arms races and dispute escalation: resolving the debate', *Journal of Peace Research* 34: 7–22.

—— (2000) 'Military buildups: arming and war', in J. Vasquez (ed.) *What Do We Know about War?*, Lanham, MD: Rowman and Littlefield.

Sanderson J. (2002) 'The changing face of peace operations: a view from the field', *Journal of International Affairs* 55: 277–88.

Sandole, D. (1999) *Capturing the Complexity of Conflict: Dealing with Violent Ethnic Conflicts in the Post-Cold War Era*, London: Pinter.

Sayles, M. (1984) 'Relative deprivation and collective protest: an impoverished theory?', *Sociological Inquiry* 54: 449–65.

Schelling, T. (1960) *The Strategy of Conflict*, Cambridge, MA, Harvard University Press.

Scheper-Hughes, N. (1996) 'Small wars and invisible genocides', *Social Science and Medicine* 43: 889–900.

Schilling, W. (1962) 'The politics of national defense: fiscal 1950', in W. Schilling, P. Hammond and G. Snyder (eds) *Strategy, Politics and Defense Budgets*, New York: Columbia University Press.

Schmid, H. (1968) 'Peace research and politics', *Journal of Peace Research* 5: 217–32.

Schoenewolf, G. (1989) *Sexual Animosity between Men and Women*, Northvale, NJ: Jason Aronson.

Schumpeter, J. (1934) 'Depressions: can we learn from past experiences?', in D. Brown, E. Chamberlin and S. Harris (eds) *The Economics of the Recovery Program*, New York: McGraw-Hill.

Schwebel, M. (1997) 'Job insecurity as structural violence: implications for destructive inter-group conflict', *Peace and Conflict: Journal of Peace Psychology* 3: 333–52.

Schwebel, M. and Christie, D. (2001) 'Children and structural violence', in D. Christie, R. Wagner and D. Winter (eds) *Peace, Conflict and Violence: Peace Psychology for the 21st Century*, Upper Saddle River, NJ: Prentice-Hall.

Scott, J. C. (1977) 'Protest and profanation: agrarian revolt and the little tradition', *Theory and Society* 4: 1–38.

Scott, J. P. (1958) *Aggression*, Chicago, IL: University of Chicago Press.

Scott, J. P. and Fuller, J. (1965) *Genetics and the Social Behaviour of the Dog*, Chicago, IL: University of Chicago Press.

Segall, M. (1989) 'Cultural factors, biology and human aggression', in J. Groebel and R. Hinde (eds) *Aggression and War: Their Biological and Social Bases*, Cambridge: Cambridge University Press.

Sen, A. (1998) 'Mortality as an indicator of economic success and failure', *The Economic Journal* 108: 1–25.

Shalit, B. (1988) *The Psychology of Conflict and Combat*, New York: Praeger.

Shaw, M. (2000) 'The contemporary mode of warfare? Mary Kaldor's theory of new wars', *Review of International Political Economy* 7: 171–92.

Shaw, R. and Wong, Y. (1989) *Genetic Seeds of Warfare: Evolution, Nationalism and Patriotism*, Boston, MA: Unwin Hyman.

Shawcross, W. (2000) *Deliver Us from Evil: Warlords and Peacekeepers in a World of Endless Conflict*, London: Bloomsbury.

Sheehan, M. (1996) *The Balance of Power: History and Theory*, London: Routledge.

Sherman, J. (2003) 'Burma: lessons from the cease-fires', in K. Ballentine and J. Sherman (eds) *The Political Economy of Armed Conflict: Beyond Greed and Grievance*, Boulder, CO: Lynne Rienner.

Silber, L. and Little, A. (1995) *The Death of Yugoslavia*, Harmondsworth: Penguin.

Silverman, I. (1987) 'Race, race differences, and race relations: perspectives from psychology and sociobiology', in C. Crawford, M. Smith and D. Krebs (eds) *Sociobiology and Psychology: Ideas, Issues and Applications*, Hillsdale, NJ: Erlbaum.

Simon, H. (1958) 'The decision making schema: a reply', *Public Administration Review* 18: 60–5.

—— (1960) *The New Science of Management Decision*, Englewood Cliffs, NJ: Prentice-Hall.

Simons, A. (1999) 'War: back to the future', *Annual Review of Anthropology* 28: 73–108.

Singer, J. D. (1958) 'Threat-perception and the armament-tension dilemma', *Journal of Conflict Resolution* 2: 90–105.

Singer, J. D. and Small, M. (1982) *Resort to Arms: International and Civil Wars 1816–1980*, Beverly Hills, CA: Sage.

—— (1994) *Correlates of War Project: International and Civil War Data, 1815–1992*, Ann Arbor, MI: Inter-university Consortium for Political and Social Research.

Singh, A. (2002) 'Aid, conditionality and development', *Development and Change* 33: 295–305.

Sion, L. (2006) ' "Too sweet and innocent for war?" Dutch peacekeepers and the use of violence', *Armed Forces and Society* 32: 454–74.

Sivard, R. (1993) *World Military and Social Expenditures*, Washington, DC: World Priorities.

Siverson, R. and Diehl, P. (1989) 'Arms races, the conflict spiral, and the onset for war', in M. Midlarsky (ed.) *Handbook of War Studies*, Boston, MA: Unwin Hyman.

Siverson, R. and King, J. (1979) 'Alliances and the expansion of war, 1816–1975', in J. D. Singer and M. Wallace (eds) *To Augur Well: Early Warning Indicators in World Politics*, Beverly Hills, CA: Sage.

Skillen, J. (1982) 'Security and morality in planning for U.S. defense', *Journal of the American Scientific Affiliation* 34: 85–9.

Skinner, B. F. (1938) *The Behavior of Organisms: An Experimental Analysis*, New York: Appleton-Century.

Small, M. and Singer, J. D. (1982) *Resort to Arms: International and Civil Wars, 1816–1980*, London: Sage.

Smillie, I. and Todorovic, G. (2001) 'Reconstructing Bosnia, constructing civil society: disjuncture and convergence', in I. Smillie (ed.) *Patronage or Partnership: Local Capacity Building in Humanitarian Crises*, Bloomfield, CT: Kumarian.

Smith, B. (2004) 'Oil wealth and regime survival in the developing world 1960–1999', *American Journal of Political Science* 48: 232–46.

Smith, J. M. (1995) *The Republic of Letters, The Correspondence between Thomas Jefferson and James Madison 1776–1826*, New York: Norton.

Smith, S. (1980) 'Allison and the Cuban Missile Crisis: a review of the bureaucratic politics model of foreign policy decision-making', *Millennium: Journal of International Studies* 9: 21–40.

—— (1997) 'Epistemology, postmodernism and international relations theory', *Journal of Peace Research* 34: 330–6.

Smith, T. (1979) 'The underdevelopment of development literature: the case of dependency theory', *World Politics* 31: 247–88.

Smith, T. W. (1984) 'The polls: gender and attitudes toward violence', *Public Opinion Quarterly* 48: 384–96.

Smoke, R. (1977) *War: Controlling Escalation*, Cambridge, MA: Harvard University Press.

Snow, D. (1996) *Uncivil Wars: International Security and New Internal Conflicts*, Boulder, CO: Lynne Rienner.

Snyder, D. (1978) 'Collective violence: a research agenda and some strategic considerations', *Journal of Conflict Resolution*, 22: 499–534.

Snyder, D. and Tilly, C. (1972) 'Hardship and collective violence in France, 1830–1960', *American Sociological Review* 37: 520–32.

Snyder, G. (1961) *Deterrence and Defense: Toward a New Theory of National Security*, Princeton, NJ: Princeton University Press.

Snyder, G. and Diesing, P. (1977) *Conflict Among Nations: Bargaining, Decision Making and System Structure in International Crises*, Princeton, NJ: Princeton University Press.

Snyder, J. (1990) 'The concept of strategic culture: caveat emptor', in C. Jacobsen (ed.) *Strategic Power: USA/USSR*, Basingstoke: Macmillan.

Snyder, J. and Ballentine, K. (1996) 'Nationalism and the marketplace of ideas', *International Security* 21: 5–40.

Snyder, R. (1958) 'A decision-making approach to the study of political phenomena', in R. Young (ed.) *Approaches to the Study of Politics: Twenty-Two Contemporary Essays Exploring the Nature of Politics and Methods by which it can be Studied*, Evanston, IL: Northwestern University Press.

Solomon N. (2005) 'Judaism and the ethics of war', *International Review of the Red Cross* 87: 295–309.

de Sola Pool, I. (1966) 'Communication and development', in M. Weiner (ed.) *Modernization: The Dynamics of Growth*, New York: Basic Books.

Somers, M. (1999) 'The privatization of citizenship: how to unthink a knowledge culture', in V. Bonnell and L. Hunt (eds) *Beyond the Cultural Turn: New Directions in the Study of Society and Culture*, Berkeley, CA: University of California Press.

Somit, A. (1990) 'Humans, chimps and bonobos: the biological bases of aggression, war and peacemaking', *Journal of Conflict Resolution* 34: 553–82.

Somit, A. and Peterson, S. (1997) *Darwinism, Dominance and Democracy: The Biological Bases of Authoritarianism*, Westport, CT: Praeger.

Sorensen, T. (1965) *Kennedy*, New York: Harper and Row.

Sorokin, P. (1957) *Social Change and Cultural Dynamics*, Boston, MA: Porter Sargent.

de Soysa, I. (2000) 'The resource curse: are civil wars driven by rapacity or paucity?', in M. Berdal and D. Malone (eds) *Greed and Grievance: Economic Agendas in Civil Wars*, Boulder, CO: Lynne Rienner.

—— (2002) 'Paradise is a bazaar? Greed, creed, and governance in civil war, 1989–99', *Journal of Peace Research* 395–416.

de Soysa, I., Oneal, J. and Park, Y.-H. (1997) 'Testing power-transition theory using alternative measure for national capabilities', *Journal of Conflict Resolution* 41: 509–28.

Starbuck, W. (1985) 'Acting first and thinking later: theory versus reality in strategic change', in J. Pennings (ed.) *Organizational Strategy and Change*, San Francisco, CA: Jossey-Bass.

Starn, O. (1998) 'Villagers at arms: war and counterrevolution in the Central-South

Andes', in S. Stern (ed.) *Shining and Other Paths: War and Society in Peru*, Durham, NC, Duke University Press.

Starr, H. and Most, B. (1978) 'A return journey: Richardson, frontiers and war in the 1945–1965 era', *Journal of Conflict Resolution* 22: 441–62.

Stein, A. (1976) 'Conflict and cohesion: a review of the literature', *Journal of Conflict Resolution* 20: 143–72.

Steinberg, G. (2004) 'The thin line between peace education and political advocacy: towards a code of conduct', in Y. Iram (ed.) *Educating Towards a Culture of Peace*, Greenwich, CT: Information Age.

Steinbruner, J. (1974) *The Cybernetic Theory of Decision: New Dimensions of Political Analysis*, Princeton, NJ: Princeton University Press.

Steiner, M. (1977) 'The elusive essence of decision: a critical comparison of Allison's and Snyder's decision-making approaches', *International Studies Quarterly* 21: 389–422.

Sterling-Folker, J. (2002) 'Realism and the constructivist challenge: rejecting, reconstructing, or rereading', *International Studies Review* 4: 73–97.

Stinchcombe, A. (1995) *Sugar Island Slavery in the Age of the Enlightenment: The Political Economy of the Caribbean World*, Princeton, NJ: Princeton University Press.

Stohl, M. (1976) *War and Domestic Political Violence: The American Capacity for Repression and Reaction*, Beverly Hills, CA: Sage.

Storey, A. (1997) 'Non-neutral humanitarianism: NGOs and the Rwanda crisis', *Development in Practice* 7: 384–94.

Stouffer, S., Suchman, E., DeVinney, L., Star, S. and Williams, R. (1949) *The American Soldier: Adjustment during Army Life*, Princeton, NJ: Princeton University Press.

Strachey, J (1964). *The Standard Edition of the Complete Psychological Works of Sigmund Freud, Vol. 16*, London: Hogarth Press.

Strauss, L. (1965) *Natural Right and History*, Chicago, IL: University of Chicago Press.

Strizek, H. (2004) 'Central Africa: 15 years after the end of the cold war. The international involvement', *Internationales Afrikaforum* 40: 273–88.

Sumner, W. (1906) *Folkways*, Boston, MA: Ginn.

Swift, L. (1973) 'Augustine on war and killing: another view', *Harvard Theological Review* 66: 369–83.

Tambiah, S. (1996) *Leveling Crowds: Ethnonationalist Conflicts and Collective Violence in South Asia*, Berkeley, CA: University of California Press.

Tammen, R., Kugler, J., Lemke, D., Stam, A., Abdollahian, M., Alsharabati, C., Efird, B. and Organski, A. (2000) *Power Transitions: Strategies for the 21st Century*, New York: Chatham House.

Tannen, B. (1990) *You Just Don't Understand: Women and Men in Conversation*, New York: Ballantine.

Tanter, R. (1966) 'Dimensions of conflict behaviour within and between nations, 1958–1960', *Journal of Conflict Resolution* 10: 41–64.

Tapper, K. and Boulton, M. (2005) 'Victim and peer group response to different forms of aggression among primary school children', *Aggressive Behavior* 31: 238–53.

Tarrow, S. (1998) *Power in Movement: Social Movements and Contentious Politics*, Cambridge: Cambridge University Press.

Taylor, A. and Beinstein Miller, J. (1994) 'The necessity of seeing gender in conflict', in A. Taylor and J. Beinstein Miller (eds) *Conflict and Gender*, Cresskill, NJ: Hampton Press.

Taylor, A. J. P. (1954) *The Struggle for the Mastery of Europe, 1848–1918*, Oxford: Oxford University Press.

Taylor, M. (1988) 'Rationality and revolutionary collective action', in M. Taylor (ed.) *Rationality and Revolution*, Cambridge: Cambridge University Press.

—— (2002) 'Fraternal deprivation, collective threat, and racial resentment: perspectives on white racism', in I. Walker and H. Smith (eds) *Relative Deprivation: Specification, Development and Integration*, Cambridge: Cambridge University Press.

Tellis, A., Bially, J., Layne, C. and McPherson, M. (2000) *Measuring National Power in the Postindustrial Age*, Washington, DC: Rand.

Temple, R. (2002) 'The modern world: a joint creation of China and the West', Paper presented at the Chinese Academy of Engineering and the Chinese Academy of Science, Beijing. Available online: http://www.robert-temple.com/papers/theModernWorldAJointCreationOfChinaAndTheWest.pdf (accessed 20 March 2006).

Tessler, M., Nachtwey, J. and Grant, A. (1999) 'Further tests of the women and peace hypothesis: evidence from cross-national survey research in the Middle East', *International Studies Quarterly* 43: 519–31.

Thayer, B. (2000) 'Bringing in Darwin: evolutionary theory, realism, and international politics', *International Security* 25: 124–51.

Thérien, J.-P. and Lloyd, C. (2000) 'Development assistance on the brink', *Third World Quarterly* 21: 21–38.

Thompson, J. and Tuden A. (1987) 'Strategies, structures and processes of organizational decision', in J. Thompson, P. Hammond, R. Hawkes, B. Junker and A. Tuden (eds) *Comparative Studies in Administration: Management and Technology*, New York: Garland Publishing.

Thompson, W. (1992) 'Dehio, long cycles, and the geohistorical content of structural transition', *World Politics* 45: 127–52.

Thompson, W. and Zuk, L. G. (1982) 'War, inflation, and the Kondratieff long wave', *Journal of Conflict Resolution* 26: 621–44.

Thorndike, E. L. (1898) 'Animal intelligence: an experimental study of the associate processes in animals', *Psychological Review Monograph Supplement* 2: 1–8.

—— (1932) *The Fundamentals of Learning*, New York: Teachers College.

Thorpe, W. (1974) *Animal Nature and Human Nature*, London: Methuen.

Tickner, J. A. (1992) *Gender in International Relations: Feminist Perspectives on Achieving Global Security*, New York: Columbia University Press.

—— (2002) 'Feminist perspectives on 9/11', *International Studies Quarterly* 3: 333–50.

Tilly, C. (1973) 'Does modernization breed revolution?', *Comparative Politics* 5: 425–47.

—— (1975a) 'Revolutions and collective violence', in F. Greenstein and N. Polsby (eds) *Handbook of Political Science, Vol. III*, Reading, MA: Addison-Wesley.

—— (1975b) 'Reflections on the history of European state making', in C. Tilly (ed.) *The Formation of National States in Western Europe*, Princeton, NJ: Princeton University Press.

—— (1978) *From Mobilization to Revolution*, Reading, MA: Addison-Wesley.

Tilly, C., Tilly, L. and Tilly, R. (1975) *The Rebellious Century, 1830–1930*, Cambridge, MA: Harvard University Press.

Tobias, S. (1990) 'Shifting heroisms: the uses of military service in politics', in J. Elshtain and S. Tobias (eds) *Women, Militarism, and War: Essays in History, Politics, and Social Theory*, Savage, MD: Rowman and Littlefield.

de Tocqueville, A. (1856) *The Old Regime and the French Revolution* (trans. J. Bonner), New York: Harper.

Toynbee, A. (1954) *A Study of History, Vol. IX*, Oxford: Oxford University Press.

Travaglianti, M. (2006) 'The role of the state in the natural resources and civil war paradigm', Catania: Jean Monnet Working Papers in Comparative and International Politics 61. Available online: http://www.fscpo.unict.it/EuroMed/jmwp61.pdf (accessed 15 November 2006).

Treadwell, M. (1954) *United States Army in World War II: The Women's Army Corps*, Washington, DC: Office of the Chief of Military History.

Trivers, R. (1971) 'The evolution of reciprocal altruism', *Quarterly Review of Biology* 46: 35–57.

Tuastad, D. (2003) 'Neo-orientalism and the new barbarism thesis: aspects of symbolic violence in the Middle East conflict(s)', *Third World Quarterly* 24: 591–9.

Tullock, G. (1971) 'The paradox of revolution', *Public Choice* 11: 89–99.

Turner, R. (1969) 'The theme of contemporary social movements', *British Journal of Sociology* 20: 390–405.

Tuzin, D. (1996) 'The specter of peace in unlikely places: concept and paradox in the anthropology of peace', in T. Gregor (ed.) *A Natural History of Peace*, Nashville, TN: Vanderbilt University Press.

Tyler, T and Lind, E. A. (2002) 'Understanding the nature of fraternalistic deprivation: does group-based deprivation involve fair outcomes or fair treatment?', in I. Walker and H. Smith (eds) *Relative Deprivation: Specification, Development and Integration*, Cambridge: Cambridge University Press.

UNESCO (1986) 'Seville statement on violence'. Available online: http://portal.unesco.org/education/en/ev.php-URL_ID=3247&URL_DO=DO_TOPIC&URL_SECTION=201.html (accessed 23 July 2005).

UNICEF (1986) *The Children and the Nations: The Story of UNICEF*, New York: UNICEF.

Uphoff N. (1995) 'Why NGOs are not a third sector: a sectoral analysis with some thoughts on accountability, sustainability and evaluation', in M. Edwards and D. Hulme (eds) *Non-Governmental Organisation: Performance and Accountability – Beyond the Magic Bullet*, London: Earthscan.

Uvin, P. (1998) *Aiding Violence: The Development Enterprise in Rwanda*, West Hartford, CT: Kumarian Press.

Valenzuela, J. and Valenzuela. A. (1978) 'Modernization and dependency: alternative perspectives in the study of Latin American underdevelopment', *Comparative Politics* 10: 535–57.

Vanneman, R and Pettigrew, T. (1972) 'Race and relative deprivation in the urban United States', *Race* 13: 461–86.

Vasquez, J. (1976) 'Toward a unified strategy of peace education', *Journal of Conflict Resolution* 20: 707–28.

—— (1987a) 'The steps to war: toward a scientific explanation of Correlates of War findings', *World Politics* 20: 108–45.

—— (1987b) 'Foreign policy, learning, and war', in C. Hermann, C. Kegley and J.

Rosenau (eds) *New Dimensions in the Study of Foreign Policy*, Winchester, MA: Allen and Unwin.
—— (1993) *The War Puzzle*, Cambridge: Cambridge University Press.
—— (2000a) 'Preface', in J. Vasquez (ed.) *What Do We Know about War?*, Lanham, MD: Rowman and Littlefield.
—— (2000b) 'Reexamining the steps to war: new evidence and theoretical insights', in M. Midlarsky (ed.) *Handbook of War Studies II*, Ann Arbor, MI: University of Michigan Press.
Vaux, T. (2006) 'Humanitarian trends and dilemmas', *Development in Practice* 16: 240–54.
Väyrynen, R. (1987) 'Global power dynamics and collective violence', in R. Väyrynen, D. Senghaas and C. Schmidt (eds) *The Quest for Peace: Transcending Collective Violence and War Among Societies, Cultures and States*, London: Sage.
Venugopal, R. (2003) 'The global dimensions of conflict in Sri Lanka', Oxford: Queen Elizabeth House Working Paper Number 99. Available online: http://www.qeh.ox.ac.uk/pdf/qehwp/qehwps99.pdf (accessed 25 January 2006).
Volgy, T. and Imwalle, L. (1995) 'Hegemonic and bipolar perspectives on the new world order', *American Journal of Political Science* 39: 19–34.
Wagner, H. (1974) 'Dissolving the state: three recent perspectives on international relations', *International Organization* 28: 435–66.
Walker, I. and Smith, H. (2002a) 'Fifty years of relative deprivation research', in I. Walker and H. Smith (eds) *Relative Deprivation: Specification, Development and Integration*, Cambridge: Cambridge University Press.
—— (2002b) 'Preface', in I. Walker and H. Smith (eds) *Relative Deprivation: Specification, Development and Integration*, Cambridge: Cambridge University Press.
Wallace, M. (1973) 'Alliance polarization, cross-cutting, and international war, 1815–1964', *Journal of Conflict Resolution* 17: 575–604.
—— (1979) 'Arms races and escalation: some new evidence', *Journal of Conflict Resolution* 23: 3–16.
—— (1982) 'Armaments and escalation: two competing hypotheses', *International Studies Quarterly* 26: 37–56.
Wallensteen, P. and Sollenberg, M. (2000) 'Armed conflict, 1989–99', *Journal of Peace Research* 37: 635–49.
Wallerstein, I. (1974a) *The Modern World System*, New York: Academic Press.
—— (1974b) 'The rise and future demise of the world capitalist system: concepts for comparative analysis', *Comparative Studies in Society and History* 16: 387–415.
—— (1984) 'The three instances of hegemony in the history of the capitalist world-economy', *International Journal of Comparative Sociology* 24: 100–8.
Walt, S. (1987) *The Origins of Alliances*, Ithaca, NY: Cornell University Press.
Walters, R. and Brown, M. (1963) 'Studies of reinforcement of aggression: transfer of responses to an interpersonal situation', *Child Development* 34: 563–71.
Waltz, K. (1959) *Man, the State and War*, New York: Columbia University Press.
—— (1967) 'International structure, national force, and the balance of world power', *Journal of International Affairs* 21: 215–31.
—— (1979) *Theory of International Politics*, New York: Random House.
Walzer, M. (2006) *Just and Unjust Wars: A Moral Argument with Historical Illustrations*, New York: Basic Books.
Warren, K. (2000) *Ecofeminist Philosophy: A Western Perspective on What it is and Why it Matters*, Lanham, MD: Rowman and Littlefield.

Wayman, F. W. (1996) 'Power shifts and the onset of war', in J. Kugler and D. Lemke (eds) *Parity and War: Evaluations and Extensions of The War Ledger*, Ann Arbor, MI: University of Michigan Press.

—— (2000) 'Rivalries: recurrent disputes and explaining war', in J. Vasquez (ed.) *What Do We Know about War?*, Lanham, MD: Rowman and Littlefield.

Wayne, S. (1993) 'President Bush goes to war: a psychological interpretation from a distance', in S. Renshon (ed.) *The Political Psychology of the Gulf War: Leaders, Publics and the Process of Conflict*, Pittsburgh, PA: University of Pittsburgh Press.

Webb, K. (1986) 'Structural violence and the definition of conflict', in L. Pauling (ed.) *World Encyclopaedia of Peace 2*, Oxford: Pergamon Press.

—— (1992) 'Science, biology and conflict', *Paradigms* 6: 65–96.

Weede, E. (1980) 'Arms races and escalation: some persisting doubts', *Journal of Conflict Resolution* 24: 285–7.

Weede, E. and Muller, E. (1998) 'Rebellion, violence and revolution: a rational choice perspective', *Journal of Peace Research* 35: 43–59.

Wehler, H. (1985) *The German Empire: 1871–1918*, Dover, NH: Berg.

Welch, D. (1992) 'The organizational process and bureaucratic politics paradigms: retrospect and prospect', *International Security* 17: 112–46.

—— (1997) 'The "clash of civilization" thesis as an argument and as a phenomenon', *Security Studies* 6: 197–216.

Wendt, A. (1994) 'Collective identity formation and the international state', *American Political Science Review* 99: 384–96.

Werner, S. and Kugler, J. (1996) 'Power transitions and military buildups', in J. Kugler and D. Lemke (eds) *Parity and War: Evaluations and Extensions of The War Ledger*, Ann Arbor, MI: University of Michigan Press.

Whelan, D, and Donnelly, J. (2006) 'The West, economic and social rights, and the global human rights regime: setting the record straight', *Human Rights & Human Welfare: An International Review of Books and Other Publications* 40. Available online: http://www.du.edu/gsis/hrhw/working/2006/40-whelan_donnelly-2006.pdf (accessed 23 December 2006).

White, R. (1999) 'The epistemological basis for evolutionary politics: three alternative research programs', Paper presented at the Annual Meeting of the American Political Science Association, Atlanta, September.

Wilkenfeld, J. (1972) 'Models for the analysis of foreign conflict behaviour of nations', in B. Russet (ed.) *Peace, War and Numbers*, Beverly Hills, CA: Sage.

Wilkenfeld, J. and Brecher, M. (2000) 'Interstate crises and violence: twentieth century findings', in M. Midlarsky (ed.) *Handbook of War Studies II*, Ann Arbor, MI: University of Michigan Press.

Wilkinson, R. (1969) *Governing Elites: Studies in Training and Selection*, Oxford: Oxford University Press.

Willhoite, F. (1971) 'Ethology and the tradition of political thought', *Journal of Politics* 33: 615–41.

Williams, R. (1975) 'Relative deprivation', in L. Coser (ed.) *The Idea of Social Structure: Papers in Honor of Robert K. Merton*, New York: Harcourt Brace Jovanovich.

Willoughby, J. (1995) 'Evaluating the Leninist theory of imperialism', *Science and Society* 59: 320–38.

Wilson, E. (1975) *Sociobiology – The New Synthesis*, Cambridge, MA: Harvard University Press.

—— (1978) *On Human Nature*, Cambridge, MA: Harvard University Press.

—— (1998) *Consilience: The Unity of Knowledge*, New York: Alfred A. Knopf.

Wilson, J. (1973) *Political Organizations*, New York: Basic Books.

Wimmer, A. (2004) 'Introduction', in A. Wimmer, R. Goldstone, D. Hotowitz, U. Jones and C. Schetter (eds) *Facing Ethnic Conflict: Towards a New Realism*, Lanham, MD: Rowman and Littlefield.

Winter, J. (2005) *The Experience of World War I*, London: Macmillan.

Wistrich, R. (1997) *Who's Who in Nazi Germany*, London: Routledge.

Wittner, L. (2003) *Toward Nuclear Abolition: A History of the World Nuclear Disarmament Movement, 1971–Present*, Stanford, CA: Stanford University Press.

Wolfgang, M. and Ferracuti, F. (1967) *The Subculture of Violence*, London: Tavistock.

Wolstenholme, G. (1963) 'Eugenics and genetics: discussion', in G. Wolstenholme (ed.) *Man and His Future*, Boston, MA: Little, Brown and Co.

Wood, E. (2003) *Insurgent Collective Action and Civil War in El Salvador*, Cambridge: Cambridge University Press.

Woolf, V. (1938) *Three Guineas*, New York: Harcourt Brace.

Wright, Q. (1965) *A Study of War*, 2nd edn, Chicago, IL: University of Chicago Press.

Wright, G. and Czelusta, J. (2004) 'Mineral resources and economic development', Stanford, CA: Stanford University Center for International Development Working Paper No. 209. Available online: http://scid.stanford.edu/pdf/scid209.pdf (accessed 26 January 2006).

Wylie, N. (2002) 'The sound of silence: the history of the International Committee of the Red Cross as past and present', *Diplomacy and Statecraft* 13: 186–204.

Wynne-Edwards, W. (1962) *Animal Dispersion in Relation to Social Behaviour*, New York: Hafner.

Yule, P. (2000) *Babitsky's War* (Documentary film – producer T. Charles), London: Channel Four.

Zillmann, D. (1979) *Hostility and Aggression*, Hillsdale, NJ: Erlbaum.

Zorpette, G. (1999) 'The mystery of muscle', *Scientific American* 10: 40–8.

Index